Hors de Combat
The Falklands-Malvinas Conflict in Retrospect

Edited by Diego F. García Quiroga and Mike Seear

Critical, Cultural and Communications Press
Nottingham
2009

The military is a great matter of the state.
It is the ground of death and life,
The Tao of survival or extinction.
One cannot but examine it.

The Art of War
Sun Tzu, 6th Century BC

Dedication

To the fallen of both sides and to those who survived
but continue to fight the battle in their lives.

Contents

Page

Acknowledgments

The editors wish to acknowledge the support given by the Centre for the Study of Post-Conflict Cultures of the University of Nottingham throughout the planning and implementation of the International Colloquium *The Falklands-Malvinas Conflict Twenty-Five Years On* and also to the Humanities Research Centre for its funding support. A key person who worked behind the scenes in the administration of the event was Beverly Tribbick, the secretary of the Centre. Without her there would have been no colloquium. Other players whose decisive interventions were crucial to the eventual participation of all the invited Argentine delegates were Eduardo Gerding, María Fra Amador, Lucrecia Escudero Chauvel and Ambassador Archibaldo Lanús. They each came to understand the meaning of crisis management and the need to trouble-shoot diplomatically when certain issues arose prior to the encounter.

During the colloquium the inevitable English-Spanish language barrier was brilliantly overcome by the many interpreters, under the expert eye and guidance of Dr Jean Andrews, who worked ceaselessly both in the colloquium room and during the various social events. Thanks and admiration for their considerable translating skills are owed to Victoria Ríos Castaño, Esther Villegas, Pablo Valdivia, Iona Macintyre, Chris Hull, Meesha Nehru, Emilse Hidalgo, Jeremy Lawrance and Stephen Roberts and, for their technical, logistical and organisational input, Rui Gonçalves Miranda, Laiz Chen Capra, Catherine McGuirk and Ana Cláudia Lessa. During the editing process, the critical acumen and eye for detail of Elizabeth McGuirk were invaluable.

Editors' Preface to the Second Edition

The success of the first edition of *Hors de Combat* has been reflected not only in the need, within two years of publication, to reprint it, but also in the international response to its capturing – in the words of the Vietnam War veteran and eminent psychologist Mark Sandman – of a "magical moment". The impact of the first coming together, twenty-five years on, and the publication of the deliberations of the veteran ex-combatants from both sides of the 1982 war demanded a considerable supplementing of the original version. Thus, transcriptions of, for example, several BBC Radio interviews; an extract from the leading Argentine daily newspaper *Clarín*, on "How British Academics See Us", and the responses to it of the distinguished novelist Carlos Gamerro; reminiscences of the editors' subsequent encounters with Baroness Thatcher; and contributions to the event held precisely one year after the colloquium marking the launch of the original book, including the remarkable testimony of the film-director Stuart Urban on the making, in 1992, of *An Ungentlemanly Act*; all have been added to the second edition. The editors extend their thanks to the Centre for the Study of Post-Conflict Cultures of the University of Nottingham and to the Buenos Aires-based Grupo Nottingham-Malvinas, under the auspices of the military historian and Medical Coordinator of the Malvinas War Veterans, Eduardo Gerding, for their continued support.

Diego F. García Quiroga and Mike Seear
Geneva/Oslo, April 2009

Editors' Preface

As editors of this book, which brings together the contributions from the University of Nottingham's International Colloquium on *The Falklands-Malvinas Conflict Twenty-Five Years On* (18-19 November 2006) we were not only active contributors but also enthralled spectators. Professor Bernard McGuirk and Mike Seear, at a meeting in December 2005, initiated the idea of holding such an historic event, which took months in design, planning and organising.

Deeply moved many times during this unprecedented meeting of former adversaries, we marvelled that it took place with such respect, warmth and friendliness. Nearly twenty-five years ago, many of those present were professionally contemplating and planning to manoeuvre into positions in order to kill each other. Indeed, if given the chance, they would have carried out these intentions effectively and efficiently. Yet now we were able to shake hands, enjoy new-found friendships, and wonder in awe at the bizarre nature of war.

We also met in a shared respect for our dead and our painful memories as we praised the courage and determination of each other, reviewed those brutal hours and days that we spent on the battlefield, and pondered on the life or death choices that combat made available to each side.

Tactfully avoiding discussion of the political issues that still set us apart, each of us shared sincere laughter with many a former opponent as we wondered on the wrongness or otherwise of assumptions both sides made when on those distant Islands. We also noted at the colloquium an immediate, and almost automatic, acceptance to combine the names "Falklands" and "Malvinas" with the literary device of a simple hyphen. Thus the "Falklands-Malvinas conflict" rolled off the tongue quite easily. Such a combination also had to be represented in the proceedings.

The compelling Anglo-Argentine theme of the extraordinary events in the South Atlantic of 1982 was a fascinating experience, whether from the perspective of those professional soldiers who had been presented once in their careers with a rare opportunity to exercise their skill at arms in a highly intensive but short-duration limited war, or from that of the other delegates in the discussion of an historical event that has proved so decisive a watershed for both Argentina and Britain in the following post-war decades of the twentieth century and, indeed, beyond.

It is only natural that the chosen co-editors are an Argentine, Diego F. García Quiroga, and a Brit, Mike Seear, who had both fought in the Falklands-Malvinas conflict or, as Mike prefers, war. He was given Diego's telephone number by Colonel Peter Reynolds (the Defence Attaché at the British Embassy in Buenos Aires) as someone with whom, apart from the war, he had something in common: a home in Oslo and a Norwegian wife. Following an initial pub rendezvous, a friendship formed where frank discussions brought new perspectives to memories and the realization that experiences ought to be shared. In particular, lessons identified and learned should not be lost. Diego also translated for Mike numerous Spanish e-mails from Argentina, which were incorporated into Mike's book *With the Gurkhas in the Falklands: A War Journal*.

Such a process has also been repeated in the way in which we have rapidly worked together on this book. We decided to structure it so that the first part features the recollections, experiences and effects of the war. The second part contains academic reflections and analyses. However, numerous themes were covered in the twenty-one contributions made and each deserves an acknowledgment. Diego starts this anthology. The vivid description of events around Government House on the Islands during 2 April 1982, his actions and their brutal consequences possess a realism difficult, if not impossible, to match. Indeed Diego's narration is (according to Mike) unique, riveting and sheer poetry: just as Mike's post-war story is (according to Diego) incredibly moving. Indeed this second contribution is of personal trauma enmeshed with a desire to find out more of the "other" and achieve an eventual reconciliation, all of which have a happy ending.

Another Argentine, Nicolás Urbieta, tells in a simple but effective way his hesitant response to Mike's attempts to meet him. It was not easy for Nicolás, a soldier of proven courage. Neither was the Battle of Two Sisters or its aftermath for his wounded platoon commander, Jorge Daniel Pérez Grandi, because here is yet another tale of personal trauma. However it is also about positives: leadership, caring for his men as Nicolás confirms, discipline and initiative.

We move back again to the "other" side. Mike Scott, the Scots Guards Commanding Officer, gives an in-depth look at the culture of his Battalion and, not least, the important roles that teamwork, leadership and regimental tradition and history played in the infantry battle of the Tumbledown. His Argentine opposite number, Carlos Hugo Robacio, follows by providing his perceptions and a concise impression of how his Marine Battalion, after preparing for sixty-eight days on the Islands and enduring heavy sea, land and air bombardments, defended the Tumbledown and its surrounding area against Mike Scott's Guardsmen in the final twenty-four hours. It is also the first time that two opposing Commanding Officers in direct combat during the war recount their battle in the same book. Their immediate subordinates also weigh in with narrations of the vicious close-quarter battle. Simon Price tells of his Right Flank Company's assault in the final phase and, once again, how teamwork, leadership and trained commanders were paramount to success. His meticulously illustrated presentation at the colloquium with many excellent pictures of the difficult terrain was one of the highlights for the professional soldiers present. Furthermore Eduardo Villarraza, his direct Argentine opponent, adds more interesting detail and analysis to his company's defensive preparations and battle actions on this key mountain in the Inner Defence Zone overlooking the Islands' capital.

Based on his Tumbledown experiences, Alan Warsap, the Scots Guards Regimental Medical Officer, provides a logical concept of how combat veterans should be handled in the post-battle period to reduce the possibility of traumatic stress in all its forms. David Morgan, the

Hors de Combat: the Falklands-Malvinas Conflict in Retrospect

Commandant of the 7th Gurkha Rifles, focusses instead on the extreme background, British Army selection methods and strengths of his Battalion's feared warriors from Nepal. Always on the periphery of the Tumbledown battle, the Gurkhas' potential was never given a chance to be unleashed and, correspondingly, their disappointment was huge. In contrast the Scots Guards' Chaplain, Angus Smith, reflects not only on the spiritual needs of soldiers about to be committed to combat and of their support afterwards, but also on good leadership at all levels, teamwork and a caring attitude. This is also evident with Jeremy McTeague's insights as a 7th Gurkha Rifles platoon commander when confronted with personal emotions before, during and after combat, and his succinct discourse on the need to examine their impact with a view to creating and implementing new British Army training policies on this important issue.

Jeremy's closing comments on trauma are then enlarged by Eduardo Gerding, the Malvinas War Veterans' Medical Co-ordinator. He analyses comprehensively the psychological injuries that war can have on soldiers of both sides and how such injuries can affect combat veterans later in life. In some ways, this common denominator is also mirrored in the war experiences and aftermath as recounted by Martin Reed, the former Chief Officer of the cruiseship-cum-troopship SS *Canberra* and now Chairman of the South Atlantic Medal Association 82. Likewise María Isabel Clausen de Bruno, an Argentine who has been dubbed by some in her country as "the Mother of the Malvinas War Veterans", underlines once more these needs of combat veterans with her passionately poetic contribution.

Two international experts complete the first part of this book. Mark Sandman was a "neutral" delegate, being a Vietnam War veteran and psychologist. He specialises in setting up veteran peer support programmes worldwide, and discusses in a most convincing fashion how this particular concept can be of benefit to veterans. The second is Lars Weisæth, a world authority on traumatic stress. In his glittering contribution, he argues most convincingly that the old concept of "forward psychiatry" should be practised in modern defence forces in a more balanced way by combining both the need to preserve combat strength, as well as protecting the mental health of personnel at risk.

In the much shorter second part of *Hors de Combat*, four more distinguished participants provide their viewpoints. Lucrecia Escudero Chauvel, a semiotician from Argentina, not only describes her initial personal experiences of Buenos Aires in that heady month of April 1982, but goes on to examine in great detail the Argentine and United Kingdom media coverage of the war. Then the French barrister Sophie Thonon-Wesfreid looks at the 1976-83 "Dirty War" in Argentina and the Falklands-Malvinas War, before discussing the national attempts to reconstruct Argentina and the bringing to justice those guilty in the aftermath of these two events. In the penultimate contribution, and from an anthropological and historical perspective, María Fra Amador reviews the 1982 conflict in the context of the genesis of aggression. Finally, in the book's coda, Bernard McGuirk utilises his profound intellect in debating representations of war with a brilliant dissection of two stunning Falklands-Malvinas War Argentine poems.

Yet it was Mark Sandman who placed the proceedings in an important reconciliation context when, on return to his Californian home, he e-mailed Mike spontaneously in the immediate colloquium aftermath:

> You assembled a world-class group of people and structured a wonderful programme. The flow of information and the emotional build-up were accomplished in a no less world-class fashion. I am proud and feel honoured to have been a small part of such a historically significant event as this. I have been intimately involved in reconciliation projects that have occurred for the Vietnamese and American veterans of the American Vietnam War. This occasion has arrived as a monumental success and necessary first step in the process of reconciliation. The concept of reconciliation is no small issue and can *only* really be accomplished at the most significant level. That is at the ex-combatant level. This was an extremely important event. It is not to be gauged by on-going business connections or any other related method. This event is what should be accomplished by politicians but never is. You have created a "magical moment" for the two sides. Do not lose sight of that.

However, what will be missing for you, the reader of *Hors de Combat*, is that tenor, that irony, that warmth and the choked voices of more than a few of those who either had the privilege of being able to speak formally or were able to ask a question and enter into dialogue with the speaker at the end of his or her presentation. These contributions have been edited, some of them being translated from their original Spanish into English. They are now published as a written record of what, for many, had been a unique moment and an immense step forward for humanity.

Diego F. García Quiroga and Mike Seear
Oslo, May 2007

Chronology of the Falklands-Malvinas Conflict (1982)

18-19 March Argentine scrap-metal merchants land at Leith Harbour, South Georgia, and raise the Argentine flag.

2 April Operación Rosario: Argentine troops land and re-capture the Falkland-Malvinas Islands.

3 April Argentine Marines land at Grytviken, South Georgia. United Nations (UN) Security Council adopts Resolution 502. Operation Corporate: the British Prime Minister, Margaret Thatcher, announces the dispatch of the British Task Force to re-capture the Islands.

5 April Lord Carrington resigns as the UK Foreign Secretary and is replaced by Francis Pym.

6 April Argentine 9th Infantry Brigade (comprising the 8th Infantry Regiment and 25th Infantry Regiment) starts deploying to the Islands from Comodoro Rivadavia.

7 April Fleet replenishment ship RFA *Stromness* departs Portsmouth with most of the Royal Marines' 45 Commando on board. The British Government declares a Maritime Exclusion Zone of 200 miles centred on the Islands to come into effect at 04.00Z hours on 12 April. Brigadier-General Mario Benjamín Menéndez assumes his appointment as Argentine Military Governor of the Islands.

8 April Argentine 5th Marine Infantry Battalion is deployed from Río Grande to the Islands and Sector Bronce (Bronze) of Tumbledown and Mount William. This unit's O Company is also initially deployed onto Mount Longdon. US Secretary of State for Foreign Affairs Alexander Haig begins his diplomatic shuttle between Washington DC, London and Buenos Aires.

9 April P&O cruise ship SS *Canberra* departs Southampton with the Royal Marines' 40 and 42 Commando, and 3rd Battalion, Parachute Regiment on board.

11 April Argentine 10th Infantry Brigade (comprising the 3rd Infantry Regiment, 6th Infantry Regiment and 7th Infantry Regiment) starts deploying by civil Boeing 707 aircraft from El Palomar, Buenos Aires to Comodoro Rivadavia. These Brigade units are then flown from there by military aircraft to the Islands. They are in position by 16 April, the 7th Infantry Regiment replacing the 5th Marine Infantry Battalion's O Company on Mount Longdon.

24 April Argentine 3rd Infantry Brigade starts deploying to the Islands with the 5th Infantry Regiment and 12th Infantry Regiment flying from Comodoro Rivadavia. The latter Regiment deploys onto Mount Challenger and later moves to Goose Green, whilst the 5th Infantry Regiment is based at Port Howard.

25 April Operation Paraquet: Royal Marine Commando forces land at Grytviken, South Georgia and the Argentine garrison surrenders. The Roll-on/Roll-off Ferry MV *Norland* departs Portsmouth with 2nd Battalion, the Parachute Regiment on board.

26 April After initially being deployed to Patagonia from their Monte Caseros base in the northern Corrientes province to protect the Argentine border with Chile, the other infantry unit of 3rd Infantry Brigade, the 4th Infantry Regiment, flies from Río Gallegos to the

Islands in aircraft of Austral airline. The following day, this Regiment's B and C Companies deploy to Wall Mountain and start preparing defensive positions.

29 April Argentine 3rd Infantry Brigade is in position.

30 April British Total Exclusion Zone of 200 nautical miles around the Islands comes into effect. US President Reagan announces support for the UK.

1 May Operation Black Buck 1: pre-dawn raid carried out by a single Vulcan bomber on the airfield north of Stanley. Afterwards Task Force Harrier aircraft carry out first air strikes on the airfield and elsewhere in the Islands.

2 May Peru offers a new peace plan for resolving the crisis. UN offers similar services. The Royal Navy submarine HMS *Conqueror* torpedoes and sinks the Argentine cruiser ARA *General Belgrano* outside the Total Exclusion Zone.

4 May Royal Navy destroyer HMS *Sheffield* is hit by an air-launched Exocet missile within the Total Exclusion Zone and eventually sinks. Operation Black Buck 2: second pre-dawn raid carried out by a single Vulcan bomber on the Stanley airfield.

6 May British Government formally accepts offer of UN mediation.

7 May The British Total Exclusion Zone is extended to within twelve miles of Argent-ina's coastline. The UN Secretary-General Javier Pérez de Cuéllar announces a new peace initiative.

12 May UK decision made to land troops at San Carlos Water. The Cunard cruise liner RMS *Queen Elizabeth 2* departs from Southampton with the 5th Infantry Brigade aboard.

21 May Operation Sutton, Phase I: the reinforced British 3 Commando Brigade of 4,000 men carry out an amphibious landing virtually unopposed at San Carlos, East Falkland. Heavy attacks by the Argentine Air Force and Navy aircraft are launched against British shipping in this first day of the overall five-day Battle of San Carlos Water. The frigate HMS *Ardent* is bombed, set on fire and abandoned. Other British vessels are also damaged.

24 May The frigate HMS *Antelope* sinks after an unexploded bomb on board detonates as it is being defused.

25 May The destroyer HMS *Coventry* is sunk by bombs from an Argentine air attack, and aircraft transport containership SS *Atlantic Conveyor* is hit by two air-launched Exocet missiles. The latter vessel is set on fire and eventually sinks. The Battle of San Carlos Water ends. Argentine Air Force Commander Brigadier-General Lami Dozo sends a peace envoy to New York.

26 May UN Security Council adopts Resolution 505. 2 Para advances towards Darwin and Goose Green.

27 May RMS *Queen Elizabeth 2* and other vessels carrying the 5th Infantry Brigade rendezvous at South Georgia. Transfer of troops commences. 2nd Battalion, Scots Guards and 1st Battalion, Welsh Guards cross-deck to SS *Canberra*, whilst 1st Battalion, 7th Duke of Edinburgh's Own Gurkha Rifles cross-deck to MV *Norland*.

28 May 2 Para commences its attack on Darwin and Goose Green. Cross-decking of the 5th Infantry Brigade is completed at South

Georgia by late afternoon of 28 May. The Brigade sails for San Carlos, East Falkland.

29 May Argentine garrison at Goose Green surrender to 2 Para. Approximately 1,000 prisoners are taken. 3 Para reaches Teal Inlet and 45 Commando begins its advance on Douglas.

30 May Major-General Jeremy Moore arrives at San Carlos and assumes command of British land forces in the Islands. 45 Commando and 3 Para secure Douglas and Teal respectively.

31 May UN Secretary-General proposes a new peace plan.

1 June Operation Sutton, Phase V: 1st Battalion, 7th DEO Gurkha Rifles land at San Carlos and are flown by Chinook helicopter Bravo November to Darwin. 3 Commando Brigade forward base established at Teal Inlet. Argentine 4th Infantry Regiment re-assigned new positions at Two Sisters (C Company) and Mount Harriet (Battalion Headquarters and B Company).

2 June Remainder of the 5th Infantry Brigade land at San Carlos. Surrender leaflets are dropped over Stanley. 2 Para elements are airlifted by Chinook Bravo November to Bluff Cove.

3 June 1st Battalion, 7th DEO Gurkha Rifles garrison Goose Green. Versailles Summit opens. President Reagan presents a five-point plan to the British.

5 June 2nd Battalion, Scots Guards embark on RFA *Sir Tristram* for transport to the Fitzroy-Bluff Cove area.

6 June 2nd Battalion, Scots Guards land at Fitzroy, East Falkland and establish a 5th Infantry Brigade forward base. 1st Battalion, Welsh Guards start moving up to Fitzroy by sea. Landings at San Carlos completed with about 8,000 British troops on the Islands.

7 June 1st Battalion, 7th DEO Gurkha Rifles start moving up to Fitzroy, initially by sea, and later by helicopter. The UN Secretary-General announces another peace plan.

8 June RFAs *Sir Galahad* and *Sir Tristram* attacked by Argentine aircraft whilst anchored at Port Pleasant, near Fitzroy. Fifty men are killed and one hundred and thirty-two wounded. *Sir Galahad* is crippled and, after the war, is towed out to sea and torpedoed.

10 June By midnight, 1st Battalion, 7th DEO Gurkha Rifles are in position at Wether Ground.

11-12 June On the night of 11-12 June, 3 Para attacks Mount Longdon defended by elements of the Argentine 7th Infantry Regiment, 45 Commando attacks Two Sisters, which is defended by elements of the Argentine 4th Infantry Regiment, and 42 Commando attacks Mount Harriet and Goat Ridge also defended by 4th Infantry Regiment elements. All objectives are captured by first light on 12 June.

13-14 June On the night of 13-14 June, 2 Para attack Wireless Ridge which is defended by elements of the Argentine 7th Infantry Regiment, whilst 2nd Battalion, Scots Guards attack the Tumbledown and 1st Battalion, 7th DEO Gurkha Rifles attack the north-east spur of Tumbledown and Mount William. These latter objectives are defended by elements of the Argentine 5th Marine Infantry Battalion, and are captured by 16.00Z hours on 14 June. The Gurkhas seize their two objectives unopposed.

14 June After negotiations, Brigadier-General Mario Benjamín Menéndez surrenders all Argentine forces on East and West Falklands.
12 July UK announces that active hostilities over the Falkland Islands are regarded as ended. Argentina does not make a similar Malvinas Islands statement.
22 July The British Total Exclusion Zone around the Islands is lifted.

Part 1
Recollection and Support

First In, First Out:
A Casualty of War and Coping with Life Post-Conflict

Diego F. García Quiroga

On the early afternoon of 26 March 1982 I was ordered to gather a group of eight men from my Special Forces unit for a mission. I was then serving as the operations officer in the APBT (Agrupación de Buzos Tácticos). Although in the previous few days the wardroom had been buzzing with rumours about the developments in South Georgia, no hint of the upcoming operation had yet reached us. That night,

together with a group of Comandos Anfibios led by Lieutenant (Junior Grade) Bernardo Schweitzer, we travelled down to the Puerto Belgrano Naval Base, some 400 kilometres south of our units' location. On arrival we met Lieutenant-Commander Pedro Giacchino, who was to be our group commander. We amounted to sixteen all in all, a mix of BBTT (Buzos Tácticos) and Comandos Anfibios.

The Task Force sailed on 28 March, and the first men to land on the islands were our group's scouts, Lieutenant Schweitzer and a corporal from the Comandos Anfibios. This happened, contrary to the description

of the operation in several books on the war, with the help of rubber boats and shortly before midnight on 1 April. Led by Lieutenant Commander Giacchino, we navigated the distance from Mullet Creek to Government House at the islands' capital in the dark and reached our target before first light. Thus on the morning of 2 April, as we were fighting to overcome the resistance put up by the Royal Marine

Commandos who were shooting at us from inside the house, Lieutenant Commander Giacchino was hit in the chest and fell to the ground. I was shadowing his movements, and was also then hit by three different aimed shots: one went through my right elbow, another through my lower torso and the third was stopped by a Swiss Army pocket knife that was fastened to my belt over my left groin. All these three bullets were fired from different weapons. I was immediately stunned, but nevertheless remained conscious.

More than one and a half hours later we were finally assisted, once the firing had stopped and the area was secured. By then, Corporal Urbina had been seriously wounded while trying to help us, and Lieutenant-

Commander Giacchino had lost so much blood that he died before reaching the hospital at Stanley.

Once in the hospital, my injuries were inspected by a team of doctors. I clearly remember a female doctor providing me with a confusing diagnosis. "You're through, baby," she said. I wondered for a long time whether this had meant that I was alive or already dead. After this came a ride on a stretcher lashed up to the side of a helicopter that landed on the deck of ARA Almirante Irizar, our designated hospital ship, followed by another flight back to the airport where I was lifted on board a plane, still strapped down on the same stretcher, and evacuated to Comodoro Rivadavia on the mainland. I arrived in the local hospital once again via a helicopter and was already very weak, everything reaching me through a dense fog that grew increasingly darker. Whilst my wounds were being X-rayed I heard a nurse ask my name and on hearing my answer, the radiologist asked whether I was related to a friend of his who, indeed, happened to be my father. Happy at the unexpected coincidence, he then told me that none of my vital organs seemed to be severely damaged. Those words are the last thing I remember having heard before waking up several hours later, after three consecutive surgeries.

My wife and my parents were at my side, having been flown in by the Navy. My executive officer was also there, still dressed in his combat clothes. He told me about Lieutenant Commander Giacchino's death and the outcome of the mission. It took me months to recover completely from my wounds and the conflict was already over when I was declared fit for duty. From an almost perfectly executed military operation engineered to place Argentina in a better bargaining position concerning the islands, it had evolved into a full-fledged confrontation killing hundreds of men, plunging their families into grief and filling them with hatred that had not been there before the conflict.

I was decorated as a hero before the conflict ended. At the time my feelings were that I did not deserve it and I still think that way. I have been told that a nation needs heroes, but it still feels unfair, as many braver people died on the islands. I was perfectly prepared for this "first in" as a career officer and member of an elite unit. Indeed this operation met all the expectations I had about the way of life I had chosen to pursue. At twenty-eight and having married just three months before, I felt I was already a member of the prototypical band of brothers. The same elation with which Shakespeare coloured King Henry V's words just before Agincourt was in the air, although there was nothing that could have been called patriotic in my attitude. I was as skeptical as ever about the soundness of the decision and cannot recall many of us there as having had intense feelings about the islands.

Speaking only for me, the whole idea of fighting was a personal challenge. We were to spearhead an operation directed against an enemy I had learned to admire. As a young man, my concepts of courage and duty were shaped after a mixture of Argentina's own war-waging tradition and many of Rudyard Kipling's characters, probably because I had been formed at an English school in Buenos Aires. Combat was the perfect arena to find out the type of stuff I was made of. And there I was, going in with a group of men who were as brave as or possibly braver than myself. We were perfectly honed for the mission, fit as fiddles, and happy as partygoers. I trusted each and everyone, as I had not trusted anyone before.

Others may discuss whether the cause of this campaign was evil or just, but as a young officer it was not for me to analyze the politics behind the decisions. Today I am convinced that the fog of war as defined by Clausewitz had a significant role in the escalation of the events that followed, but such is the danger of waging war and such is the nature of men. The Clausewitzian statement that "war is not only a political issue but more precisely a political instrument, or a continuation of political relations; a way of handling these through other means" applies in my view to both the Argentine and British governments, who not only sought to put an end to their diplomatic differences but also to overcome their respective internal political situations. I marvel in retrospection at the inability of our government to realise at that time that Great Britain had already embarked on a war. Well into the campaign I remember our leaders' political objective still being to try to induce the international community into voting for a diplomatic solution allowing Argentina to regain sovereignty over the islands. Mrs Thatcher's objective was only to punish the aggression.

I make this digression in order to introduce an anecdote told to me shortly after the war . It is, apparently, true: In the early planning stages of the invasion-probably early December 1981- a highly respected retired Argentine admiral was called in by the planners of Operation Azul (later re-named Rosario) to express his views on the issue. As soon as he learned about the invasion, he asked to see the plans they had prepared for attacking London. Aghast, everybody turned to look at him, and one of the senior officers present exclaimed "London! With all due respect, sir, are you out of your wits?" The retired Admiral looked back at him and said: "If you are planning to make war on the Brits and do not have made plans to attack London, then it's not me who's the mad man in this room ".Nonetheless, the sad result was that from both sides a grand total of nine hundred and four lives were lost in the conflict: a ratio of precisely one war fatality for every two inhabitants of the islands at that time. This is a unique statistic. Thirty warships and support ships were sunk or damaged, and one hundred and thirty-eight aircraft were either destroyed or captured. As for that morning, all of this was still part of the future. Life was beautiful and everything exciting in a way I have never experienced since. The examples of our heroes were in our minds and with them the feeling of playing a small, but meaningful, role in the history of our nation. It was a great moment, and I have never since felt a similar intensity from life.

As I mentioned above, I was physically powerless after having been hit three times by the enemy's bullets. Lieutenant-Commander Giacchino lay at my side. I recall witnessing what appeared to me as being his death, when he was being lifted onto something that resembled a stretcher. I was somehow confused and felt weird rushes of pain from my injured back. My right arm hurt terribly. However, by and large, I appeared to be all right even though I was feeling very light-headed after an injection of morphine that was given to me by a quick-thinking Royal Marine commando. Using my blood as makeshift ink, he daubed the letter "M" on my forehead to indicate that morphine had already been injected. An additional dose administered by error could have had fatal consequences.

It was extremely cold. I remember a bundle of funny details from those moments which were probably filled with utmost gravity and drama. Nevertheless, I retain a feeling of having lived through them all not only from a certain distance, but also through some sort of gauze curtain. There were, of course, flashes of family and personal memories. But most of my thoughts were monopolized by things that were happening there and then, as if I had entered another reality which possessed its own particular separate urgencies. Questions about life or death were not at all on my mind. I can understand perfectly that these types of thoughts torture the minds of men who are unlucky enough to come under heavy shelling or bombing. This mind-shattering nightmare did not apply to me. I was incredibly lucky by being wounded as fast and clean as it can possibly be. All my memories from the moment I was hit until collapsing at the hospital X-ray room remain vivid. Things seemed to be happening in a strange, quieter rhythm. Lieutenant-Commander Giacchino was speaking to me in an urgent and obviously painful way. The Governor's geese were walking clumsily around us. Oblivious of the bullets, I heard Corporal Urbina's cry of frustration when he was hit. All this was happening while I gradually slid from fantastic excitement into a peaceful quietness. I could not move and had lost the grip on my weapon, the sun was quickly coming up and I could still hear the voices and the firing, but was sinking away very fast. I heard the rotating blades of a chopper, but could not see it. The sky was blue and I remember thinking that it was not bad to die on such a beautiful morning, amongst friends and lying on the grass. The Royal Marine commando who gave me morphine snapped me out of my reverie. I could not speak or move and my vision was already tunnelling. I nevertheless could interpret he was not one of us and, for one endless moment, was convinced that he had come to finish me off with his combat knife. Under the effect of morphine, I clearly remember my desperation at feeling unable to draw enough air into my lungs.

While at the hospital ship, I remember the sailors were having difficulties in getting my stretcher through the arrow passages on board. There was blood pouring from it and, as it was tilted at every door entrance, a mess was made of the deck. All the faces I saw were talking to me – but I could not hear them. Once again, one question came to mind. Was I still alive? A classmate recognized my face under the camouflage and grasped my wounded arm passionately. It hurt like hell, but I could not tell him to let go, I could not speak at all. Members of my unit were standing on the tarmac as I was being lifted inside the aircraft and my Commanding Officer was there with them. As the stretcher went by, I saw they were looking at me, their faces grey with exhaustion and eyes lowered. Nobody spoke, nobody reached to touch me. I was certain that death had incurred And it did not feel too bad.

The interior of the aircraft had been stripped bare of all seats and throughout the flight to Comodoro Rivadavia a soldier kept slapping my face to prevent me from losing consciousness. I would not have survived without him. I was angry with myself for being unable to get back to the front. The war was certainly to end soon and I felt the opportunity of experiencing it had been missed by my being shot on its very first day. However when the war did eventually end I was still unable to return to military service, my right arm being still useless. I rejoined my unit in November and performed a couple of parachute jumps in order to leave no doubts about my recovery. Life kept on. Again, I consider myself very lucky. I have enjoyed the privilege of fighting alongside brave men and surviving almost unscathed. It could be said that I was just a visitor to the front having, through my wounds, escaped the long and dreadful hours of vigil, the bombing, the freezing nights, the darkness, the hunger and the horror of seeing men killed, blown to pieces or gruesomely dismembered at my side.

I cannot speak as a war casualty. I do not know what these extremes do to men's minds but still, war is part of our nature. It is also a terrible affair. Yet life can be quite hard even in the absence of war, and many veterans of terrifying situations are able to suppress their emotional experiences in order to become functional again. It is widely accepted that the effects of combat on men have a direct relationship with several factors regarding each individual, for example heredity, upbringing, the way he and his immediate group "feel" about the war, the relationship with his comrades, or the harmony of his private life. Some of these factors can be overshadowed by those instruments of collective influence that are common in the military, such as discipline. I was very well equipped in these areas, and it was this foundation, along with the briefness of my combat experience, that provided no chance for my world to crack.

No doubt the excitement of that day magnified my impression of everything happening around me. I believe this explains the bright aura that surrounds each of my memories of that morning. The sounds were louder, the light brighter, the deeds worthier. As regards to any negative effect I may have suffered as a consequence, then virtually every new experience results dull in comparison. On the other hand I became oversensitive to trivialities that before would have not prompted me to react. Another possible effect is that some of my memories have become quite scrambled, while others have disappeared leaving no trace at all. There are some periods of my life of which I can't recall hardly anything. Most of these are very short but some become significant deficiencies, as when I meet people I have met in the past yet cannot remember them. Many of those who knew me before that morning in the Malvinas agree by saying that the war affected my personality radically, a fact which I find difficult to either accept or deny. According to these opinions, patterns of thought that I am convinced had always been with me were not there before at all. If anything, I feel the experience strengthened me. Along with the pride I felt immediately from having been part of re-taking the islands on 2 April 1982, I gained the satisfaction of proving my faithfulness to my comrades, profession and country. I cannot imagine a better deal. If I were to pinpoint oddities of my character possibly emerging from some sort of post-war trauma, then the following ought to be highlighted: a tendency to downplay the urgency or graveness of situations, a deeper lack of interest in competition, and an enhanced scepticism about almost everything. Yet I still have dreams of glory.

Seeking "The Other" in the Post-Conflict 1982-2006

Mike Seear

And so in the military –
Knowing the other and knowing oneself,
In one hundred battles no danger.
Not knowing the other and knowing oneself,
One victory for one loss.
Not knowing the other and not knowing
 oneself,
In every battle certain defeat.

Sun Tzu, 6th Century BC

On the eleventh day after cessation of the Falklands-Malvinas War, I was on duty at 04.00 hours in the small Goose Green operations room set up in the bunkhouse for bachelor shepherds. The previous day, 24 June, was a dreadful one for 1st Battalion, 7th Duke of Edinburgh's Own Gurkha Rifles. Whilst back-filling some Argentine trenches north of the settlement, Lance-Corporal Budhaparsad Limbu had hit his spade on an unexploded, but buried, M-79 grenade that a paratrooper of 2 Para had fired during the battle there on 28 May. The grenade now exploded, killing the Lance-Corporal and wounding two other Gurkha soldiers. Indeed Budhaparsad was the formal two hundred and fifty-fifth and final British Task Force fatality of the war. As the Battalion's Operations and Training Officer, I had been on duty in the operations room at the time and became fully involved in the immediate crisis management of this unpleasant incident.

More than twelve hours later there was little to do, but even at this "dead-man's hour" thoughts about the accident kept me fully alert. It was also the event that started a long-term project as I turned over a pad of signal message proformas and began jotting down on the rear blank page a few notes of my experiences in the previous tumultuous twelve weeks which represented and still remain, in my view, the greatest single-nation crisis management operation since the Second World War. I had been in the category of "last in, last out", having landed on the Islands for the war's final fourteen days and soon would depart in nearly three weeks time. But on this night that single pad page would become the embryo of a book manuscript that would require an accumulated period of eight years to complete and publish (Seear, 2003). Even on that particular night, as the idea grew, I decided there had to be an Argentine dimension to my book which must include a particular representative of "the other" we had confronted in the war.

Corporal Nicolás Urbieta, an Argentine 4th Infantry Regiment support section commander, was the natural choice. His helmet, weapon, webbing, large pack, kit bag, training manuals, five unposted letters and roll of film had been found by my Battalion Tactical Headquarters'

British radio operator, Corporal Chris Aslett, and some Gurkha soldiers when, post-war, they had been scouring the Two Sisters' and Mount Harriet battlefields for Argentine souvenirs. In the kit bag was also half a sheep's carcass that indicated the extent of the Argentine soldier's predicament: a desperate shortfall of rations. All these items, less the carcass, were brought into my little Goose Green operations room. I intervened when one Gurkha was about to throw the letters into my wastepaper basket. Although they were written in Spanish, I rescued them and, indeed, they would become my personal souvenirs of the war. Thus a couple of nights later, when starting to write those book notes, I remembered the Argentine soldier's letters. There was no hesitation. The letters had to be incorporated into my book project.

My initial writing was combined with the interesting task of editing for many hours the two Gurkha Battalion post-operational reports of the war: one at the settlement of Goose Green and the other on board the British Task Force's former Naval Ocean-going Surgical Hospital Ship SS *Uganda* en route back to the United Kingdom. But those untranslated letters still intrigued me as the book's first draft manuscript of fifty-five pages typed up by two ever-faithful Gurkha clerks in the makeshift Battalion orderly room on board was completed by the time of our arrival at Southampton.

In the autumn, I visited my Aunt Nancy at her flat in London to tell her of my book plans and ask for help in translating the letters. Otherwise known as the Baroness Seear of Paddington and soon to be leader of the Liberal Peers (1984-88) in the British Parliament's House of Lords, she sought a Spanish-English translator from her impressive network. When the English versions of the letters were eventually returned to me, they were accompanied by a note from the translator. She opposed my idea that these letters be published, commenting that they described a terrible situation which faced the Argentine soldier, who was suffering so much. I shrugged at these objections of a civilian who would never be able to understand the thought processes of any combat veteran and, instead, avidly read Urbieta's letters. I could empathise immediately with this graphic account of how one Argentine soldier was waiting at the end of May in his section defensive position on Wall Mountain, East Falkland, for the British to attack.

His moods ranged from bravado to downright depression. As a war veteran I sympathised with "the other's" roller-coaster emotions. I also had his roll of film developed. Some of the photographs had been ruined by the hostile wet Falklands' climate, but some were of surprisingly good quality and showed the young Nicolás Urbieta as a section commander in training with his men at Rio Gallegos. The Regiment had been sent south from its Monte Caseros base in the sub-tropical northern province of Corrientes to counter the threat posed by Chile against Argentina's southern border. But plans had changed suddenly and the 4th Infantry Regiment were to be deployed direct from Río Gallegos in civil aircraft to the Islas las Malvinas.

Dark and short, but stocky in build, Urbieta seemed to have a charismatic leader's air about him. In November 1982, I mailed the originals to the British Red Cross, requesting that they be returned to

Urbieta. A few days later I received back a letter informing me that they had been forwarded to the International Committee of the Red Cross in Geneva for eventual onward transmission to Argentina and Urbieta.

In the next two years of my Gurkha secondment from the Light Infantry, which included a Battalion move to Hong Kong in April 1983, I continued with my writing. However, at the end of this final fourteen-month period with the Gurkhas, it was obvious that the manuscript was not of sufficient literary quality to be published. I was posted to Norway and that imperfect 200-page manuscript of my war experiences from the worm's eye-view of the Gurkha Operations and Training Officer was put in a shoebox. Storing this in the cellar of my home on the outskirts of Oslo, I concentrated instead on my new staff appointment at the Kolsås NATO headquarters and my young family which now included my third daughter born in Hong Kong the previous year. A baby of my war's aftermath, she had Downs Syndrome. There were greater priorities in my life than writing, with her two open-heart surgeries during the two successive years and the beginning of turbulence within the family. Nonetheless, I adopted a philosophical attitude: my book project remained alive, and patience would be required to realise my ultimate publication aim.

In 1988 I became a civilian in Norway and Head of Security and Emergency Response in Scandinavian Airlines. The start of this latter venture had remarkably similar parallels to my Gurkha secondment six years previously: the requirement to learn a new culture, language, job and become acquainted with new people: albeit civilians. I threw myself at the challenges. The only difference was that my next "war" would come years later in this job. With the benefit of hindsight this was also a subconscious second bite at the "Falklands-Malvinas apple" which might rectify my non-optimal performance during that war. At an early stage in my emergency response training with airline personnel I enlisted Professor Lars Weisæth, a world authority in traumatic stress, to assist. He was to teach me, in an enlightening yet simple way, the theory of traumatic stress and psychosocial support after my practical experiences from the Falklands-Malvinas War.

My home life deteriorated. My marriage survived two separations. Burning the candle at both ends with additional demands due to my daughter's condition, I collapsed at Easter 1993. The diagnosis was chronic fatigue syndrome, and six months sick leave. Yet on return to my job I continued at the same reckless work pace as before. There were more crises both privately and professionally: another short separation in my marriage, and an aircraft hijack successfully crisis-managed. But by then my post-traumatic growth and existential authority had begun to grate on some airline superiors. I knew too much, certainly more than them, and was therefore being perceived as a "threat" to the system. The climax came in May 1996 at a London international civil aviation symposium where two questions I posed in open forum were interpreted, incorrectly, by a Norwegian with power, and less than perfect English as being too provocative towards him and his organisation.

Within two months I was jobless, the victim of an "unlawful dismissal". My second bite at the "apple" had turned rotten, completely crushing my professional ego. Refusing to accept the fact that, in reality, I had grown out of my job, this event also proved to be that much talked-about war veterans' "trigger in later life" which re-awakens past battlefield traumas. I endured a prolonged sense of powerlessness, just like that on the last night of the war when we came under intensive enemy artillery and mortar fire behind the Tumbledown. My current predicament resulted not only in twenty months of unemployment, but a severe depression combined with multiple symptoms of post-traumatic stress disorder. Eventually this culminated in a nervous breakdown, ensuing three-week hospitalisation, eventual marriage break-down and loss of my family home. It is what psycho-traumatology experts label a "multi-event". However, this implosion of my professional and personal life did have one positive effect: it produced a subconscious cathartic need to re-examine my life. That twelve year-long objective to publish a book was resurrected with a return to the old shoebox in which lay my uncompleted project. It was to bring back a much-needed focus amidst all the personal wreckage in my life, as the re-writing of *With the Gurkhas in the Falklands: A War Journal* started to gather pace.

All this increased the need to seek out in a more active way my chosen "other" of the 1982 Falklands-Malvinas War. But was Nicolás Urbieta alive? I decided to attack the problem on two fronts. One was the formal route. A letter was written to the International Committee of the Red Cross in January 1997, with a reply from Geneva on 13 March 1997 confirming that Urbieta had been repatriated to Argentina after the war. (He was one of the 4,144 Argentine prisoners of war transported by the P&O cruise liner SS *Canberra*.). Although not normal practice, attempts would be made to locate him in Argentina.

I had also chosen an informal route. Amongst other items I had retained from Urbieta's kit was a piece of toilet-paper. On this he had written the names and addresses of the ten men in his section. So I also wrote a letter asking for Urbieta's whereabouts in Argentina and had this translated into Spanish. Then, rather like Robinson Crusoe throwing bottles containing hopeful messages into the sea, these ten identical letters were posted to the ten toilet-paper addresses. I succeeded with only one. But it was enough. The recipient obviously thought that the contents were unusual and passed it to Marcela Bordenave, an Argentine National Congress representative whose political advisor asked for an interview about my connection with Urbieta and the war in view of the forthcoming fifteenth anniversary of its cessation. I received Urbieta's address and a one-page article written about Urbieta and Seear that was published on 15 June 1997 by *Clarín*, the largest national newspaper in Argentina. The main theme of the article was that the British officer wanted to meet "the other", whilst the Argentine Sergeant (Urbieta was still serving in the Army with the 24th Mechanised Infantry Regiment at Río Gallegos in the southern province of Patagonia) most certainly did not. Indeed "the other" did not seem to want to talk about the war at all, and most definitely not to his former enemy. Curiously, there was one phone call from Nicolás to me a week or so after the article had been published. Alas, our conversation did not last long as he did not speak English, nor I Spanish.

The article hit a raw nerve elsewhere in Argentina. *Clarín* had also published a letter I had written in May 1997 to Urbieta which displayed my address in Norway. Many Argentines subsequently wrote to me. Some were Malvinas War veterans. Others were civilians. One was María Emilia Bosio, a student of English who helped me considerably by translating many of these letters and the *Clarín* article. Another was Alberto Peralta Ramos, a freelance TV producer of the cultural programme *Astrolabio* (Sextant). He informed me that he had produced a TV programme on the Gurkhas, and had also given a briefing to the Argentine Army HQ in Buenos Aires about the Gurkhas when it was made known that the latter would be deployed to the South Atlantic in May 1982. He became an invaluable and generous ally in my quest to find out more about "the other" and Argentine culture during my subsequent three visits to Buenos Aires in 2002 and 2003.

Late in 1997, an angry letter came from an Argentine woman who lived in the little country town of General Roca in Córdoba province. María Isabel Clausen de Bruno berated me severely for belonging to the Gurkha war machine which had been intent on killing the young conscript boys of the Argentine Army in the Malvinas War. However, this bad start did not last long. I was now living on my own in a thirty-five square metre basement flat in Oslo, had been unemployed for sixteen months and was still licking my wounds after a most difficult time. "Marisa", as she liked to be known, was a staunch supporter of the Malvinas War veterans and, paradoxically, also provided me with much written psychosocial support after I sent her several long letters explaining my predicament.

By now I had worked up a head of steam in writing my book without having secured a publisher and, at last, acquired a job in April 1998 as a security and crisis management consultant. I deemed that more material for the Argentine dimension to my book was needed as publishing Nicolás's letters did not give my potential readers enough information about "the other" and his war. A meeting between Nicolás and myself was therefore imperative. But first my life reconstruction would continue with marriage to another Norwegian in 2000. I made a comeback in Scandinavian Airlines and was engaged as a part-time crisis management consultant in a project that lasted thirty months with re-writing plans, holding seminars, and designing, writing and implementing a number of major exercises mainly at the Head Office in Stockholm, Sweden. The project was closed in June 2001. But its results would be put to the acid test in a uniquely horrifying way nearly four months later at Linate Airport, Milan when 118 people were killed in the airline's early morning aircraft accident there on 8 October 2001. I heard the news at lunchtime, and the remainder of my day was inevitably one of many personal reflections and reactions at the tragedy.

Another four years had passed by before the time seemed right for me to travel to Argentina. Many friendships were to be made in this surreal odyssey. My two facilitators on that first trip at the end of March 2002 were Alberto in Buenos Aires and Marisa in General Roca. Alberto met me at the airport and hosted me with much generosity in the capital. He engineered my meeting, in a Buenos Aires restaurant and over a cup of coffee, with retired Brigadier-General Mario Benjamín Menéndez, the former 1982 Malvinas Military Governor who was also the Commander of the Argentine Land Forces on the Islands. A second meeting was arranged with Lieutenant-Colonel Tomás ("Tommy") Jorge Fox in the latter's Buenos Aires apartment. He was the artillery forward observation officer perched on top of Mount Harriet in the war who directed that Argentine 155mm artillery fire against the Gurkhas for nearly three days when we were dug-in at a place called Wether Ground on the southern coastline of East Falkland. After four hours of swapping stories about the war, "Tommy", his wife, who was an English teacher, Alberto and I enjoyed a delightful midnight meal at a Buenos Aires restaurant.

I also met Marisa and her husband, Roberto, at the iconic Plaza de Mayo, scene of General Galtieri's speeches from the balcony of Government House, otherwise known as the Casa Rosada (Pink House), to the Argentine crowds during those heady post-Falklands invasion days of April 1982. From there we visited the impressive pink stone Malvinas War Memorial in the Plaza San Martín, where inquisitive Guadalupe Barriviera, a *Clarín* journalist, interviewed me about my quest for Nicolás.

The *Clarín* article was published the following day, forty-eight hours before the veterans' Malvinas Day on 2 April, and Marisa's and Roberto's home where I was staying was besieged by the local media. A national radio programme conducted a ten-minute live interview between Nicolás in Río Gallegos and me. Nicolás seemed a solid person who, despite his previous hesitation, did not appear during the broadcast to have an aversion to speaking to me. But there was to be no meeting with "the other" on that particular trip. Nonetheless a breakthrough had been made. I returned to Buenos Aires to watch the impressive Malvinas War Veterans' Day military parade with Alberto. That evening, before my flight home on the following day, I received a phone call in my hotel room from a Jorge Pérez Grandi. He had read the *Clarín* article published a few days previously and wanted to meet me as soon as possible. He had been Nicolás Urbieta's platoon commander in the war.

An hour later I met Jorge in the hotel lobby, and for the next three hours he told me about his platoon's experiences and the fighting at the Battle of Two Sisters against the Royal Marine 45 Commando unit on the night of 11-12 June 1982. He also gave me some startling information about the modest Nicolás Urbieta. An extract from my book is pertinent:

> After they ran out of ammunition Pérez Grandi ordered Urbieta to lead his platoon off their position. Not shirking his responsibility, the officer then covered their withdrawal alone. But, as they began to move down Moody Valley, a mortar bomb exploded by Pérez Grandi.

Shrapnel tore into his right arm, legs, and thighs – smashing bones and slicing off chunks of flesh. He ordered his men to continue their withdrawal, but one volunteered to remain with him. Pérez Grandi's men managed to escape but, on reaching an Argentine Army artillery battery three kilometres away near Moody Brook bridge, south-east of Mount Longdon, Urbieta asked for a stretcher and, accompanied by nine men, made his way back to Dos Hermanos (Two Sisters). Like frozen mutton, his platoon commander's bleeding had been slowed down by the cold. Pérez Grandi was put on the stretcher, covered with combat kit and, despite lack of morphine, survived the agonizing trek to a waiting truck at the artillery battery. Urbieta had tabbed more than nine kilometres to rescue his officer who, that same day, underwent an emergency operation in Puerto Argentino's military hospital before being flown out on the last Hercules to Río Gallegos. Pérez Grandi contracted gangrene and was hospitalised for a year. Urbieta remained in defence around the battery, only to withdraw to Puerto Argentino's Racecourse just before the ceasefire – but would receive no decoration for his outstanding bravery.

In December 2002 I made a second visit to Argentina accompanied by my Norwegian colleague and friend, Professor Lars Weisæth. By then I had established a further contact in Buenos Aires, Dr Eduardo Gerding, the Malvinas War Veterans' Medical Co-ordinator. There was the possibility of establishing a traumatic stress project, so Lars and I interviewed eight Malvinas War veterans, assisted by Eduardo. I was intrigued to discover that two of them had been through a similar "unlawful dismissal" process as me. As a result they were still unemployed. I tried to encourage them by sharing my experience.

Lars and I then travelled to General Roca to interview another six veterans in Marisa's home. The exchange was most positive, and I became convinced that veteran peer support is a most effective concept for assisting veterans who continue to suffer with traumatic stress reactions. Indeed I thought then, and still do, that a potential opportunity has been squandered by government and experts alike in not attempting to organise a unique bilateral project between Argentina and the United Kingdom on Falklands-Malvinas combat veterans' issues. Focus on the concrete challenges of humanity rather than the abstract notion of sovereignty might have brought the two countries closer together on the Falklands-Malvinas issue.

Although more material was gathered for my book as a direct result of this visit, including a subsequent valuable exchange of e-mails between Rear-Admiral Carlos Hugo Robacio, the former Commanding Officer of the 5th Marine Infantry Battalion which fought in the Battle of Tumbledown two nights after the Two Sisters battle, I did not manage to make any contact with Nicolás. But Marisa travelled to Río Gallegos in March 2003 to persuade him that it might be a good idea for us two veterans to meet. After my book had been published in July 2003, Marisa invited me to return to Argentina in September of that year. She had also just published a book that documented our correspondence and my initial visit to Argentina in the previous year. *Entre tu mano y la mía* (*Between Your Hand and Mine*) was the title and appropriate symbol that cultural friendship and understanding with "the other" can be successfully achieved post-conflict. The annual Córdoba City Book Fair was to be held that month and she had been asked by "La Solapa" (a cultural organisation) if we might be interested in presenting our books jointly at this event. It would be a unique occasion.

But there was something more. Alberto arranged a second meeting between Brigadier-General Menéndez and me. The aim was simple: to keep my promise and present him with a copy of my book. But the retired Brigadier-General did something for me which I was to discover during my visit to General Roca three days later. The General had arranged through the Argentine Army to have Nicolás flown up from Río Gallegos so we could finally meet. This long-awaited meeting took place in Marisa's kitchen on the morning of 20 September 2003. Through an interpreter Nicolás and I talked for a long time. It was then I learnt of the error in my book. For carrying out his rescue of the wounded Jorge Pérez Grandi from the Two Sisters battlefield, Nicolás had indeed been awarded his nation's second highest award for gallantry – the Medal for Valour in Combat.

Nicolás accompanied, next day, Marisa and me to the Córdoba City Book Fair. This event also produced another highly personal meeting for him. When questions were being asked by the large audience at the end of the two book presentations, a woman raised her hand to speak. She stood up. A minute later Nicolás was embraced by her. She was the mother of Jorge Pérez Grandi. Twenty-one years after the war, she had met her son's rescuer at last. This visit will not be my last to Argentina. The next will be to coincide with the Veterans' Malvinas Day Commemoration event in Buenos Aires on 2 April 2007, and is one of numerous other journeys during the twenty-fifth anniversary year of the war that will include the veterans' commemoration parade in London, the South Atlantic Medal Association 82's Pilgrimage to the Islands, and presentation of six lectures about the war and its aftermath aboard the Cunard Liner RMS *Queen Elizabeth 2* which had transported the Gurkhas to the South Atlantic in 1982.

My future writing will be about going to war, battlefield survival, post-conflict cultures, post-traumatic growth, existential authority, traumatic stress, life reconstruction, combat veteran peer support and reconciliation after the Falklands-Malvinas War. Maybe that and the telling of the tale at this colloquium might help those Falklands-Malvinas combat veterans on both sides who still suffer from the dark side of the post-conflict aftermath.

As for Alberto Peralta Ramos, sadly he died in June 2006 but, had he known, would have wholeheartedly approved of the Nottingham colloquium.

References

Seear, M. H. (2003) *With the Gurkhas in the Falklands: A War Journal*, Barnsley, Pen and Sword Books.

Meeting "The Other" in the Post-Conflict 1982-2006

Nicolás Urbieta

My story

To speak about the Malvinas-Falklands conflict after nearly twenty-five years is also to tell of things that perhaps did not happen quite as we recall them, but it does make it possible to analyze the different personal experiences entailed and to examine the positive and the negative in each war veteran in relation to his life then and since.

This was especially so in the case of the British officer, Mike Seear, and for me, because, to begin with, it was not easy for either of us to talk about things that had happened twenty-one years prior to our meeting, and to me the conflict meant, and still means, a feeling which cannot be transmitted nor, indeed, transferred to others. From the start, there were those who grew richer through our pain and impotence, causing many veterans not to speak about their experiences. Those of us who fought and still bear the burden of memory are aware that only God knows what we feel for all those who were left behind and for all those who returned.

I want to highlight that this moment, this presentation, would not have been happening had it not been for a lady who cherishes a feeling for the Malvinas which is as strong as that of any veteran: the writer and author María Isabel Clausen de Bruno, who both defends the Islands and teaches about them like no other.

She taught me that resentment is not a good companion and that I had to change my attitude, that sticking to my hate and rancour, after so many years, had brought and would bring no good, given that after the conflict we all returned to be basically normal and simple persons, with our own ideals and values; that each one has his experiences, that each one defended in his moment what he had to defend, and that I needed to open my heart to a friendship that could appear from out of the distance.

She taught me that this war veteran had the same problems as our veterans and I had had; that he too wanted to be able to close a chapter of his history together with the person who had refused to meet him as another individual for such a long time, and for having felt the mother country in a different way. Today, after many years, the time has come to end this story. I am not giving up our rights, but simply acknowledging that a friendship may be born through understanding Mike Seear as a person like me, who has a family, who is a father, a son and a brother, just as I am, and that in both our memories the shooting and the bombing still resound.

Mike and I are simply friends; if God has given us this possibility, may His will be fulfilled.

My story with the officer Mike Seear

In 1983, five letters that I had posted from the Malvinas and which had never made it to their destination arrived at my billet, shipped by the International Red Cross. Until fourteen years later, I never got to know who had taken the trouble to get these letters back to me. The fact is that it had been Mike Seear who, after those fourteen years, had cared to look into whether I had made it back from the Islands and how I might, eventually, be doing. He even brought back to me some of my personal gear that I had left behind, an act which filled me with happiness. I have treasured it, as I have treasured his great generosity, ever since.

It is because of him, because of this "British Officer Mike", that I then also began to recover part of my history. Even when he travelled to Argentina, I still refused to meet him. However, he then met other veterans and even made friends with some of them.

Nevertheless, he insisted on meeting me, and this encounter was finally made possible through the intervention of Señora María Isabel Clausen de Bruno, who arranged things so that we could meet each other at her home and during a presentation of their books at the Córdoba City Book Fair. Her book *Entre tu mano y la mía* (Between Your Hand and Mine) was written for the veterans, and I was happily surprised when reading its contents and found that much of the experience and many of the feelings of the veterans were synthesised there.

You have already heard from Mike Seear of the full story of that long and obstacle-strewn pursuit of his that eventually brought us together. There are echoes even in the not always easy process that has brought me here today. I do not even know how it was achieved, but here I find myself, amongst comrades, former adversaries and new friends, in an English University.

You will also hear from my former platoon commander, Lieutenant Jorge Pérez Grandi. I can, and shall, add no more to what he has to say about his and my part in the battle of 1982 – except to say that he was, and is, the officer and the human being that would have done no less, and indeed perhaps more, for me or for any of the men under his command and care. It has been an honour for me to have met him again in such very different circumstances and after so many years.

Because We Are Alive!

Jorge Pérez Grandi

Before beginning my story, I would like to thank Mike Seear, who invited me to this event in which, though it is still hard for me to believe, our former enemy on the battlefield is taking part. Also Bernard McGuirk, for choosing the Peruvian name of the painter Juan de la Cruz Machicado for this room in the University. I want to mention here that Peru was the only country to show Argentina unconditional support during the conflict.

I was severely wounded by mortar shrapnel that resulted in several leg fractures, broke my right arm, and started a gaseous gangrene in my left thigh. I was also admitted to, and spent almost one year, in the military hospital at Buenos Aires. I was twenty-two years of age at the time, and did not expect my father would have to hold me again in his arms to help me walk in the same way as when I took my first steps in life. It was hard to get away from my problems and it is still difficult to bear the sequels of war.

I continue fighting – although today I am not in the war – to keep alive and struggle against the 1982 war being with me today, so as to avoid sinking back into 1982. Yet I am here without finding an end to my psychological problems. I know this is not easy, but I will not surrender. I have integrity and strength, thanks to the education received in my home as well as during my military life, and these make me able to talk about my experience.

I try to prevent the problems I bear from the war affecting those I love and live with. At any rate, I try to minimize their effect. It is not easy. I know perfectly well where I am, and where I want my war to follow me without being deprived of the desire to live and to feel useful. Without doubt, we must employ a lot of strength to avoid falling into a void of depression that will gradually suffocate and immerse us in a labyrinth of darkness from which we shall not be able to find the exit and, with it, the hope with which to start a better life.

It is necessary to look at our veterans in order to understand them. It is our families who suffer the most for us. We have a duty not to transmit our problems to them because their suffering is stronger than our anguish. Sometimes we are not aware of the damage we can do when we feel bad. In this sense, I remember very well my mother's words when we were going to the Islands: "You do not know what a son means to his mother!"

To be honest, I did not appreciate those words then. Or, rather, did not appreciate the dimension of their meaning, for I was young and wanted to be in the Islands. Now that I am a father, I understand the scope and value of those words uttered by my mother. We are alive and must keep on fighting so that our previous battles do not bury us in the darkness of the slit trench. I returned and must continue to breathe as before, even though still carrying the weight of the war on my back.

Who failed to have a moment of depression once the conflict was over? All of us suffered, at least almost everyone. Who can boast never to have been through those experiences, or that they do not lie out there in the future? Nevertheless in the many situations where I have felt depressed, I have resorted to the bathroom mirror and begun talking into it, searching for the answers to my questions. After ten or fifteen minutes, I would once again feel well and tell myself, "Don't waste your time, go away and have a drink, you're alive!"

I know that I am alive, but what is the purpose of my life? I know I am still breathing, but what is it that helps me to continue breathing this contaminated air? The answers are not easy, but we must try to feel well. We live and die for the sake of God. Cannot it be that it is God who is asking us for an extra effort, in order to revert to being what we once were? I believe this is correct. In short, it is not easy. On the other hand, my current profession (I am a lawyer now) helps me to feel well too, as do some concepts which I used daily during the war. If you wonder why I do this, it is because I am alive.

Leadership: In my brief professional military experience, I led with a commitment of responsibility over my non-commissioned officers and soldiers. Had I not exercised command over my soldiers in 2 Platoon, I would have died in the Malvinas. Isn't this true, Urbieta? My Corporal, who returned to rescue me, and I am so thankful to him for having saved my life! This is of great use to me daily, for I try to work independently. That is to say, I thrive on imposing my own working conditions while choosing, at the same time, the direction of my professional performance.

Personal example: One should always provide an example, and even more when exercising command. I always knew exactly that if anyone had to die, then the first to go must be the senior rank. When realising that the British troops were about to start their assault and, as I had almost no ammunition left, I began to fall back. Then I met Lieutenant Luis Carlos Martella who asked me what was happening. I replied, "All the English are over-running my position!"

I then asked him, "My Lieutenant, fall back with my soldiers and I will stay here alone to cover the withdrawal." So I took care of this during the first withdrawal when I covered personally my soldiers' retreat and that of Lieutenant Martella. Later, once I met up again with my platoon near C Company's command post at one end of Two Sisters, I spoke to Martella again. But at that very moment I received the order to take under my command Lieutenant Mosquera's 1 Platoon as he had been injured while returning to find out what was happening to me (we were fighting at the time, but they did not realise this). We tried to set up a new defensive position, but after half an hour I received the order to fall back to Major Oscar Jaime at his B Company, 6th Mechanised Infantry Regiment's position. Second-Lieutenant Nazer, who was also wounded by grenade shrapnel, informed me that Martella died on Two Sisters, killed by machine-gun fire. Urbieta fell back before me and I followed him. Just after this I was hit by the mortar bomb shrapnel.

Lying wounded on the ground I saw a white light all around me, a near-death experience. Then I heard a voice: "My Lieutenant, you will not die alone."

It was Barosso, one of my soldiers, who volunteered to stay with me until Urbieta and some other soldiers in my platoon returned some time later to carry me back towards Puerto Argentino and safety. So now I try to apply my personal example daily as a (private) person and a professional. We have to show respect to our veterans and our dead through our own personal actions in our society.

Discipline: I use this as a fundamental factor for achieving an objective. Thanks to my pestering of the sentries, my section positions were never taken by surprise by British troops (of the Royal Marine 45 Commando unit), because we found out in advance when the latter were going to attack. This went well for me because I saved the lives of my soldiers. Returning to my current daily experience, it was, and still is, extremely useful and important to overcome my human weaknesses. From the start, I know that I must keep to my own course of action if I want to be comfortable and useful.

Initiative: This has to be applied rationally and without abuse in order to avoid it being played against one. In many combat situations I analysed the alternatives and consequences, and then decided to risk the odds for the benefit of my platoon. For example, when we started to withdraw by transport via Puerto Argentino from Wall Mountain to the Two Sisters feature, I realised that the logistics were not proceeding according to the planned schedule. Therefore I decided to march to Two Sisters with my soldiers, and we took our backpacks and our own logistical resources and re-started again in the direction of this objective. This resulted in my platoon being the only one to reach the assigned position, whereas the remainder of C Company (of the 4th Infantry Regiment) had to camp at the base of Two Sisters. In projecting myself now as a private person and a professional I also attempt to be proactive towards certain things so as to protect myself from falling into voids of depression.

Another issue related to leadership is fear. So I ask myself, who would not have been scared? By this I mean that certainly beyond our love for the mother country and flag, doubt visits us. Personally, I confess to having felt fear the very moment that the fighting began as I had not imagined it would be so intense and violent. It takes some moments until one gets over this and returns to command and lead one's soldiers. I repeat, it is hard to bear the consequences of war, but we must overcome this and realize we are alive. This is difficult but not impossible. I remember the experiences endured during the war, but try to utilise them and have them help me so as to be kept alive. In my professional life, I always try to apply what I practised during the war. It is for this reason that the practice I like most in my profession is litigation, because then I can compare it with the extreme experiences of a soldier on the battlefield.

Nowadays, when looking back at those extreme moments of our lives during the war, I realize that a part of my life never returned. It just died. I only know that I must continue living and breathing to keep being in my world, but I long to breathe for my country and my flag. It made much sense and was valid to breathe for them (my country and my flag). I do not believe I will breathe that air again. It is more probable that the human misery daily surrounding me in these times is attempting to stop my recovery and leads me to understand that life, no matter how simple, always offers us the chance to live peacefully with ourselves and those we love. I am aware of this, but must continue breathing in order to allow myself the opportunity of being alive and turn the mirror into a friend.

For that reason, whenever I make a toast it is to say "For we are alive!" and then breathe to feel that we will always be given another opportunity.

Post-colloquium note

On 12 January 2007 Jorge Pérez Grandi sent to Mike Seear the following e-mail:

Now I shall probably meet Urbieta next weekend (20 January) because I have organized a veterans' meeting with my platoon soldiers in La Esquina, Province of Corrientes. I am taking a couple days free. My goal is to find Barroso (the soldier who was with me when I was wounded). He did not leave me and stayed with me until Urbieta came back and took me to Puerto Argentino. I never saw Barroso again after the war.

Culture in Battle: 2nd Battalion, Scots Guards
at Tumbledown Mountain – 14 June 1982

Mike Scott

Before looking at culture in battle, it is, I think, important to paint a backcloth of the culture of the British which, of course, underpins all that we do, including fighting in a war. What is that? Fish and chips, roast beef, the Beatles, cricket, the Royal Family, James Bond, the pub, the last night of the Proms, or poppies on Remembrance Sunday? However, you might think all that is a little superficial and we should dig deeper. Although multi-culturalism has been much in the news in this country of late, in truth the British Isles have been multi-cultural since the earliest arrivals of Celts, Vikings, Romans, Saxons, the Norman French and so on. We are the people of an Island comprising English, Irish, Scottish and Welsh nationalities – and I have deliberately put those in alphabetical order! These four nations share a great deal, but each has its own ideas of identity and particular cultural heritage. Our long history, our geography and our weather are but three examples of major contributors to our culture.

But the average inhabitant of the United Kingdom, despite his well-developed sense of humour, attaches enormous importance to his equally well-developed sense of fairness. When roused, he will stand up with thousands of others to demand what is fair and, if he has to, fight for it.

While not critical to the outcome of any tactical battle, success in war is largely dependent on belief in the justification for conflict and support of the home population. In the case of the Falklands Conflict, while historians and academics could argue the ownership rights of the Islands, there was no doubt, in the minds of the British general public, including the Armed Forces, that the Falkland Islands were a dependency of the United Kingdom. The Islanders did not see themselves as an offshore province of Argentina. Galtieri's troops were a force occupying against their will and Britain had a contract to defend them. So my first point on culture in battle is that all my soldiers understood and believed in the cause for which they were to fight.

My Regiment is composed of volunteer professional soldiers. The normal contract for a warrant officer or non-commissioned officer (NCO) can be up to twenty-two years, so senior ranks in my Battalion had served for many years. Officers can serve in a battalion up to the rank of Lieutenant-Colonel. I was forty-one years old in 1982, but did not retire from the British Army until the age of fifty-five. (Mind you, the average age of my Guardsmen was only twenty-two).

We are also a family Regiment. Often men follow their fathers or brothers into the Regiment and some have forbears going back to the Battle of Waterloo in 1815. Officers and soldiers who have served together for years know each other very well and establish a close relationship seldom understood by those outside. All this combines to create an insuperable strength and depth of confidence in each other. My second point therefore is the inestimable value of a disciplined and tightly bonded team to which every individual feels a profound sense both of duty and of personal loyalty. This is a battle-winning factor.

We are a Regiment proud of our traditions and our close affiliation to the British Royal Family. We are jealous of our privilege of guarding the Sovereign and, because of our ceremonial public duties in London, we have less time for tactical training than other units. While this is an obvious disadvantage, it does not prevent us from carrying out our operational tour responsibilities. In the years prior to 1982 we had had long periods of counter-terrorism operations in Northern Ireland. We were not as physically fit, nor as well-trained for war-fighting, as the Parachute Regiment or Royal Marine Commandos, but then they are specialist shock troops, expensively and specifically trained for impact operations. While our critics sometime see our lack of training or physical fitness as an inadequacy, I have yet to meet anyone who has suggested that more fitness or training would have altered the final outcome of the Battle of Tumbledown. In practice, our considerable experience of Northern Ireland operations, highly dependent on low-level section and platoon command tactics, leads to my third point. Whilst the minute-to-minute requirements of a full-scale night Battalion deliberate attack and ensuing battle might be different, all my junior commanders – from the Majors commanding companies of about 100 Guardsmen, down to the Corporals commanding perhaps only three or four Guardsmen – were self-confident, trusted by those under their command, and used to making quick decisions on their own.

While the plan and execution of our attack on Tumbledown is now well known, what is less apparent is that its strength lay in the fact that it was designed, considered, and enthusiastically endorsed by my command team. It was not, therefore, a plan autocratically imposed by me. It was, however, my responsibility to persuade the 5 Infantry Brigade Commander, who originally had some different ideas, to approve it. My fourth point then is that we have a very well rehearsed system for planning, and an equally well-practised system for ensuring that the plan, once agreed, is known and understood by all. Every man knew what was expected of him immediately prior to the Tumbledown battle.

It goes without saying that leadership, my fifth and final point, is vital. In this battle, once contact was made, it became the company and platoon commanders' operation, coupled with the efforts of their NCOs. My influence on the battle was, in the end, reduced to adapting the direct and indirect fire support, encouraging and guiding the company commanders, maintaining a deployable reserve, anticipating alternatives if things went wrong, and keeping the Brigadier calm! Our records of the battle demonstrate our commitment to leadership from the front at all levels. Overall, we suffered eight dead and forty wounded – over fifty percent of these casualties were officers, warrant officers and NCOs.

A final brief word on the aftermath, although I realise it is being examined at this University International Colloquium in much more detail and depth. We acquired considerable self-confidence, personally and militarily, having succeeded in accomplishing a difficult battalion-level night attack of a scale not seen since the Korean War, which had occurred some thirty years before. The six weeks in which we were left behind in the Falklands after the war, whilst difficult and frustrating, had the long-term advantage that we bonded even closer together. Platoon commanders were accommodated with their men. We had no family or media intrusion. Camaraderie, at a level no other experience can create, was established amongst those who had seen real battle at close quarters. These important bonds were made which will last for the rest of our lives. When we returned to the United Kingdom there was not for us any of the swaggering *braggadocio* of the conquering hero, but the quiet confidence that we, and others, knew our worth. We resumed our duties and got on with life.

In conclusion, I am intensely proud of all the men of my Battalion. They are the true inheritors of those who defended Hougoumont.

Summary of the Actions of the 5th Marine Infantry Battalion Ec. (BIM5) in the Malvinas Conflict

Carlos Hugo Robacio

Once the Malvinas were re-taken by the Amphibious Task Force, the Landing Force returned immediately to the mainland, leaving behind a small garrison of the Argentine Army. Meanwhile the national government began handling the crisis with the clear intention of discussing seriously and through diplomatic channels the litigation of sovereignty between both contenders. Sadly the British Government put all its effort into recovering the archipelago through force of arms. This required the reinforcement of the garrison that had been left behind, for which the 5th Marine Infantry Battalion (BIM5) was deployed in addition to other units belonging to the Army, Air Force and the Navy.

The unit arrived on 8 April 1982 and, with the purpose of providing direct support to BIM5, B Battery of the BIAC and a platoon of Amphibious Engineers was added later, as was a 12.7mm Machine Gun Company of which a single platoon was assigned. On 16 April, the definitive defence order was distributed to the unit, assigning responsibility over Mounts Tumbledown and William, and Sapper Hill. O (-) Company was constituted as a reserve and prepared for counter-attacks on these features. The positions were occupied from the first day of arrival, given the capacity of the British Task Force for executing large incursions.

The baptism of fire began at dawn on 1 May 1982, and there was one fatality and five wounded on Sapper Hill from naval support fire. From 15 May, naval bombardments and naval aircraft attacks grew more intense, with ground-based shelling being added later. The logistic suffocation of the unit increased because both sea and air were in possession of the attacking naval force. The landing at San Carlos took place on 21 May 1982 and the duel between patrols from each side began. As elements of the coastal defence, and to raise morale by acquiring firepower to respond to the enemy's bombing, an Exocet launching ramp was incorporated, as well as 155mm Sofma guns.

On 5 June as the Battalion's area of responsibility was increased, O (-) Company was detached forward to the area of Pony's Pass to set up a delaying battle to interdict the line of approach through Mount Harriet and Sapper Hill into the town (of Puerto Argentino). During the night of 11 June, the first phase began on the heights of Mount Harriet, Two Sisters and Mount Longdon, all of which were attacked by the Royal Marine Brigade and 3 Para.

BIM5 was then in the front line as the remaining troops fell back to Puerto Argentino and only some men voluntarily joined the Battalion, as was the case of Army Second-Lieutenant Silva and five conscripts, who would fight alongside 4 Platoon in the Tumbledown. Attention has to be drawn to an inexplicable diversionary attack in the direction of Mount William which was against the pattern of doing this at night. Performed during last light on 13 June, the attacking sub-unit was (according to us) practically annihilated by fire from our defensive locations.

It is worth mentioning that BIM5 both integrated and directed supporting fire from the two Army Artillery Battalions who provided total and indiscriminate support at critical moments of the battle. On the other hand, B Company of 6th Infantry Regiment, which linked the rear of Two Sisters with the troops on Longdon, and should have fallen back to the Tumbledown's western salient, unfortunately did this some kilometres to the east, thus weakening the anticipated plan for the defence of Mount Tumbledown which had already been co-ordinated and laid out. Nothing was done by higher command to correct this error, leaving those troops to cover Moody Valley.

During the night of 13-14 June the attacking forces set out on their final offensive from the south-west at approximately 22.15 hours. On the one hand they did it straddling the road running south of Mount Harriet that leads directly to Puerto Argentino, and on the other they did it going directly over the Tumbledown where it coincided with the positions of 4 Platoon, N Company, BIM5. Initially the attack was repulsed and restrained by bloody and intensive fighting with well-coordinated fire support on the attacking sub-units and determined action from the men of O (-) Company – until finally the latter was ordered to initiate a withdrawal and re-group in the proximity of the Battalion's command post, thereby allowing freedom to M Company, BIM5 and permitting us to carry out all our efforts on the Tumbledown. This was possible since C   (-) Company of the Army's 3rd Infantry Regiment – which had been put under BIM5's command – flanked the access to the attacking forces that straddled the road.

Meanwhile 4 Platoon was being attacked in the Tumbledown by the Scot Guards and managed to repulse the latter's first attack. Combat at this position would, within hours, acquire a totally epic meaning for both contenders. There was long and fierce fighting there. The Scots Guards Battalion assaulted and then retreated time and time again, concentrating their effort on the heroic 4 Platoon. They fought hand to hand with grenades and using everything that was available. Fire support from both sides was accurate. 4 Platoon was still resisting, their men would shout out victory and challenging words as they repulsed the first attacks. At dawn the assault continued with the Scots Guards pouring over our positions and beyond. The platoon commander called for friendly shelling onto his positions to stop the advancing attack, and requested a counter-attack to restore his position. Troops from another Argentine Marine platoon and one from the Army were thrown in, without achieving the success expected due to the prevailing situation. The attitude and aptitude of this platoon commander, as well as those of his men, turned them into role models. The commander, for leading his men in combat, personally engaging in the greater risks and contributing with his fighting spirit, made his subordinates fight decisively. These men are an example that the Marines must treasure with pride.

To the North, across the Moody Brook, the attack of 2 Para had neutralised the remaining positions of the 7th Infantry Regiment, thus threatening – along with 3 Para – our logistics area and command post.

At about 03.00 hours a counter-attack was considered using M and O (-) Companies. This possibility was refused by order of our higher command, thus preventing our last possibility for breaking the assault. At about 05.00 hours the assault was re-initiated in an intense and brutal way in spite of the shelling of our own positions. This was interrupted when 4 Platoon exhausted its ammunition and lost part of its force. Once the Scots Guards held on fast in the Tumbledown, the 7th Gurkhas climbed to attack Mount William and take the 81mm mortars.

At 06.15 hours on 14 June, the Battalion received the order to fall back to Puerto Argentino. It did not do this. Relevant orders were issued to cease combat and fall back on Sapper Hill to establish – given the remaining ammunition of M Company/BIM5 – the last defence. This was achieved approximately at 11.00 hours when new intentions to surrender were received from higher command. This happened at around 13.00/14.00 hours. The Battalion entered Puerto Argentino, marching past with arms at the shoulder, leaving a sixteen-strong rearguard on Sapper Hill with two general purpose machine guns (MAG) and a 12.7 mm Browning heavy machine gun. These made contact with an enemy wave of approximately six helicopters, and such were the circumstances in which the final combat took place.

Thus ended the action of a unit which – although trained to attack – had to fight in the heart of the defence at the Battle for Puerto Argentino.

The Close-Quarter Battle: Right Flank Company, 2nd Battalion, Scots Guards on Tumbledown Mountain – 13-14 June 1982

Simon Price

General

Close-quarter fighting at night is amongst the most challenging of tasks that an infantry sub-unit can be called upon to undertake in war. Add to that the immensely difficult terrain of the Tumbledown and, in particular, the crag and rock terrain of its eastern summit, combined with poor communications and lack of training in night attacks, then all these factors resulted in a task that confronted the Guardsmen of 2nd Battalion, the Scots Guards as being one of gargantuan proportions. The difficulties were further compounded on that 13-14 June night of the Scots Guards' assault by a most inhospitable austral winter climate of a force six wind with snow and temperature of minus six degrees centigrade which, when combined, meant soldiers were being exposed to a dangerous chill factor of minus twenty-two degrees centigrade.

What then were the factors that enabled the Battalion to be so successful in its night attack against the Argentine 5th Marine Infantry Battalion and some other sub-units of the Argentine Army? Using the story of Right Flank Company's deliberate third and final phase attack of the Battalion's difficult night battle, some of the key ingredients will be identified that led to an eventually successful outcome to the operation after brutal fighting.

Clear orders

At night the unexpected invariably occurs in a close-quarter battle. A tactical system is essential to overcome this problem and enable more junior commanders at platoon and section level to work around apparently insurmountable obstacles and then be able to exploit the ensuing opportunities. Today all these procedures are encapsulated in the British Army's concept of "Mission Command". Back in 1982 such a concept was not as clearly articulated. In Right Flank Company's night battle the final objective could not be viewed from the Scots Guards' positions near the Mount Harriet area because it was in complete dead ground to the observer. The consequence was that a final assault plan could not be presented at the formal Right Flank Company Orders Group for this particular deliberate company night attack prior to the Battalion's tactical advance to battle on the entire Tumbledown feature. To obviate this potentially damaging shortfall, a much fuller than normal "Concept of Operations" was given out which stipulated, unless countermanded later during the battle, what the Company Commander expected from each platoon commander and his platoon on arrival at the Company's final objective on the Tumbledown's eastern end.

Decisive leadership

Uncertainty in battle is one condition that any commander, whether it be at battalion, company, platoon or section level, simply cannot afford to have within his unit or sub-unit. It is, by far, better to do something, even if it is wrong or perhaps unconventional at the time and in the unbelievably noisy chaos of an infantry night battle, than to be indecisive and do nothing at all. This was personified by Sergeant Robert Jackson's individual hand-grenade attack on an enemy machine-gun nest perched high in the rocks. The senior NCO discarded his Self-Loading Rifle and climbed up a rock pinnacle to a position that overlooked this enemy position so as to throw a number of grenades accurately onto it and thus neutralise its effectiveness. Right Flank Company's battle provided a number of other outstanding examples in which such leadership, at all levels, enabled difficult obstacles to be overcome and ensuing situations exploited to the best possible advantage.

Surprise
Surprise during any battle, whether it takes place during daylight or at night, is quoted often as being a "battle-winning factor". It is believed that Right Flank Company's battle produced one such example when the Royal Artillery's gunfire support that had been promised for the Company's assault became unexpectedly unavailable at a crucial point in the fighting. The resulting action, to the best of my knowledge, led to the Company having to conduct the only British infantry assault on an enemy Argentine objective without any higher-level supporting fire of any type in the entire Falklands War. Paradoxically this, in turn, resulted in the enemy being taken completely by surprise as to exactly when the Company's final assault would take place.

Maintenance of the momentum
This key principle was amply demonstrated during Right Flank Company's battle. During the initial lodgement onto the objective, and when the Company's momentum became stalled due to Argentine defensive placements that had been cleverly located, the Company Commander had to intervene personally on the first of three such occasions so as to restore momentum to the Company's attack. If this had not been done then Right Flank's attack might well have continued to stall throughout the valuable remaining limited time of darkness available. Obviously the latter is a key advantage to any attacking unit that wishes to maintain an effective assault on the enemy. The arrival of first light and then subsequent gradual increase of daylight would have probably started to work in the enemy's favour.

The Company Commander's intervention was required a second time when 2 Platoon became pinned down by a small group of the enemy in the central group of crags within the final objective. Then, when Lieutenant Robert Lawrence received a serious head wound from an enemy sniper bullet as he led his platoon in a decisive right-flanking attack on enemy Marine positions, the third and final Company Commander intervention was needed in order to resolve this difficult situation and, once more, regain the all-important sub-unit's momentum of their assault.

Teamwork

At night, and during the noise and chaos of close-quarter battle when vision is restricted to a bare couple of metres, both teamwork and confidence in your fellow soldiers, junior commanders and more senior commanders is absolutely essential for success. This final phase of the Battalion's battle was eventually reduced to pairs of men carrying out basic infantry fire and movement attacks on enemy dug-in defensive positions. Such a tactic was loosely, but successfully, controlled by both Section and Platoon Commanders. Effective teamwork and confidence in each other's abilities enabled such dispersed action to succeed against enemy bunker positions which had been prepared thoroughly by the Argentine Marines for sixty-seven days prior to the Scots Guards' assault. Such were the strength of these enemy bunkers that the Argentine casualties from the Royal Navy and Royal Artillery bombardments and British Harrier aircraft air strikes as from 1 May were exceptionally limited prior to the Battalion's assault in the final twenty-four hours of the campaign

Trained commanders

Primarily due to its traditional ceremonial role of London Public Duties, the Household Division also has had an accompanying tradition of obeying orders quickly and accurately. This stood the Battalion and Right Flank Company in good stead during the Tumbledown battle. When this asset is combined with properly trained and highly-capable junior officers and non-commissioned officers, then the result is that Guardsmen are capable of applying their basic skills to areas they are either not well-versed in, or have not been trained to tackle. The Battle of Tumbledown was just such an occasion which the Battalion, including Right Flank, had never been trained for or carried out such a conventional and complex operation. However, because the unit had confidence in its commanders at all levels, all sub-units were most effective when the moment of truth arrived and they were put through a gruelling test of stamina and courage.

Artillery

The effective use of artillery is essential in limiting one's own side's casualties and, on the other hand, unbalancing and thereby neutralising an enemy in their defensive positions. Lack of artillery, when initially requested on the Tumbledown by Right Flank Company, triggered a major alteration in the Company's battle plan. Also there was uncalled for, or misdirected, British artillery fire that almost caused a major "blue-on-blue" incident and significant own Right Flank casualties. On the credit side, however, the failure of effective Argentine artillery made our troops' tasks infinitely easier. As a final point, the effective use of accurately controlled artillery fire from Right Flank's newly won defensive positions onto the Moody Valley area immediately west of the capital of Stanley, contributed to bringing the war to a rapid conclusion. It also probably saved many lives – both British and Argentine.

Tumbledown and Mount William

Eduardo Villarraza

The 5th Marine Infantry Battalion (BIM5) – and therefore its N Company of which I was the Company Commander – was made up of both enlisted men and conscripts, the latter having been called up after their eighteenth birthday to fulfill the mandatory military duties required by law in Argentina at the time of these facts. N Company consisted of ten percent enlisted personnel and ninety percent conscripts. The enlisted personnel held the command appointments, except for a few cases in which these were held by outstanding conscripts because of a shortfall in regular military personnel.

In terms of training, N Company had achieved a high standard aided by the fact that it was possible for us to carry out training in different environments and extreme conditions, for Tierra del Fuego is a region with a very cold climate, steppes and mountains, dense woods and trees of great height. The terrain includes large lakes and it is surrounded by sea. N Company also had access and proximity to different terrains suitable for exercises and the use of ground, airborne and naval artillery. The strong focus of the training plan developed in 1981 called for a large number of out-of-barrack days, with multiple exercises at Battalion level which included support weapons firing live ammunition, exercises with naval gunfire support and attack aircraft providing fire support.

Deployment and defence planning

Given the distribution of the units in the proximity of Puerto Argentino and the organization of the defensive system, the (Joint) Argentine Command was convinced that the British offensive would come from the sea and that there would be landings on the southern coast. This idea was not shared neither by us nor by the Commanding Officer of BIM5, for as Marines we knew that landing on a defended coast is extremely costly and we were also aware of what it takes to establish military presence starting from zero and then launch operations. Furthermore, the CO of BIM5 alerted the (Joint) Argentine Command that British troops would seek to land anywhere on Soledad Island (East Falkland) and then execute their attack from their land bridgehead. Indeed the British manoeuvre was developed based on this concept.

In spite of the addition of regiments – particularly Infantry Regiments – the area of responsibility and the sectors assigned to BIM5 were never modified, the exception being the role of O Company which was originally deployed onto Mount Longdon. This Company was relieved by the 7th Infantry Regiment and the Battalion then recovered it so as to form a reserve. With the addition of C Company (Fusiliers) of the 3rd Infantry Regiment placed next to M Company at their position between Sapper Hill and Mount William, N Company adopted its final defensive system by occupying Mounts Tumbledown and William with a tactical area of responsibility covering from the edge of the sea up to Moody Valley.

The final defence organization was drawn with 1st Platoon located south-west of Mount William, 2nd Platoon north-west of Mount William and south of Tumbledown, and 3rd Platoon north-east of Tumbledown. Each of these units consisted of three infantry rifle sections of thirteen men each, a nine-man group of machine guns (7.62 mm) with a platoon commander and two to four additional men to man the communications and act, if so required, as medical assistants. This added up to a total of fifty-two or fifty-four men. In addition there was a 60mm mortar group with three mortars that consisted of fifteen to eighteen men located in an area to the east of Tumbledown; an 81mm mortar group (six mortars) north-east of Mount William at a location roughly equidistant between the latter and Tumbledown, and N Company Headquarters located on the east end of Tumbledown; plus Communications and logistics personnel and a medical assistant, and a rocket launcher group of four men. This last group was placed under the command of N Company Headquarters and could be used wherever a threat materialized which was suitable for a counter-attack by these weapons.

This disposition answered to the initial plan set up with organic means, i.e. personnel and weapons. Afterwards, using the reinforcements received, weapons and troops were placed in the following sectors: a 105mm Recoilless Gun Group with two weapons, a Bantam Missile Group with two launchers, and a 12.7mm Browning Machine Gun Group were placed at Mount William and 4th Platoon, consisting of a well-trained Battalion Scout Group of approximately twelve men, and another group commanded by a Sergeant-Major (approximately ten men with limited training, for they belonged to the logistics sub-unit) took positions at the western end of the Tumbledown.

Altogether this amounted to about twenty-five men. They were armed with assault rifles, an automatic rifle (FAP), two 7.62mm general purpose machine guns (MAG) and one 60mm mortar. Although all were Marines the composition of the platoon was not organic, and therefore their training had not been systematized or included in the rest of N Company's training. There was also a sub-unit of Amphibious Engineers of about twenty-five men who would fight in their infantry role.

The total personnel of N Company plus its reinforcements added up to about two hundred and fifty men. The first tasks implemented were to place the weapons according to their selected main and secondary firing directions, the construction of their positions and, as a final item, the construction of shelters for the men. It is worth pointing out that in spite of the short time we had available for this task, excellent shelters and positions were built which were soon to prove their worth once the British attack and the bombing began.

A fact which also needs to be highlighted is the structure of the communications system at Company level, as well as that at Battalion level, for between landline and radio links we managed virtually to triple the circuits. Seven kilometers of cable were used by N Company alone to establish landline communications. Another important point to emphasize is the amount of ammunition issued per weapon, which was calculated at about twenty to twenty-five days supply depending on the weapon system. With regard to rations and because of the scheme adopted, hot food was distributed in the form of three daily meals until noon on 13 June.

Operations Begin

On 1 May the British forces began their operations with air and naval bombing. Since my position was located on one of the relevant heights I was able to observe with absolute clearness the moment when the first warships of the Royal Navy appeared on the horizon sailing in from the east, the naval gunfire support they executed from their southern flank and the Argentine aircraft raids that were launched against them. From this day (1 May) on, naval bombardments were carried out systematically and would take place nightly . Although not effective in relation to the losses they produced, at least within BIM5, they nevertheless resulted inan understandable mental wearing-down of our personnel, for it was impossible to know when they would take place or what area they would target.

On the tactical side, one of my main worries from the beginning up to the very end of the operations was the extension of the front assigned to N Company which, if judged by its dimensions and terrain features, should have been taken up by the Battalion. So extensive was this front for the three platoons I had available that it was not only hardly possible to cover it visually from a standing point, but nor did it allow for the establishment of a minimum reserve force. All this made it extremely difficult to defend and questions may arise as to why was it like that: a logical action would have been to occupy and maintain the main heights, but doing this would have opened very extensive distances between them. As a result of this, the British forces would have attacked our positions from the rear placing fixed weapons on the heights and then perform surrounding manoeuvres with serious consequences for our troops. On the other hand, we were convinced from the first moment

that operations would be carried out during the night. We were not mistaken. An intermediate solution was then chosen with the idea of employing mutual support between platoons or receiving support from the Battalion. Once the attack of 11-12 June on the Argentine troops placed at Mount Harriet and Two Sisters took place, I had not the slightest doubt about it continuing immediately onto our positions; neither did I have any doubts that it would happen during the night.

The battle

On the morning of 13 June I gathered my junior commanders together. I was sure the enemy would attack that night and that this could possibly be the last time I would see some of my subordinates. But, thank God, this did not happen. I conveyed my message to them saying that the moment had now come to show what we really were and what we Marines were worth. I also said that a praiseworthy performance was expected in the hours of combat to come. From that evening of 13 June onwards, firing grew more and more intense. I believe that we were attacked in the Mount William-Tumbledown area by several thousand projectiles since five artillery batteries, two ships and the mortars of the Gurkhas and 42nd Commando supported the assault on our positions. According to information collected from different media, some 14,000 rounds of ammunition of high-calibre weapons (mortars, artillery, and naval gunfire support) were fired.

At approximately 22.30 hours (local time) Lieutenant Vázquez of 4th Platoon informed me that he was being attacked by British troops and the situation was confusing because his forces were becoming intermingled with the British. At around 24.00 hours, the Engineer subunit began its withdrawal towards the East, but communications with 4th Platoon to co-ordinate actions between the two sub-units could not be established as planned. Given the intensity of the fight, Lieutenant Vázquez requested friendly fire over his position, which was provided by both the Company's 81mm and 60mm mortars. At approximately 01.30 hours I was informed the fighting had stopped.

Battalion Headquarters was kept permanently informed, and due to developments in the fight, ordered M Company to prepare for a counter-attack. This was not carried out. At approximately 02.00 hours, a new offensive began on 4th Platoon's positions. The situation became very complicated for them because the British troops had taken positions to their rear. Mortar and artillery rounds were ordered again onto the platoon's position, reinforcements for M Company were required once again, and the Engineer sub-unit was sent away to support them. At this point an Argentine Army sub-unit of about twenty men arrived, commanded by Second-Lieutenant Lamadrid.

Neither this nor the Engineer sub-unit could make it to the position occupied by 4th Platoon for, after having advanced half the way, they met British troops who stopped them.

Therefore between 02.00 hours and 03.00 hours on 14 June, the situation was that 4th Platoon had been engaged at the eastern end of Tumbledown without being able to break contact. The Engineer sub-unit was still in the Tumbledown and in contact with British troops, but found itself unable to advance. 1st and 2nd Platoons were at Mount William, with limited possibility of being used due to a concrete threat from Mount Harriet and Pony's Pass after fighting had taken place in that area a few hours before. We knew that on the northern flank there were no more Argentine troops, as we had heard on the radio that the 7th Infantry Regiment had fallen back with a great number of personnel heading towards the town. Lastly, M Company remained in its position and had not initiated any movement. The conclusion was that the last line of defence towards the west comprised N Company and that it was being penetrated. I took the decision therefore to hold the position for as long as it was possible.

This was the situation when at about 06.00 hours Lieutenant Vázquez informed me that he could not hold his position anymore and was about to surrender. It was then that I realised we had a short time to remain in the Tumbledown. Meanwhile the Engineers, the Company's mortar groups and Army sub-unit were engaging British troops. The latter exerted so strong a pressure that they forced our troops to fall back towards the eastern end of Tumbledown. Between 08.00 hours and 08.30 hours, it had already become impossible to hold the Tumbledown and I ordered the withdrawal to start. It did so in a somewhat disorganized way but, after the line had retreated a few metres, the commanders were able to regain control over their subunits. At this point we were having problems communicating with 1st and 2nd Platoons, which were then ordered from Battalion Headquarters to fall back onto Sapper Hill, this marking therefore the end of N Company's actions.

Conclusion
From my point of view, the following factors accounted for N Company's overcome:

- The front that N Company had been assigned to cover was extremely large when, in fact, that sector should have been the entire Battalion's responsibility.
- The main effort of the defence was originally pointed towards the southern coast of our area, thus weakening the defensive positions towards the west.
- The defensive system always gave the initiative to the British troops, therefore everything the Company was called upon to doamounted , in reality, only to just sit and wait.
- The defensive system was, in general terms, static. We lacked mobility and this, in practical terms, prevented any offensive operations from being carried out, especially counter-attacks.

On the other hand, I believe the following to have been positive aspects of the defence:

- The high degree of training the Battalion had achieved during the previous years and its ability to operate in cold weather.
- As a result of this training, the significant confidence which permeated throughout the chain of command, with superiors and subordinates trusting each other in the roles to which each had been appointed.
- The construction of effective defensive positions.
- The guidance which platoon commanders, at all levels, exerted over their personnel.
- The excellent communications system which allowed the continuous exercise of appropriate leadership over sub-units on the basis of precise and timely information.

As a conclusion, it might be stated that although ninety percent of the Battalion's troops were conscripts, its performance demonstrates that effective combat-ready units can be achieved through suitable training in techniques, tactics and use of weapons, and, most importantly, through appropriate leadership.

2nd Battalion, Scots Guards – The Tumbledown Legacy

Alan Warsap

Introduction

It is close to twenty-five years since the Falklands-Malvinas War. My personal, retrospective observations are made not only from the events of 1982, but are influenced by fifty years of involvement with the British Army from 1954 until 2004. This contact has included time as an Army General Practicioner, Regimental Medical Officer (RMO) and, lastly, as the President of an Army Medical Board responsible for examining, grading and sometimes medically discharging many men and women from service. An increasing number of boards involve at least some element of mental ill-health, mainly in men who had served in Bosnia and the Gulf War. Even today, working for The Tribunals Service, I still have contact with the medical and social problems of ex-servicemen.

As for the 2nd Battalion, Scots Guards' medical arrangements and training, I acknowledge the full support received from my Commanding Officer, the then Lieutenant-Colonel Mike Scott, my Medical Senior Non-Commissioned Officer, Colour-Sergeant Baird and our Padre, the Reverend Angus Smith. At the time of the Falklands I was, in addition to being the Battalion's RMO, on the staff of the Royal Army Medical College. The Professor of Military Psychiatry at the College was the then Colonel Peter Abraham. He guided me as to what might be possible with regard to the recognition and management of immediate battle shock casualties. This information I shared with my CO and, having just been warned for Falklands duty, it focussed our minds.

The Falklands

On Tumbledown during the night and morning of 13-14 June 1982, eight Scots Guardsmen and a Royal Engineer were killed or reported missing and forty wounded. Psychological casualties at that stage were virtually invisible, or at least battle-shock had not led to defeat. I recall only three possible battle-shock casualties at this early stage, one not of our unit, and one who recovered so quickly that he was an efficient soldier for the rest of the battle and afterwards. The third cannot be discussed – even now. He did not engage with any part of our unit medical team, but may well have been such a casualty. After post-tour leave I recall one Junior NCO who exhibited classical symptoms of post battle stress adjustment reaction. He declined psychiatric referral – I hope he did well.

Recently I was encouraged to hear from retired Commodore Toby Elliott from the Ex-Servicemen's Mental Health Society and "Combat Stress" organisation that of the eight hundred servicemen from the Falklands conflict known to him, only four were ex-Scots Guardsmen (Elliott, 2006). However I am now aware that everyone, including myself, probably sustained a highly variable permanent mental scarring. In many this is dormant, but can be activated by life events in the future. What hides this scar is the great variability of individuals to cope with the mental damage sustained.

The natural tendency in many to deny or unconsciously suppress the psychological effects of battle trauma is what medical and command authority is unwittingly endorsing (and I understand this). As a result stoicism is mistaken for absence of mental scarring and only manifest psychiatric illness acknowledged. Variability in individual soldiers' reactions to the same battle trauma is mistakenly seized on to deny that mental scarring has occurred. For example, a heavy mortar round bursts near to and equidistant from two soldiers. One with poor resilience has a life dogged by intermittent mental ill health and dependency, often with a war disability pension to help support him. His comrade may appear at first successfully to have avoided mental scarring only to suffer partially hidden handicaps of suppressed symptoms which may or may not break through into mental ill health later in life. Variability is such that it is not unknown to me that some soldiers claim traumatic events in their careers that they have not witnessed themselves but heard about from comrades. They cannot identify what makes them now feel different but feel altered by their experiences compared to the person they used to be.

I emphasise the great importance attached to the psychotherapeutic benefit gained by everyone in the Battalion from the opportunity to "wind-down" collectively after the battle as the unit rested up in the sheep sheds at Fitzroy. Here, all ranks were jammed together out of the wind for about three days. We then spent long weeks, less closely confined, but still very much together in sub-units on a ship, and then on garrison duty on West Falkland at Port Howard. We travelled back to UK, still all together, by ship to Ascension Island, and then flew back to post-tour leave.

The dominating medical condition we had to deal with after 13-14 June was, for many, the pain and disability of trench foot. All through that time until we returned from leave "sick parade" numbers were very low indeed, apart from the trench foot. There were no psychological casualties at this time – that is, none were evident. Late on 14 June, after the ceasefire, our Regimental Aid Post (RAP) treated some dozen Argentinian soldiers for minor injuries on their way back to a holding facility in Stanley. I saw many acts of spontaneous kindness shown to them by our Guardsmen.

From the RAP on Goat Ridge on the morning of 14 June, during hostilities, elements of the RAP staff and I went forward in a Navy Sea King helicopter to start the casualty pick-up. As we took off we crossed the Gurkha mortar line which was close by and preparing to fire on a forward target, probably Mount William. The mortars erupted, and at least one mortar bomb must have passed through the helicopter's rotor blade motion. We picked up, I believe, seven or eight Gurkha casualties. All were semi-comatose, sleep deprivation combining with the pain of their wounds. They were typically stoical, and we took them to the 16 Field Ambulance Advanced Dressing Station at Fitzroy. At this point helicopter evacuation formally ceased. Friendly-fire incidents, inevitable in war, take their own special toll – and we had been lucky to escape such a fate on this occasion.

Lessons learned

Medical first-aid training for everyone, bolted on to all the pre-operational work-up training, was most important. It was realistic and often confrontational, including the practising of burials and watching uncut films of casualties from the Vietnam War. This latter was the idea of the then Captain Tim Spicer, our Operations and Training Officer. With this the men were made first-aid reliant in pairs and small groups. However, it is important to de-select for combat any soldier with unresolved mental health or drugs problems, and also only fair to inform recruits about the full military significance for them of voluntary service in the Army.

Casualty evacuation plans must be very flexible and always a primary command responsibility. Delayed evacuation was inevitable, depending as it did on scarce helicopter availability. Here, the sustaining treatment given by the Pipes and Drums Platoon first-aid trainers was of key importance, embedded as they were in all sub-units. The extent of long term mental scarring and acute shell-shock, that is, battle-immediate casualties, is directly related to the number of physical casualties and the intensity and character of the conflict.

Following the initial shock-effects of battle from fear, fatigue, explosions and sights, there follows a degree of 'post-battle adjustment reaction' for weeks and months afterwards, characterised by over-arousal feelings, family and social maladjustment, anger and aggressiveness. Our CO warned the Battalion about such difficulties before we all dispersed on leave. It helped us recognise such reactions as almost normal, and to be expected, when irrational anger welled up in the post-battle months. "If you feel angry you have nothing to prove," I remember the CO saying. After battle and trauma you cannot help but experience irrational extreme irritation to the point of violence with the seemingly trivial concerns of those at home in the United Kingdom.

I now know, years later, that there is further, hitherto hidden mental damage for some to live with when post-battle mental damage leads to a tendency to develop ordinary mental illness in those vulnerable: I mean depression, suicide and even violent and criminal behaviour. Other burdens include alcoholism, drug misuse, family breakdown, nightmares, flashbacks, unemployment and destitution in extreme cases. Long-term, past exposure to battle seems to facilitate the early development of mental ill-health which might, anyway, have surfaced in the fullness of time in some subjects.

I recommend that the way to reduce battle stress in all its forms, short- and long-term, is to be found in the example of 2nd Battalion, Scots Guards: that is, allowing for a wind-down period to be made possible after high intensity warfare, perhaps along the formula of three days' whole unit close-proximity living, resting, hearing how others got on, how they feel and their worries, talking through guilt and blame together, self-directed and in no way structured. This should be followed by three weeks' less intensive interaction and debriefing. It would be helpful at this time for officers to brief the whole unit on how the operation or battle worked out (or otherwise) overall. Let everyone view the big picture so that the individual can understand how his contribution fitted in. At the same time,   reassure the men that their contribution did help their fellow soldiers.

There should then be a total period of three months away from the end of hostilities, to include post-tour leave, in which soldiers should be relieved of any serious military responsibility and activity. There should be no enforced or organised counselling for all – especially not by non-unit personnel. In any large body of men, closely confined, there are always enough talkers and listeners to guarantee lively discussion and thought.

Long-term
So, long-term, what should be done? Of course, emerging mental ill-health should come under the care of military or veterans' mental health teams with welfare back-up. For those whose lives are faltering as the result of their mental scarring, value is likely to be had, not from opening the mental wounds of past traumas, but by helping those affected to climb a tower, as it were, above their troubles and be motivated to look out toward a series of personal goals, aiming to re-launch them into stable life.

This type of therapy was first proposed, or something much like it, by Captain Arthur Brock of the Royal Army Medical Corps. He was a psychiatrist in the Great War at Craiglockhart, wartime military hospital for officers in Edinburgh. Apparently the building still exists. It had been a Spa Hotel and is now student accommodation. Here were treated officers, most from the Somme era, who were suffering from battle neurasthenia or shell-shock, which was the terminology of the time. This is a key part of the history of battle-induced mental ill-health, and famous among its patients were Wilfred Owen and Siegfried Sassoon, the Great War Poets (Hibberd, 2002). As patients they were visited by Robert Graves, the poet and author, who also had post-war neurasthenia. He finally attempted to put his past on record and behind him when, ten years after the war, he wrote his autobiography, *Goodbye to All That*, and headed for a new life abroad (Graves, 1957).

One way to help deal with post-battle mental adjustment once and for all is to write down one's experiences, good and bad, and one's reactions, whether in the form of a notebook, tape or book, and, as it were, lock it away in the past before moving on. As such, it could be suggested by units after returning from action. The Craiglockhart trio, as we can now regard them, remain the great communicators from their war generation, with messages which will endure for Great Britain. I met Robert Graves very briefly just before he gave his first lecture as Professor of Poetry at Oxford University in the 'sixties.

As you get older the past has a curious quality of becoming closer to your own life. I can well remember London match-sellers on street corners, often with a crutch and Great War medals; being told that a neighbour had "shell-shock"; being taught to fish by a man who had been gassed on the Western Front. At a recent Parochial Church Council meeting, of the eleven souls present, two had had fathers who survived the Battle of the Somme. With such reminders is it not reasonable in our more psychologically vulnerable age to make long-term military mental health and support provision for those affected by combat?

Practical help must include money. The current compensation for losing a finger in battle is £2,559 (single payment). Soldiers should not receive lump sum payments. They will need the money later in their lives and long-term, regardless, and rightly so, of whether the victim shows his hand proudly to his grandchildren or to the examiner for incapacity benefits. We all cope differently. There is no logic in giving compensation for a little finger and not for mental scarring. The scar must be compensated for, not allowed to develop into some long-term mental illness which the scarring may predispose the soldier to. How do we do this? A war pension based on the number of days in combat and intensity of that combat as judged from measures such as physical casualty rates, death rates, ammunition expenditure, etc? In this way, retrospectively, scores are produced for each day, the worst possible day being 100 points, e.g. the first day on the Somme (but no day will ever equal that). An agreed formula calculation could be arrived at so as to produce a modest pension increment to retirement pay for those exposed to agreed significant battle-trauma.

Practical help might also include regular, if brief, long-term follow-up of those becoming the mental health casualties of battle or those with high "Somme" scores, e.g. by Internet or text, and organised by the Veterans Welfare Organisation with Regimental and British Legion input. This idea was, in part, promoted by a conversation I had with Lieutenant Robert Lawrence, who was very badly wounded in the Tumbledown attack. Robert went furthest forward of any officer before he fell. I know also now that his Company, led by Major Simon Price, carried out an exemplary night attack in mountainous terrain, the worth of which I only recently came to appreciate.

Recently I have had a glimpse of medical advances which indicate a possibly more sound method of diagnosing and treating different types of mental health illness with the help of brain-scanning and imaging. There is hope here for the future casualty. However, I have two postscripts.

What is the Tumbledown legacy of the 2nd Battalion, Scots Guards? It is the intense low murmuring roar that was so distinctive and memorable as the Battalion wound-down during the time in the Fitzroy sheep sheds, exchanging their experiences, worries and fears. I shall never forget it and neither should the Army Medical Services. This points the way to bring practical clarity of action to the part-prevention and long-term military medical care and support for those damaged by war.

Finally, about five years after the war I was doing a short locum duty with the United Nations Forces in Cyprus (UNFICYP). Along the camp road I encountered the first Argentinian serviceman I had seen since the war. His unit was newly arrived in Cyprus. I was unsure of his rank and no doubt he felt the same. Each off us saluted early, only to salute exactly together. We were very much on the same side. For me the war was over.

Note
The main suggestions in this paper were first touched on during a briefing to the Treasury Solicitors' Council in the Spring of 2001 on another matter.

References
Elliott, Toby (2006) personal communication (November)
Graves, R.R. (1957) Goodbye to All That : a*n Autobiography*, London, Jonathan Cape.
Hibberd, D (2002) *Wilfred Owen : A New Biography*, London, Weidenfeld and Nicolson.

Gurkhas in the Falklands

David Morgan

Introduction

The 1st Battalion, 7th Duke of Edinburgh's Own Gurkha Rifles did not take part in any great battles during the Falklands Campaign of 1982. The Battle of the Tumbledown was fought and won by 2nd Battalion, the Scots Guards, and when the Gurkhas had reached their objective on Mount William, the enemy had already retreated. There was no battle for Mount William.

However, either by clever design or by pure accident, the British Forces found that their strongest battalion was, at the end of the fighting on the Tumbledown, facing Stanley with three powerful rifle companies, fully manned (less eight wounded who had been injured by shell-fire during the approach march and one wounded in a "blue-on-blue" incident), heavily armed, fit and angry. More, perhaps, by chance than design, the Gurkhas would have been exactly the right unit in exactly the correct place, to have fought any final rearguard, or defensive battle for either Stanley or, perhaps, the Airport. Their reputation had preceded them, but had their bluff been called, the remaining demoralised Argentinian forces would have faced an infantry enemy whose standards of loyalty to their officers, courage and sheer professionalism were second to none.

Each rifleman carried 100 rounds of ammunition for his own personal Self-Loading Rifle. In addition the Battalion carried forward all its complete complement of anti-armour (anti-bunker) weapons including the Carl Gustav 84mm anti-tank rocket launcher, 66mm Light Anti-Tank Weapon and six Milan anti-tank missile launchers, and a total of three .50 inch Browning Heavy Machine Guns. All this meant that on occasions men in the Battalion were carrying anything up to seventy kilograms – more than their own body weight, but the upshot was that they were ready for whatever the future held. A Gurkha is normally a most passive man but, in action, and particularly when his fellow soldiers have been wounded or killed, he can generate a cold anger that is only held in place by his over-riding professionalism. So, what is it about these men that gives them their well-earned reputation? How is it that such high standards can be reached?

Nepal

One of the answers lies in the country of their birth. Nepal is a small land-locked country situated at the southern edge of the largest mountain mass in the world, the Himalayas. It is some 500 miles long and 125 miles wide. However, the astonishing fact about this country is that, in section, the land rises from almost sea-level to 30,000 feet in a space of approximately sixty-five kilometres. This enormous height differential throughout the country means that it is inherently unstable. Monsoon rains and melted snow combine to produce frighteningly powerful rivers that can wash away houses and roads and, in fact, do so on a yearly basis. The main access routes into the Hills are

42

frequently closed for repairs. This means that anything of value needed in the Hills must be carried in on a man's back. Lack of good communications in the Hills means that there is no ambulance service for the sick or injured, no fire service, few hospitals of even poor to moderate standard, few schools and an inefficient police force. People in mountain villages must travel down several thousands of feet just to get their daily water. There are no natural resources; no oil, coal or gas. The only fuel available is wood, and that is in ever-decreasing supply.

In short, life is tough. A young man grows up independent, a hunter for food, capable of living off the land, and is used to carrying very heavy weights day in, day out, over some of the most atrocious terrain in the world. The seventy kilogram weight mentioned previously would be a commonplace load in the Hills of Nepal. Many young men join an Army (either the Nepalese Army, Indian Army or British Army) in order to escape the trials of life in the Hills. But their background produces a character that is just what any Army is actually looking for, and provides the clay to fashion the best of infantry soldiers.

Recruiting

The problem comes at the recruiting season which normally lasts for about six months. In 1989, in order to select 238 recruits, the Recruiting Teams that searched the country within fairly limited areas, looked at some 40,000 to 50,000 hopeful volunteers. To whittle this huge number down, the Teams ran a succession of highly complex tests. The first set, which is designed to be "man against test", consists of basic educational, intelligence, medical, eyesight and physical tests. This process is known as "Hill Selection". Amongst the many tests that each young man must pass include the ability to carry out twelve "heaves" to a bar. Another of the basic tests requires the potential recruit to lie on a board which is then raised to an angle of sixty degrees with his feet held by a rope in the air and his head on the floor. He has to touch his forehead to his knees thirty times in a minute. If any of these tests are failed, and if he is young enough, he will be asked to return the following year.

After passing Hill Selection the boy is called forward to the main Recruiting Depot in Pokhara. Here he is subjected to a further two weeks of tests, this time "man against man". Amongst the various tests, the Team will see who is beaten at running, carry out interviews and judge the candidates' reactions to "murder ball". The candidates are then subjected to the "doka test". They are lined up and made to run as fast as they can over a course that starts at the far end of a football pitch. They have to run the length of the pitch, and then on down a sheer escarpment to a river, through it and then up a hill to a height of about 3,000 feet above the water, round a marker pole, and then back again. He must do all of this with an eighteen kilogram load of bricks on his back.

After this type of testing the Recruiting team believe that they have obtained the best young men from the country, and those who are selected are then trained for three weeks at the Depot before they appear on a parade in front of their Commander to swear an oath of allegiance to Queen Elizabeth II. Once the Swearing-In Ceremony, or Kasam Khane (literally to eat an oath) parade is completed, the recruits can then be transferred to the Infantry Training Depot to begin their training as soldiers. This normally takes a year, but could well now be a much shorter period of time.

Regimental Service

Recruit training is rigorous, but the competition and desire to improve and impress is so great that the failure rate is low. Unlike most other armies, Gurkha recruit-training, whilst being extremely tough, is in many ways gentle. Few harsh words are spoken by the Instructors. They guide rather than bully and the results are astonishing. After relatively few weeks of training, recruits who but a few months previously had never flown in an aircraft or seen a television set are learning about military radios and modern weapons.

Much is made of "swearing-in", and it is taken very seriously. Having sworn the oath of allegiance to the Queen whilst still in Nepal, the recruit does this again on arrival in the Battalion of his Regiment and, because this final swearing-in is done in front of the whole of his new unit drawn up on parade, he will never be allowed to forget it. It is at this stage that the young man becomes aware, for the first time, of his responsibilities to himself, his fellow recruits, his comrades-in-arms and above all to his Section, Platoon, Company and Battalion.

The Gurkha soldier is brought up in his Battalion to obey orders without question and to live life in such a way that he is always trying to improve the "name of the Regiment". This means he will be striving throughout his career to do constantly better in whatever task he is given. He will play football to win, his civilian dress will be perfect (he has had to pass an inspection by the Guard Commander before leaving the Barracks), and he will do his utmost to ensure that he does not let down either his fellows or his parents in Nepal. It is more than likely that his family will be watching his progress keenly. It is equally likely there are many male members of his family who have already served, and will have been through the same tests and experiences. They are always of great assistance to him, but at a long distance. The young recruit, after he has joined his new Regiment, will be separated from his family for the best part of three years before he can return to his home in the Hills of Nepal for a well-earned holiday.

Courage and professionalism

Much is said and written about the courage of the Gurkha. It is expected. The Gurkha motto is: "Kapher hunnu bhanda, marnu ramro chha", which means "It is better to die than to be a coward". But Gurkhas are very human. They may be unusually focussed soldiers, but they have feelings and fears, and it is silly to suggest that a Gurkha has been blessed with an extra dollop of bravery when he was born. No, the difference between him and many others is that he is absolutely loyal and tirelessly professional in all that he does. So, when faced with a dangerous situation he will do what his training dictates. Very often this will mean he will do something amazingly brave, but he, and his fellow soldiers, would not necessarily see it as bravery, rather it would be considered as being expected of him in his particular capacity and position.

The man
It is true that Gurkhas are exceedingly good at their business. They are intensely proud, professional soldiers. They are part of a tough, well-trained, well-drilled killing machine. However, people might be surprised when meeting a Gurkha. He is smart, generally quiet and delightfully polite even in unfamiliar surroundings. He laughs a great deal, has a lovely sense of humour, is gentle with his women-folk and adores children. He loves dancing and singing and rum. He appreciates flowers, and would think nothing of dressing up as a girl for a demonstration of a Nepalese tribal dance. In short, he is fallible and human, but he is also a highly trained soldier.

The Falklands
When it became clear in early May 1982 that the Gurkha Battalion was due to be deployed in the South Atlantic as part of the British Task Force, the mood amongst the soldiers was one of joy. Morale was high. The Gurkhas' eagerness to take part did, on one occasion, go beyond what one who did not know them might expect. One of the Battalion's rifle companies that had been training in Belize for the previous seven months was waiting at the airport for its flight to the United Kingdom one week before the Battalion's embarkation on board the Cunard liner *QE2*. When news arrived in the airport terminal building that the destroyer HMS *Sheffield* had been hit by an Argentine Exocet missile which killed twenty of her ship's company, these Gurkha soldiers cheered. Their Company Commander, who was a British Major, complained that they had clearly not understood the situation. But his Queens Gurkha Officer Second-in-Command said to him, "Saheb, they do understand because now it means there will be a war. It is no longer just an exercise!"

Very few other troops would react in this way. Morale rose on the back of a disaster because it meant that they would have a chance to exact revenge for the loss of their British comrades. The fact that the Gurkhas never actually closed in combat with their enemy in the Falklands was fortuitous. There is no doubt that had the Battalion been allowed forward into Stanley, or further towards the Airport, on that fateful morning, and if the Argentinians had had the wherewithal and will to have resisted, the battle would have been noted for its ferocity and many lives would undoubtedly have been lost. But, as was stated at the time, "If Gurkhas can win by reputation, who wants to kill people?"

The Future
The Gurkhas of today are little different from those who went to the South Atlantic twenty-five years ago. They are just as tough and, as standards have risen in Nepal, are now far better educated. Recruiting

is still as good as ever, with the keenest and the best of the young men of Nepal joining the British Army in preference to either the Indian or Nepalese Armies. The chances for active service are greater now than in the nineteen eighties and Gurkhas are playing their parts, just as well and professionally, in both Iraq and Afghanistan. It is highly unlikely that the Maoists will seriously affect the way in which Gurkhas are recruited. In time the various petty jealousies that currently exist in the Hills will diminish, and the situation will once again return to what it was in the 'eighties and early 'nineties. This augurs well for the future, and Gurkhas will no doubt continue to lead by example and conquer by reputation.

A Chaplain Reflects

Angus Smith

What are the expectations of Chaplaincy in the British Army and how do they dovetail with an organization whose aim is to achieve operational success? When the present Chaplain General held the post of Deputy Chaplain General, he defined these expectations and the dovetailing process in the following way. He focussed first on the needs of the Army. He said:

> It is an organization whose *raison d'être*, indeed whose overall motto, could be defined as "Prepare for War", and whose aim is to achieve operational success. For this it requires good leadership, teamwork and a caring approach towards, in particular, the Army's most vital asset – the soldiers. The Army's core values are courage, commitment, discipline, loyalty, integrity and respect for others. In combat characterized by hardship, fear and the ultimate possibility of self-sacrifice, soldiers are forced to face up to their own mortality. Spiritual values are therefore of great importance, as these can sustain soldiers in combat.

A basic acquaintance with biblical literature will demonstrate how close these core values really are to the values of "faith". I talk here specifically about the Christian faith, although much relates to core values of other religions and belief systems as well. Without doubt agnostics, humanists and atheists can be proficient soldiers. Many in all three services whose courage and operational successes are not only impressive but also praiseworthy have no religious background or experience. The only call they make on God's name is in the form of a passionate expletive. Despite their living by their wits and often being just one step ahead of the "law" during their adolescent and pre-service years, one could wish for no better person at one's side when penetrating closely guarded enemy positions in the crags of Tumbledown or of Mount William in the Falklands.

Yet having said all that, and explained the tradition I come from, I make no apology for saying that those whose lives are shaped by a firm belief in God and in the values of faith already have an appreciation of the core values already referred to. They are aware of the motivation for which these values provide a definite dynamic. Motivation, of course, is also powerfully manifested by the creeds and values displayed by competent commanders such as we had at Tumbledown by unit non-commissioned officers, Guardsmen and soldiers. It can come from Regimental Medical Officers and their staff. How fortunate indeed we were in the Falklands campaign to have Brigadier (then Lieutenant-Colonel) Alan Warsap as our Medical Officer, and then people of the calibre of Morgan O'Connell, the Principal Naval Psychiatrist. Their compassion, advice, wisdom and humanity were invaluable.

Motivation for the soldier engaged in military operations can also come from the confident awareness that family matters on the home front can reliably be entrusted to the Families Officer and his team. While this need has been identified and provided for in the three main British Services, and I dare say elsewhere, it is salutary to see the official recognition given to such important matters in the Introduction to the 2006 document "Operational Mental Health – A NATO Programme Adopted for the 21st Century", of which one of the co-authors was Professor Lars Weisæth. The document was sent to me by Mike Seear, who had also made various contributions to it based on his Falklands War experiences:

> The new conditions have led to a change from a one-sided focus on providing and maintaining manpower, to a more balanced doctrine to preserve combat strength while protecting the mental health of personnel at risk. In contemporary military operations and war a wider spectrum of stressor has been identified. War-related Potential Traumatic Events (PTE) exist as always, but service-related stressors and civilian stressors need to receive more attention.

Under the heading of "Professionalism" the same document quotes from the publication "Stress, Appraisal and Coping" by Lazarus and Folkman. They make the point, which is really self-evident, that professionalism and training can enable personnel to cope more adequately with their tasks. That quotation is prefaced by the following statement:

> The before-deployment phase can be a much underrated period in terms of laying a solid foundation for professionalism, in terms of supplying adequate and realistic unit training.

Shortly after receiving notification for our deployment, the newly-constituted 5th Infantry Brigade, in which the infantry components were the 2nd Battalion, Scots Guards, 1st Battalion, Welsh Guards, and 1st Battalion, 7th Duke of Edinburgh's Own Gurkha Rifles, had a preparatory military exercise in Wales. In this exercise an imaginative scenario was planned. Infantry skills and operational requirements were practised. Good leadership at all levels, teamwork and a caring attitude towards its most valuable asset – the soldiers – came into their own. One day, when I visited a company during this exercise, a young officer, who was a convinced and practising Christian, asked me: "Padre, how are you going to prepare the Battalion spiritually for war?" This really was a question which was never far from my mind but, when posed by this young and thoughtful officer, it became for me a more immediate concern.

Grateful as I was for the many opportunities to address the various companies for character-training periods and regular daily contact with members of the Battalion at all levels, this scenario was to be a new point of departure. If we were to be involved in combat, all ranks had to face up to the possibility of the ultimate sacrifice and be aware of their own mortality. I had by every means possible to give those, for whom I was responsible, some appreciation of the spiritual insights that could sustain them before, during and after combat.

How did I seek to implement this important role? Firstly by my identifying with the Battalion on the widest possible basis by taking part in the various courses on map- reading, radio procedure and first aid. By this time the Medical Officer and I had formed a natural team. Our thinking was so close at so many different levels. We were both, in our different ways, interested in making people "whole" (to quote an Anglican theologian) or in making them as "whole" as we could. Whilst each company was put through a basic first aid course, I was given the task of explaining "Burial Procedure" to each company in terms of our existing Standard Operating Procedures (SOP). Now the fact that "Burial Procedure" was changed when we got to the Falklands was really irrelevant. What was of importance was that a procedure was adopted which suited our location at the time.

When Headquarters Company came for their first aid course, the Company Commander decreed that the tallest, and possibly the heaviest, soldier in that company should act as the "dead soldier". Drill-Sergeant Wight was selected – a great character in every sense of the word. Four sweating Guardsmen brought in the Drill-Sergeant on a standard-issue sleeping bag and lowered him down into a temporary grave. Faces were sombre. To defuse the situation I gave a mock "Eulogy" for the Drill-Sergeant. I finished with the words, "OK Drill-Sergeant, you may now join the ranks of the living."

The Drill-Sergeant then flashed his usual ready smile and remarked, "By God Padre, I hope I will be fully gone when you stand at my grave. It's an awful thing to be in a grave and see people gathered around it." Much laughter ensued. His words, however, came back to me when I learned at about 01.45 hours on 14 June 1982 that the good Drill-Sergeant had been killed in the diversionary attack during the Battle for Tumbledown Mountain in the Falklands.

However, I jump ahead of myself, but the "story within the story" had to be told in its entirety. I think at this point of my reflections on events of almost twenty-five years ago it is important, particularly for this kind of audience, for me to say something about my ministry and task as a Chaplain for this venture. In the British Army, indeed in all three services, Chaplains are first and foremost ministers and priests of their Churches. We are non-combatants. We exercise our ministry in the name of our Churches on behalf of the units for which we are responsible. A realistic incarnational theology should expect that we have an intelligent awareness of the ethos, character and role of these units, not least to enable our ministry to "dovetail" into their life and work both on a spiritual and practical basis.

In our Churches, and particularly in the Churches which follow the Reformed Tradition, the expression, proclamation and commendation of faith is based upon the Bible duly interpreted and explained and applied, not only in terms of the historical dimension of faith, but also of its relevance to the contemporary scene in which one is placed. Now it would be strange if, in an audience of this nature, you would all be in total agreement with what I say here, but it is important you should at least be aware of what my thinking about my pastoral role in this scenario was. It should also serve as a useful pointer to the many correlates which undoubtedly there are, on the one hand in that document "Operational Mental Health – A NATO Programme Adopted for the 21st Century" and, on the other hand, in the theological premises on which my spiritual preparation and pastoral care of the Battalion were based. In the final analysis, of course, Professor Lars Weisæth is a Psychiatrist and I am/was a Chaplain, but I firmly believe that in future developments of theories and plans in this NATO document, an intelligent dialogue between both these areas of experience would promote even more correlatives to their mutual benefit and enrichment.

Now then, what about the spiritual preparation of the Battalion for war? Did I simply have to proclaim the simple unadulterated Biblical message, and hope that the religious message would somehow underscore the military requirement? That could very well be so. One day, however, during the exercise in Wales, I had a flash of inspiration. Some eighteen years prior to that day, I had read a book which, in a theological sense, gripped us all as students. The book was entitled *The Courage to Be* and was written by Paul Tillich. The Reverend Professor Paul Tillich was a Professor of Systematic Theology in Germany during the late 1930s. He was one of several German theologians who were forced to leave their posts as a result of the intolerable pressure put on them by the Nazis. Tillich readily found posts at various American Universities, where his teaching flourished and attracted thousands of students.

Why then go back to a book which was printed in the 'sixties in the search of a measure of light for the spiritual and pastoral task that engaged me in 1982? That certainly is a valid question. However Tillich, as his theological work developed, sought to engage with literature, philosophy, ethics, psychotherapy and several other departments of life. Tillich had, and I believe still has, much to say about our contemporary scene even if, in some respects, the book is undoubtedly dated. He has much to say about courage.

Tillich had seen that for the Existentialist School of writers "non-being" was the greatest threat and anxiety of modern man. He defined anxiety as that state in which a being is aware of its possible "non-being". Now if courage (which Tillich defined as the power of the mind to overcome fear) does not remove the awareness of possible "non-being", courage can still take the possibility of "non-being" into itself. This in turn enables courage to express itself in affirmation "in spite of", that is, in spite of the possibility of "non-being".

If that piece of theory is somewhat "meaty", let me now explain how I saw one particular example of it in action. As the Battalion made its final preparations in the Assembly Area before going into battle, I went round to each company to wish them well. As I talked to one Lance-Sergeant in his trench, a shell landed fairly close, burying itself fortunately into the peaty soil. The Lance-Sergeant said, "Better come into the trench, padre, in case the next one is closer." In fact the next shell landed some distance away. The Lance-Sergeant then looked at me and said, "Padre, if your number is on that bullet or shell, there is little you can do about it." Was that simply an expression of fatalism?

Of course it could be interpreted in that way. The more I reflect on that incident, however, the more I believe that what the Lance-Sergeant declared really amounted to courage expressing itself in affirmation "in spite of", that is, in spite of the threats and dangers of the battle that was to come. The fact that the Lance-Sergeant was awarded a well-deserved "Mention in Dispatches" for bravery that night would certainly point in that direction.

Tillich in his book also wrote that anxiety with the prospect of death increases with the spread of individualization, but that people in collectivist cultures are less open to this type of anxiety. Now, for my purposes, I defined a collectivist culture in terms of the Regimental or Battalion Spirit or, as the Commanding Officer frequently emphasized, "The Family Spirit within the Battalion". These dominant traits in the Battalion were indeed a solid basis on which to foster and develop its spiritual strength. There are many testimonies throughout history regarding the value of spiritual resources and strength for any testing episode we are to encounter. General Fromm, a General of the German Wehrmacht, in 1939 declared his support for Pastor Franz Dohrmann when the latter, as the Military Bishop for the Wehrmacht, was expecting not a few difficulties with Hitler and his regime. General Fromm stated, "All experiences of war have learned that the spiritual strength of an army is its best weapon." I endeavoured to foster an appropriate degree of spiritual strength, not only in simple applied messages from the scriptures, but also in leading prayer for matters of ultimate concern for us all and, not least, in the saying of the Regimental Collect or Prayer.

I shared Paul Tillich's insights in a much simplified version with many on a daily basis, and have every reason to believe that the sharing of these spiritual insights helped us fulfil our individual roles before, during and after the conflict. During the battle, I was mainly co-located with the Medical Officer at the Regimental Aid Post, but was also involved in the several tasks that were appropriate to my role as the Chaplain, having placed myself at the disposal of the three Company Commanders should they wish my assistance or presence at any time. The actions and progress of the Battles for Tumbledown and Mount William has been described with authority by those who were actively involved in them.

Let me refer briefly to the post-conflict phase. For various reasons it was decreed that the Scots Guards should remain in the Falklands until the relief battalion arrived from the United Kingdom. The prospect of staying for an extra six weeks was not popular. However, on balance, this period was beneficial in so many ways. The dead received a dignified though temporary burial. The wounded were visited as often as possible on board the Task Force Hospital Ship, SS *Uganda*. All ranks had the time and space to face up to, and accept, what had happened and what they had gone through. We also had the time and space to meet and give appropriate help and social support to those who required it. Company Commanders ensured that each company was involved in purposeful activities. I had a helicopter (and pilot) entirely at my disposal each Sunday and Monday morning. Church Services were held at each company location. Spiritual and pastoral support, as well as sound medical support, were available regularly. Services were often followed by impromptu "Ceilidhs" and "sing-songs". All these in their several ways contributed to normality. Good humour and laughter increased as the date of departure for the UK came closer.

The Commanding Officer had arranged for a Cross to be erected on Tumbledown; a brass plate bearing the names of the Guardsmen who had died in the battle was attached to the Cross. On Friday, 30 July 1982, a group of us went by helicopter to the top of Tumbledown Mountain for the Dedication of the Cross. Even if a Force Eight gale virtually whipped away each word as it was spoken, the performance of this – our penultimate duty on the Islands – was both poignant and significant. The Cross on Tumbledown – the memorial to our dead – also points to something beyond itself. For almost a quarter of a century it has reminded the inhabitants both of Stanley and the Islands of certain special words of Christ in the Fourth Gospel: "Greater love has no man than this, that a man lay down his life for his friends."

References

Dohrmann, F. (1983) *Feldbischof Unter Hitler*, Sutherisches Verlaghus, Hannover.

Fromm, General (1939) *Gott Lässt Sich Nicht Spotten*, Herausgeber Herman Kunst.

Tillich, P. (1963) *The Courage to Be*, Fontana Library, Glasgow.

Weisæth L., Michel P.-O. *Operational Mental Health: A NATO Programme Adopted for the 21st Century*, presented to the NATO Comeds Panel on Military Psychiatry (January 2006).

Who Cares about the Enemy?

Jeremy McTeague

> *To be prepared is half the victory.*
> Miguel de Cervantes Saavedra (1547–1616)

Introduction

Training soldiers to operate effectively in combat is the core activity of the British Army. Indeed, in the latter half of the twentieth century the priority placed on training by the Army's high command was (and may still be) the single most critical factor for its success. It is this almost religious dedication to preparation that has enabled the Army to fulfil the numerous demands made upon it without losing a war.

The Army spends enormous time and resources selecting, assessing and developing the strengths of young men and women to make them "fit for purpose". Soldiers in the "teeth arms" such as the infantry must therefore be "battle-ready". From a practical perspective this means that they must be highly competent in handling their equipment and weapons. They must know, understand and be able to act according to standard operating procedures (routines that permit men to operate in a logical way when, under extreme pressure and duress, their rational thought processes may be slow or unreliable). Finally, they must be supportive of the command structure and have the self-discipline to sublimate self-interest and act in the best interests of their sub-units.

British Army training is staggeringly effective and it reaps some important side-benefits such as the widespread development of *esprit de corps*. Nevertheless, in my experience, there are several "soft" areas where the training of leaders for combat could, and should, be improved and where failure to do so can, and will, have hard and durable personal consequences for the potential combatants. The first improvement is giving advice on what to expect regarding the emotions and concerns that arise before and during combat, and the second is dealing with the appearance of unpalatable emotions post-combat.

Emotions and concerns arising before and during combat

Dealing with indecision caused by concerns about being wrong – when the stake may be life itself or otherwise

The idea of being frozen into indecision by the fear of being wrong is neither new nor complicated. Indeed many people are able to relate to such an experience. But what most people have experienced is the need to decide an issue in the absence of critical urgency or where the penalty of error is not death or injury to self or comrades.

Just prior to the last fourteen days of the Falklands-Malvinas conflict in late May 1982, my unit, 1st Battalion, 7th Duke of Edinburgh's Own Gurkha Rifles, still at sea on board the Cunard liner RMS *Queen Elizabeth 2*, received its warning order to land at Blue Beach 2, San Carlos Water on 1 June. The orders given to the Battalion, and down through the organisation whilst on board our subsequent ship MV *Norland* on 31 May, the night before the landing, were scant. As illustrated here (fig. 1), my orders book clearly reports: "Action on beachhead – no idea".

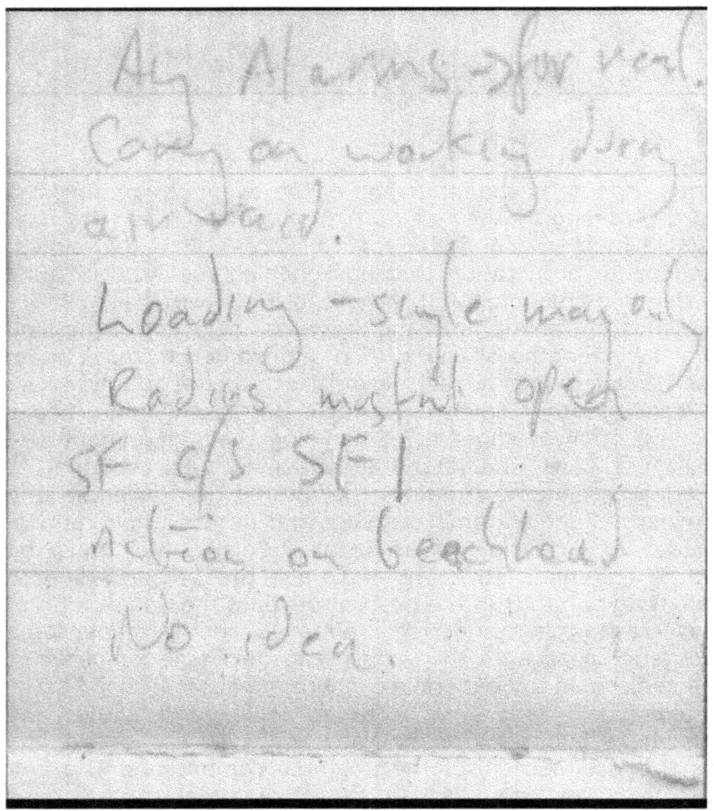

Figure 1. Extract from Jeremy McTeague's orders book depicting notes for the Battalion's landing at Blue Beach 2, San Carlos Water.

This caused my men and me real concern. We were about to enter a battle-zone and the plan to effect that act of entry was non-existent. A plan is always better than no plan, and while initiative is rightly a valued trait, it cannot and must not be relied upon as the sole factor/contributor to define courses of action. All officers and non-commissioned officers should be trained to understand why they should never use the words "no idea" in formal orders.

How to deal with being utterly powerless when under duress
On our long night approach march along Goat Ridge on 14 June towards our Company Start Line (the location from which a company deliberate attack is launched) on the eastern end of the Tumbledown, we were in single file moving through a suspected minefield when, suddenly, we came under heavy artillery and mortar fire that lasted for nearly an

hour. The standard operating procedure (SOP) in such a situation is to fall to the ground, seek cover and await orders. As the Platoon Commander, I was aware of my responsibility to get my men into safety. We could not just scatter, and yet to make an orderly exit, we would have had to keep close together in single file – a perilous action indeed in the context of the current situation. But falling to the ground was only a marginally better solution as we remained within the target area of the accurate Argentine artillery and mortar fire.

Having decided that we should remain in cover, I was still without any other options and so felt powerless to protect my men further. In that situation the realisation that there is nothing one can do is not easy to accept, and one feels a corresponding overwhelming sense of inadequacy. Indeed for some time after this frighteningly intensive and prolonged bombardment had ceased, I worried that my men thought of me as being ineffective. This was a poor state of mind for a young officer preparing to participate in the launching of a deliberate company attack on an enemy defensive position that had been prepared for sixty-seven days beforehand.

My message is crystal-clear. It is simple to teach young commanders and soldiers alike that instances of powerlessness will occur on the battlefield. So merely having that knowledge in advance will allow soldiers in a similar position to deal appropriately with it.

How to handle new, unexpected and intense emotional states personally and in one's men

No matter how long the time one has known the men under one's command, there will, in my experience, always be a change in the way that they behave and in how one behaves as combat becomes imminent and the danger grows or, indeed, is experienced. We all react in different ways and, in many instances, I was surprised by how much and in what unexpected directions my men's behaviour changed. Interestingly it was not that the men's behaviour changed for the worse *per se* – it just simply became erratic and intense.

This presented problems in command and created the need to be super-understanding and empathetic on the one hand, and firmer and occasionally more authoritarian on the other – depending on the individual and specific circumstances. Vitally, it became clear to me that I had also to examine my own behaviour to ensure that this remained as consistent as possible. I should stress that this did not mean my pretending to be unaffected by the situation – just that the manner of my being affected was consistent with the Lieutenant McTeague my soldiers knew from before. Being recognised as having a good sense of humour is invaluable in this respect.

How to manage fear in oneself and in others

Since I was a small eight year-old boy on the rugby field, I have had to deal with fear of enemy and injury – as have most of us. It is nothing new in itself, and normally we go through life without being overly perturbed when we find that we are afraid of something since our control of fear from an early age has been mastered.

What we do not normally have to face is a rapid escalation in the threat and to manage the realisation of its new enormity. At the Royal Military Academy Sandhurst we were not trained in how to deal with fear of a threat that was so large that one's death (and that of most of one's men) appeared (quite rationally) to be the only logical outcome. My orders book again (fig. 2) provides insight into my thinking on the eve of the Battalion's battle, and the D Company attack on Mount William in particular. This was to be a frontal attack across nearly 1,000 metres of absolutely open and barren terrain. There was not a tree, bush or rock in sight along the projected path of our advance to attack three Argentine Marine platoons totalling 157 men who were dug-in both on Mount William itself and just to the north east and north-west of this objective respectively. This enemy force outnumbered D Company and was similar in number to those facing the Scots Guards. The only hope of success was that the darkness of night would cloak us and our movement, and supporting fire from A Company's fire base of Browning heavy machine guns, Milan anti-tank missiles, general purpose machine guns in the sustained fire role, our Battalion 81mm mortars and the artillery would suppress the enemy whilst we were exposed in the open.

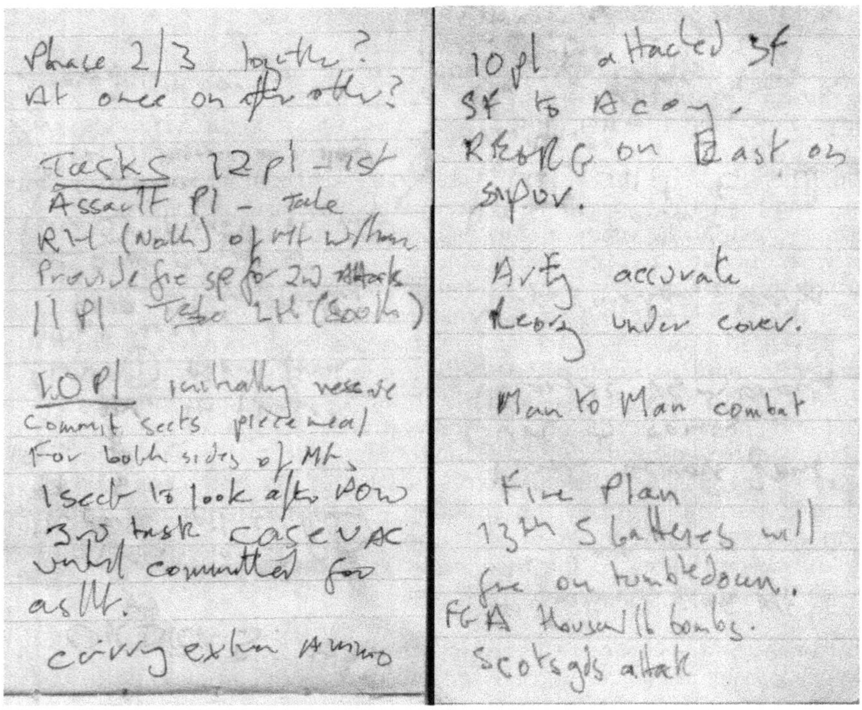

Figure 2. Extract from Jeremy McTeague's orders book depicting notes for D Company's deliberate attack on Mount William

The scene is set with an uncertainty: *Phases 2 and 3 of the attack will be together, or one after the other?*

Then the tasks: *11 and 12 Platoons will be the first attack platoons. 10 Platoon* (my command) *will initially be in reserve* (sigh of relief). But then: *10 Platoon will commit sections piecemeal to support 11 and 12 Platoons. And one section is to look after prisoners.*

Then as a third task: *another section is to evacuate the wounded until it is committed for the assault* (this was verging on the impossible, since the section could be one kilometre to the rear at the time I was meant to be putting it into the attack. Also for the record: at this point all three of my sections had now been committed to various tasks!)

Then it gets worse: *Carry extra ammo.* Ammunition is very heavy and carrying it for other soldiers, when attacking, is like sending a boxer into the boxing ring in handcuffs.

And even worse: *attached SF (general purpose machine gun in the sustained fire role) has to go to A Company* so I had also lost my only integral fire support. I was then told that *the enemy artillery is very accurate and that we must re-organise ourselves after the attack under cover.* In effect this meant treating wounded, re-supplying and dealing with prisoners whilst under artillery fire.

Finally Major Mike Kefford, my Company Commander and a man warranting great respect, advises that the fight is going to be *"man to man combat"*.

Without overstating the case, this set of orders describes a desperately difficult set of circumstances with a level of complexity that was bound to result in massive casualties, if not outright failure. The level of fear and hopelessness I felt was shared by my men and our fear was palpable, yet there was full acceptance of my orders. As I shook hands with my section commanders half an hour before crossing the Start Line (now in broad daylight because of the delay imposed on the Scots Guards' attack by fierce enemy resistance), I wished that my training had included guidance on how to alleviate the obvious fear that we all felt. It was a really unpleasant final thirty minutes whilst we waited to move.

In later life: dealing with the appearance of unpalatable emotions
How to control violent fantasies and the desire to inflict violence

This issue has been well documented and become a somewhat over-emphasised cliché. Despite this, it is a real phenomenon and remains inadequately understood by people who have experienced it, and entirely misunderstood by those who have never experienced it – rather like men knowing what it is like to give birth. When I discovered that my fellow officers also suffered from similar experiences, it was a huge relief and I immediately found myself better able to view such fantasies more objectively, so limiting their impact.

Military training establishments would be well advised to explain how these fantasies come about and how they can be dealt with. Such knowledge is enough to allow many individuals to help themselves or, in more extreme cases, to provide the impetus and "permission" to go and seek help.

How to diminish feelings of shame or humiliation
War for the combat soldier is likely to be a humiliating experience. He is on an emotional rollercoaster. He has to open himself up and prove himself to other men to such an extent that it can be, in retrospect, humiliating – rather like a teenage boy boasting or flexing his biceps in the vain hope of impressing a girl. His comrades see him terrified, hugely aggressive and even feeling guilty. Indeed they see him in a wider range of unpalatable emotional states than should his mother or wife. They witness his basest behaviour which, at its worst, is him having to kill another. The immediate reaction to such behaviour is normally positive and this can last for some time. But in the end, years later, feelings of shame and humiliation come to the fore as we judge our memories against the standards of the mature individual. Dealing with these emotions requires fortitude, and the worst thing is that they are unexpected. Forewarned is forearmed.

The emotional effect of combat and its anticipation
Combat and the anticipation or expectation of combat, unsurprisingly, causes us to experience a wide range of emotions – many for the first time, and often in a far more intense way than previously. For example, (fig. 3) anxiety is a common, balanced emotion that we often experience and which performs a useful function in our everyday lives. However, in near and actual combat situations, anxiety is heightened to fear and, *in extremis*, is intensified to outright terror. As stated earlier, fear is not uncommon. It is much rarer than anxiety but we have all generally experienced it at some time. Terror, on the other hand, is rarely experienced.

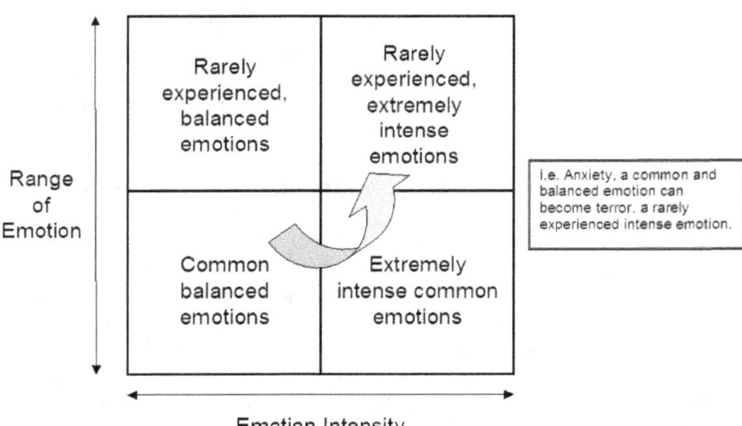

Figure 3. Combat and its anticipation create and intensify emotions.

The effect of experiencing fear for prolonged periods, or terror for even short periods, creates an emotional disjunction, with the victim losing his sense of emotional perspective in the short to medium term. Matters of routine or the mundane become beneath contempt, unworthy of consideration as they are "totally unimportant" in the victim's world, where "survival" is deemed the only issue of any importance. This is an entirely natural response. Survival is a key instinct and somebody who has cause to be extremely fearful must be able to focus on surviving to the exclusion of all else. To that end, everything else is properly relegated to irrelevance.

This phenomenon became blindingly apparent when my Battalion returned to peacetime soldiering, and officers and soldiers alike found themselves having to deal with boredom and self-discipline issues for the first time in their careers.

Emotions in the aftermath
Within a couple of days of the war ending, D Company was flown to Fox Bay on West Falkland. There we were able to keep to ourselves, rest and relax in one another's company. It was, in retrospect, an important time which allowed us to talk together about our personal experiences in an unstructured, and yet safe and comfortable way. Yet this was not the purpose of the exercise, which was to clear up the mess left by the Argentines and to mark out and clear minefields. I sometimes wonder what the effect on us all would have been if we had been taught how best to use such a period of respite.

When we subsequently returned to the United Kingdom, much of our excitement of being at war had worn off. In particular, we no longer experienced such a range of emotions. Nevertheless I was still experiencing intense emotions and mood swings. These quickly diminished, but in recent years I find that a pattern of behaviour has re-emerged (fig. 4). Common balanced emotions, such as irritation, can flash into anger with little provocation, a negative question or statement can be interpreted as an insult, causing strong reactions of insecurity, aggression or even the behaviour associated with victimisation. Feelings of low personal esteem also surface with some intensity.

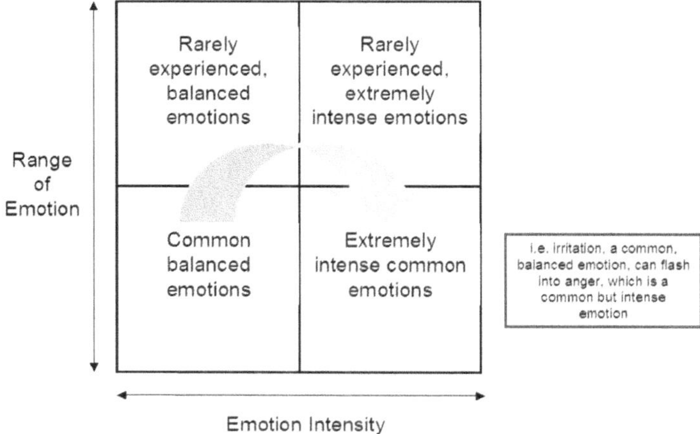

Figure 4. In the aftermath and beyond, emotions intensify erratically.

Finally, I have found recently that my ability to accept authority has weakened considerably. This may be tied up to natural ageing but, since my return from the conflict, I recognise my internally questioning the right and qualifications of each of my superiors to tell me what to do. It is very simple. They have never had to manage under the circumstances that I have experienced, and I am convinced (wrongly I am sure) that they know little about *real* management of people other than what they have been taught on courses. They have not had the ultimate hands-on experience of exercising high-stakes leadership.

The emotional intensity gap

Like many veterans, I experienced intense emotions and managed men in such heightened emotional states that their demeanour, words and actions were unacceptable to civilian society (fig. 5).

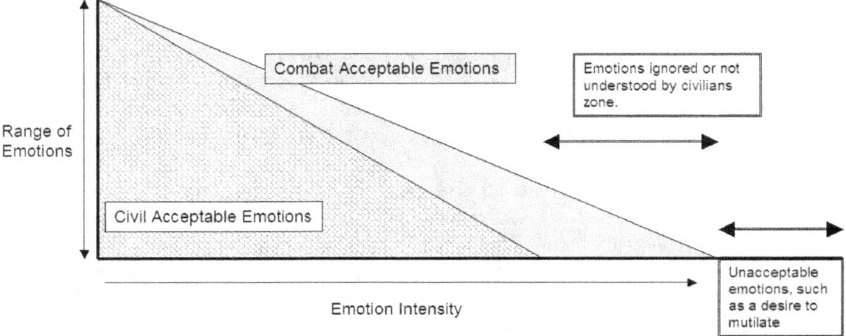

Figure 5. In the aftermath, emotions that were experienced in combat are no longer acceptable, thereby creating an emotional "gap".

As stress builds and emotions intensify, the actions and attitudes of soldiers reach a point that is generally deemed unacceptable in civilian society. Aggression is a common and relevant example. In a combat zone, aggression is not only acceptable – it is required. Even then, aggression can become so intense and unbridled that it becomes unacceptable even in military situations. An example of this might be the savage mutilations witnessed in Rwanda and Kosovo.

The gap between what is and what is not acceptable in civilian life is, in my opinion, at the root of the problems soldiers face in the aftermath of combat. The soldier who has experienced the requirement of "jumping" this gap must work hard to re-orientate his values and is likely to need assistance to do so. Once again, if soldiers were advised on this issue and taught how to identify it, they could develop coping strategies that would reduce their confusion, worry and alienation caused by them being unable to bridge "the gap".

Conclusion

If in possession years later of even a minute amount of knowledge as to what I would feel and how my reactions would be in normal interaction with others, then perhaps I would have been able to deal effectively with a number of issues, or at least seek advice. To my regret I am only now becoming aware of the many long-term effects of facing combat. To add insult to injury, it seems that many of the things described by me are well documented and a plethora of coping strategies exist.

I was on the winning side in the Falklands-Malvinas conflict and have generally dealt well with the experience and its aftermath. However, if we had lost, I hesitate to contemplate what the effects on me would have been. To have to deal with the unpalatable reality of defeat layered on top of the impact of combat must be a heavy burden indeed. I therefore strongly commend and respect those many Argentine veterans who have subsequently made a success of their lives, and sympathise with those who have suffered. It is time for all veterans of the Falklands-Malvinas conflict to look at how we care for those who have yet to regain their emotional balance – even if this means in the final analysis caring for "the enemy".

British Army officers are brought up to maintain a "stiff upper lip". That is good so far as it goes. However, stiff becomes brittle over time, and more comprehensive training policies on how to deal with the emotional issues surrounding combat and other high-stress military operations such as peace-keeping must be explored. Our society owes it to its veterans not to brush aside the issue of post-traumatic stress and its associated conditions with platitudes and parades.

With the training I advocate, it would be hoped that young commanders might be better equipped to deal with the horrors visited upon them in current non-conventional conflicts. I therefore urge the British Government to invest heavily in preventative emotional preparedness training and curative specialist post-combat care. This is definitely not a job for the National Health Service for the simple reason, of which I am personally convinced and which informal anecdotal evidence has confirmed, that people suffering from trauma require to be treated by people who have been exposed to, and suffered from, trauma.

The Anglo-Argentine Post-Conflict Common Ground: the Combat Veterans' Aftermath

Eduardo C. Gerding

Introduction

The Malvinas conflict lasted seventy-four days. There were thirty-three days of combat that caused 649 Argentine fatalities, 255 British fatalities (and 777 wounded), and three civilian fatalities. This short but intensive multi-dimensional war contained maritime engagements, air to ship combat, aerial combat, and land battles such as Darwin and Goose Green, Mount Longdon and Tumbledown that were exceptionally bloody and culminated with fixed bayonet and hand-to-hand fighting.

My aim with this contribution is to examine, by using an extensive bank of statistics, some of the Argentine and British somatic and psychological injuries from this conflict and, in particular, compare these to the American experience in the Vietnam War. I shall limit myself to describing two effects on sailors and soldiers of the extreme climate experienced during the conflict, i.e. hypothermia and trench foot, and then attempt to analyse post-conflict effects of post-traumatic stress disorder that, in some cases, lead to suicide and comorbid diagnoses. Other issues such as post-traumatic growth, existential authority, prevalent diseases, unemployment and family violence which can affect war veterans are also discussed. Finally, I shall describe the role and tasks of the War Veterans' Sub-Management Area at the *Instituto Nacional de Servicios Sociales Para Jubilados Y Pensionados (INSSJP)* in Buenos Aires where I am the Malvinas War Veterans Medical Co-ordinator.

I would like to stress from the outset that, in the Malvinas conflict, the bulk of the Argentine forces were made up conscripted servicemen, whilst the British fought with regular troops. Much has been written and talked about the war's teenage Argentine conscripts. However both sides had young soldiers and, for example, it also should be mentioned that two seventeen year-old, two eighteen year-old and three nineteen year-old British paratroopers of 3rd Battalion, Parachute Regiment were killed in the fighting on Mount Longdon. The underlying age factor therefore should not be forgotten in this presentation.

This factor's consequences have been succinctly highlighted in the Vietnam Veterans Association *Veteran* magazine published in March-April 2005 as follows:

In addition, the Vietnam veteran was our nation's youngest soldier. Whereas the average age of the World War II combatant was 26 years, the average age of the Vietnam veteran was 19. One can readily appreciate the monumental impact the brutality resulting from combat in Vietnam would have upon a 19 year-old, an adolescent with a barely formed identity still searching for suitable roles in adult life. At an age when most young men are typically forming lasting ideas about intimacy and relationships, soldiers in Vietnam were losing friends in painfully horrible ways, and perhaps learning that closeness hurts too much.

Little research has been carried out on the veterans of both sides in the Malvinas conflict. There have been a few isolated and limited projects, e.g. in 1991 a study was carried out on a group of sixty-four British Army serving Falklands War veterans. Their mean age was 27.5 years, they had 9.2 service years, eighteen had married in 1982, and fourteen suffered the death of a near one since the conflict. A significant number exhibited post-traumatic stress disorder symptoms associated with their experiences (O'Brian and Hughes, 1991). Similarly a group of 171 Argentine Malvinas War Veterans were studied in 1995. Twenty percent had lost one or more teeth, forty percent suffered some kind of accident after 1982, seventeen percent had a blood cholesterol over 240 mg %. In many cases the father died during the conflict, enhancing their sense of guilt.

It could be stated as a comment to such projects that, in spite of the several research efforts when the information is analysed with strict statistical methods, the conclusions perhaps are too fragmented to have a real and lasting value (Emerson *et al.*, 1983). Both countries have missed a wonderful opportunity to implement long-term comprehensive empirical research projects on their young combat veterans from this small war where the total number of combatants was not excessive. In the following decades post-conflict, the planning and implementing of follow-up studies on these veterans could have been conducted relatively easily. Indeed the only true common denominator pertaining to both sides from this conflict is the combat veterans, their problems and need for effective psychosocial support. Much could have been learned from such a possible pioneering study of veterans from both sides who had fought in the same war.

Hypothermia

In such extreme South Atlantic autumn and winter weather conditions, hypothermia can quickly become a killer when an individual's core body temperature drops to a dangerously low level. This became a major problem for a large number of Argentine sailors after their ship had been sunk by enemy action. Moving at thirty-five knots, the cruiser ARA *General Belgrano* (formerly USS *Phoenix*) was hit outside the Total Exclusion Zone by two torpedoes of the British Royal Navy submarine HMS *Conqueror* on 2 May 1982. This engagement would result in a total of 321 fatalities (thirty percent of a 1,091-man crew), representing fifty percent of all Argentine casualties in the war. Thirty percent who died were eighteen year-old conscripts, with eighty-four per cent of them being killed as a direct result of the torpedo explosions (Sethia, 2006).

However this was the only engagement during the conflict that had a prolific number of casualties caused by the extreme climatic conditions. As the vessel began to sink, the prevailing weather was of most concern to the crew survivors, there being gales with wind speeds in excess of 100 kilometres per hour, nine metre-high waves, and a wind-chill factor of minus twenty degrees centigrade. Approximately twenty-five percent of the survivors had to plunge into the sea that had a temperature of two degrees centigrade. Men dressed in water-permeable clothing can be considered almost "nude" when immersed in the cold South Atlantic waters, and some survivors were covered by slippery oil which made it difficult to haul them into the rafts. Ten percent of these caused great difficulties to the survivors (Gerding, 2002) and, for most, it took twenty-four hours before they were rescued. It is important in combating such conditions that clothing is layered, e.g. silk over the skin, then wool, polyester fleece and a nylon garment. But the statistics of this second phase to the disaster were grim: sixty-nine of the survivors suffered from hypothermia and eighteen died from this condition (Gerding, 1996).

Trench foot
It was Baron Dominique Jean Larrey (1766-1842), a military surgeon, who classically described the role that trench foot played in the 1812 defeat of Napoleon's Army in Poland. This non-freezing cold injury results from prolonged exposure to cold at temperatures from just above freezing to ten degrees centigrade, wetness and immobilization of the feet (Gerding, 1998). A graphic description of the condition has been provided by a First World War veteran, Sergeant Harry Roberts of the Lancashire Fusiliers:

> If you have never had trench feet described to you, I will tell you. Your feet swell to two or three times their normal size and go completely dead. You could stick a bayonet into them and not feel a thing. If you are fortunate enough not to lose your feet and the swelling begins to go down, it is then that the intolerable, indescribable agony begins. I have heard men cry and even scream with the pain and many had to have their feet and legs amputated.

Fourteen percent of all casualties on both sides in the Malvinas conflict were due to trench foot. The main reasons for British troops succumbing to this condition was a combination of the land high water table, inclement weather conditions, and appalling quality of the standard issue Direct Moulded Sole (DMS) boot which leaked like a sieve. In such a climatically hostile environment, high quality boots were vital in this classic infantryman's war. The table below is revealing with respect to the boots issued to the 707 Marines of the Argentine 5th Marine Infantry Battalion which was dug in on the Tumbledown, Mount William and Sapper Hill. The unit had also trained extensively in southern Patagonia the preceding year and was well-versed in the requirements of foot hygiene to counter bad weather conditions:

Average exposure days		Cases
Argentines	65	290
British	24	70
5th Marine Infantry Battalion	71	1

There were 173 Argentine trench foot cases treated at the Puerto Argentino Military Hospital. Thirty-four trench foot cases were treated at the end of the war at the Puerto Belgrano Naval Hospital with a hyperbaric chamber. Fifteen were severe cases, and twenty-three did not require amputation (Campana, 1987). Afterwards typical foot deformities could be observed. In third-degree injuries, the shedding like a cocoon of the shrunken gangrenous shell of epidermis leaves a pink sensitive skin similar to a baby's foot. A group of Royal Marine Commandos who were examined at the Institute of Naval Medicine suffered demyelination of medial and/or lateral plantar nerves of one or both feet. The best prognosis indicator of trench foot is the degree of damage to the peripheral nerves (Ungley *et al.*, 1946). As a result of this pathology many British soldiers who took part in the 1982 conflict suffer from cold sensitivity and will never be able to deploy to a cold environment again (Marsh, 1983).

The lessons of the past were re-learned. A good quality boot and rigid hygiene standards in the field for feet are crucial to avoiding trench foot which has the potential for crippling infantry units before they can engage the enemy.

Post-traumatic stress disorder (PTSD)

When men (and increasingly women) go to war, some are killed, some return home physically injured, whilst others return with invisible yet often equally damaging psychiatric injuries. The desirable notion that a military force deployed on operations might avoid taking somatic casualties, is a totally utopian one. This is also the case with psychiatric casualties. War provides an exaggerated, perhaps extreme, version of the entire range of human experience – not just fear, hate and guilt, but also excitement, love, friendship and achievement.

There is no single "experience of war", for good or ill. There are some for whom active service remains the best thing that ever happened to them, and for whom life afterwards is dull and monochrome. For many, though, especially those who are not part of a modern professional and volunteer military force, war is not the "best days of their lives". On return from war they appear healthy in body, but not in mind. In order to diagnose PTSD, the patient must have been exposed to an extreme stressor or traumatic event to which he or she responded with fear, helplessness or horror, and have three distinct types of symptoms. These are:

- Re-experiencing the event.

- Avoidance of reminders of the event.

- Hyper-arousal for at least one month.

Symptoms of the latter manifest themselves physiologically such as insomnia, irritability, impaired concentration, hyper-vigilance and increased startle reactions. The diagnosis is easily missed as sometimes there is an overlap with depression or other anxiety disorders.

About thirty percent of men and women who have spent time in war zones experience PTSD, whilst an additional twenty to twenty-five percent have had partial PTSD at some point in their lives.

It is estimated that between twenty-five to thirty-nine percent of Argentine Malvinas War veterans suffer from PTSD, and eighty-eight percent of them have never attended a health centre. The concept of veteran peer support which has been presented at this colloquium might well be of benefit to them, indeed the supposition that PTSD can persist for *at least* fifty years after a conflict (Herman *et al.*, 1994) is of particular significance with such a vulnerable war veteran category. In comparison, more than half of all male Vietnam War veterans and almost half of all female Vietnam War veterans have experienced PTSD. The latter has also been detected among veterans of the Gulf War, with some estimates running as high as eighty percent.

Depression is more common than post-traumatic stress disorder in UK war veterans. However only about half of those who have a diagnosis are seeking help currently, and few see specialists (Iversen *et al.*, 2005). With eighty-six years of experience in treating PTSD, the UK has Residential Treatment Centres at Ayr, Newport, and Leatherhead. The two main treatments used by psychiatrists are Cognitive Behaviour Therapy and Eye Moving Desensitisation and Reprocessing (EMDR). According to the Ex-Services Mental Welfare Society (Combat Stress), more than 85,000 veterans and their families have been helped, with forty-six percent of the referral sources come from self, friends and families and thirty-six percent from service charities, welfare etc.

Post-traumatic growth (PTG) and existential authority
War veterans can also be affected by the influence of both post-traumatic growth and existential authority. The former is an inner phenomenon which grows steadily during the remainder of the veteran's life when, with continued drive and initiative, there is constant application of the many lessons learnt and truths revealed on the battlefield. Whilst this is a positive effect, there are traps and, for some, it can lead to chronic fatigue syndrome and other problems. With existential authority, however, there is throughout the life of the veteran, a continual negative inner questioning of external authority and its capabilities. The veteran has experienced war, a major life-event that relatively few have witnessed or participated in first-hand. So the veteran's subsequent query, particularly after he has become a civilian once again, is a natural one. Could my current superior have dealt with that past situation in which I was placed? If the answer is no, the subsequent attitude might lead to reduced respect for the superior which could cause eventual problems between employee and employer.

Suicide
Suicide is a multi-dimensional concomitant of psychiatric diagnoses, especially mood disorders, and is complex in both its causation and treatment of those at risk. There have been an *estimated* 350 suicides amongst Argentine Malvinas War veterans (*La Nación*, 28 February 2006) and, according to the British Falklands veterans' South Atlantic Medical Association 82, in excess of 255 British Falklands War veterans have been *estimated* to have committed suicide, i.e. more than the

British servicemen who were actually killed during the conflict. This is claimed to be a conservative figure, but it is emphasised again that this, as well as the Argentine figure, are only most unsatisfactory estimates. Indeed the results of estimating veterans' suicide figures can vary wildly, as the following American experience demonstrates. According to one study (Bullman *et al.*, 1995) "... no more than 20,000 Vietnam Veterans died of suicide from the time of discharge through the end of 1993". However the book *Nam Vet* (Deans, 1990) states that "Fifty-eight thousand plus died in the Vietnam War. Over 150,000 have committed suicide since the war ended". The lack of comprehensive surveys both in Argentina and UK to produce reliable sets of figures for Falklands-Malvinas veterans continues to be a major drawback to understanding the problem fully. In order to measure these figures more accurately, an adequate and preferably longitudinal sample would be required.

Suicide prediction results in thirty percent false positives and, although suicide prevention is ideally primary, the reality is that most treatment is either secondary or tertiary (Maris, 2002). A recent report from Sri Lanka (Kim and Singh, 2004) described possible reasons for persons committing suicide:

- Conflict between collectivism and individualism.
- Rigid hierarchical structure.
- Repressive education.
- Influence of foreign cultures through cinema and television.

Efforts must be made to avoid normalising, glorifying, or dramatising suicidal behaviour, reporting "how-to" methods, or describing suicide as an understandable solution to a traumatic or stressful life event. Inappropriate approaches could potentially increase the risk for suicidal behaviour in vulnerable individuals, particularly youth. Applicable protective factors are:

- An individual's genetic or neurobiological makeup.
- Attitudinal and behavioural characteristics.
- Environmental attributes.
- Measures that enhance resilience.
- Effective and appropriate clinical care for mental, physical, and substance abuse disorders.
- Easy access to a variety of clinical interventions and support for help-seeking.

Comorbid diagnoses
Eighty percent of people who commit suicide have comorbid diagnoses, i.e. substance abuse etc. Fifteen percent of depressives who are admitted to hospitals will eventually commit suicide, and eighteen percent of alcoholics will die by suicide (Roy *et al.*, 1986).

According to a 1981 report of the Centre for Policy Research in the USA, the rate of alcohol problems among veterans as a whole is significantly greater than the rate for non-veterans. The association of self-reported excessive drinking in Vietnam combatants during military service, and in the first year following discharge was acknowledged in 1985, whilst six years later it was maintained that exposure to heavy combat more than doubled a Vietnam War veteran's risk of post-discharge alcohol misuse. But according to a 1992 report in the US Journal of Studies on Alcohol, the widespread incidence of substance abuse amongst Vietnam War veterans is due to PTSD, not simply the degree of exposure to combat. These statements are contradictory and illustrate the need for even more research.

Yet despite these experiences in USA with war veterans and use of alcohol (and also drugs), there are no Argentine war veterans registered at the SEDRONAR (Secretary of Prevention and Assistance).

Prevalent diseases

As a result of the average age (forty-five) of Argentine war veterans, awareness must also be made of prevalent diseases which will affect them just like the remainder of the nation. Such is the case with Chaga's disease: a tropical parasitic disease that has infected 2,300,000 Argentines, mostly in the north and north-west provinces. Coronary heart disease is the most common cause of death in the UK (125,000 deaths in 2000) but, by 2010, will be the leading cause of death in developing countries. Thirty-five percent of the Argentine population are heavy smokers, however it has been observed that the current prevalence of smoking, with all its implications for the increased risk of contracting lung cancer, was higher for veterans than for non-veterans (McKinney *et al.*, 1997).

Unemployment

In the 1995 survey, war veteran unemployment in Argentina was exceptionally high at seventy percent. This is also a deep-rooted cause of many of the subsequent problems for veterans. Long-term unemployment can cause severe depression to the affected individual which might have fatal consequences. Unemployment amongst the veterans still remains high and compares most unfavourably with Argentina's unemployment rate of 10.9 percent according to the *Instituto Nacional de Estadísticas y Censo* (INDEC), (*Clarín*, 20 September 2006). It should also be noted that, in August 2005, USA's unemployment rate among the 3.9 million veterans of the First Gulf War era (from August 1990 onwards) was 5.2 percent. Yet this was only marginally higher than the rate for non-veterans which stood at 4.7 percent.

Furthermore, a veteran exhibiting post-traumatic growth combined with existential authority can be perceived by the civilian organisation that employs the former as a major threat. In other words, the veteran has simply become too strong for the organisation's prevailing system and, in extreme cases, this can lead to dismissal (sometimes by devious means), unemployment and further negative consequences for the veteran concerned.

Family violence
According to the Argentine Judiciary, the cases of family violence have increased four- fold. Sixty-six percent of those women involved in family violence are married. Families of veterans with PTSD experience more family violence, more physical and verbal aggression, and more instances of violence against a partner (Byrne and Riggs, 1996). This represents yet another challenge for the War Veterans' Sub-Management Area at the INSSJP.

The War Veterans' Sub-Management Area at the Instituto Nacional de Servicios Sociales Para Jubilados Y Pensionados (INSSJP)
The INSSJP was founded on 13 May 1971 (Law 19.032). It has 3,200,000 affiliates (1,800,000 are older than sixty-five years of age) and represents sixty-two percent of Argentine elder people. There are thirty-six delegations and 550 nationwide offices. On 16 March 1989 (Resolution 494/89), the War Veterans' Division was founded at the INSSJP in accordance with Law 23.109 promulgated on 23 October 1984. The INSSJP tasks have been:

- Establishing the mission, objectives and personal responsibilities of the War Veterans' Sub-Management Area.
- Conducting a National Programme of Social Sanitary Control.
- Running a Health Promoters Course at the University of Buenos Aires.
- Running Self-knowledge Workshops.
- Providing free psychological assistance (John Fitzgerald Kennedy University in Buenos Aires).
- Free emergency phone call (0800).

About 150 war veterans are employed at the INSSJP and, at the Sub-Management Area, not only deal with war sequels but also the challenge of providing adequate assistance to veterans' wives and children sometimes in poverty-stricken areas. The distribution of Argentine war veterans affiliated to the INSSJP is as follows:

Province	War Veterans	Wives	Sons	INSSJP War Veteran personnel
Córdoba	1083	795	2189	10
Lanus	1061	810	2226	10
Chaco	927	677	2454 *	10
Corrientes	871	673	2298	10
San Martín	738	538	1390	10
Capital city	603	372	697	6
Moron	544	405	1101	10

* Fifty-six percent of these sons are below twelve years of age.

There is no doubt that we still have a long road ahead. With regard to this international colloquium at the University of Nottingham and paraphrasing military terminology, I would like to name our activities "Operation Healing": a true national debt towards all the brave men who went to the conflict.

References

Bell, N. "Why are people who return from war at increased risk of injury?", *EMJ Online*, Volume 175, August 2001.

Bullman, T. A., Yang, H. K. *Federal Practitioner*, 12 (3): pp. 9-13, March 1995.

Byrne, C. A., Riggs, D. S. (1996) "The cycle of trauma: Relationship aggression in male Vietnam veterans with symptoms of post traumatic stress disorder": In *Violence and Victims,* pp. 11, 213-225.

Campana, J. M. *Revista Argentina de Cirugía*, 52 (1/2)-59-65-Ene., February 1987.

Deans, C., (1990) *Nam Vet.*, Multnomah Press, Portland, Oregon, 97226.

Emerson, J. D., *et al.* "Use of Statistical Analysis", *The New England Journal of Medicine*, 22 September 1983.

Gerding, E. C. "Accidental Immersion Hypothermia in the South Atlantic", *International Review of the Armed Forces Medical Services*, Volume LXIX, 15 June 1996.

Gerding, E. C. "The 1982 South Atlantic Conflict's Aftermath", *International Review of the Armed Forces Medical Services*, Volume 75/2, 2002.

Gerding, E. C. "Trench Foot: The South Atlantic Experience", *International Review of the Armed Forces Medical Services*, Volume LXXI, 15 September 1998.

Herman *et al. Canadian Journal of Psychiatry*, 39: pp. 439-41, 1994.

Iversen, A., *et al.* "'Goodbye and good luck': The mental health needs and treatment experiences of British ex-service personnel", *British Journal of Psychiatry*, 186: pp. 480 – 486, June 2005.

Journal of Studies on Alcohol, 53: pp. 357-363, USA, 1992.

Kim, W. J., Singh, T. "Commentary", *The Lancet*, Volume 363, 3 April 2004.

"La Plata Islas Malvinas' War Centre", *La Nación*, 28 February 2006.

McKinney P. *et al. Public Health Report*, Volume 112, May-June 1997.

Maris, R. *The Lancet*, Volume 360, 27 July 2002.

Marsh, A.R. "A short but distant war – the Falklands campaign", *Journal of the Royal Society of Medicine*, Volume 76, November 1983.

National Commission of War Veterans Report, Ministry of the Interior, Argentina, July 1997.

O'Brien, L.S., Hughes, S.J. "Symptoms of post-traumatic stress disorder in Falklands veterans five years after the conflict", *British Journal of Psychiatry*, Volume 159, pp. 135-41, 1991.

Roy A. *et al. Biology of Suicide*, New York, 1986.

Sethia, N. "Hit by two torpedoes", *The Guardian,* 18 October 2006.

Ungley *et al. British Journal of Surgery*, 33: p. 17, 1946.

Wyband op den Velde *et al. Alcohol and Alcoholism*, Volume 37, No. 4, pp. 355-361, 2001.

The South Atlantic Medal Association 82

Martin Reed

The beginning

In 1982 Denzil Connick was a Corporal in the Anti-Tank Platoon of 3rd Battalion, the Parachute Regiment, which was a unit with the advancing British land forces on Port Stanley in the Falklands War. After the Battle for Mount Longdon he was wounded from artillery fire, losing his left leg and being badly injured in the other. His two companions were killed in this incident. Following a long hospitalisation and recuperation, he retired from the British Army and began to settle into the civilian environment. During the middle 1990s he became aware of the increasing number of 1982 Falklands War veterans that he was seeing as a caseworker for the Forces charity, "Soldiers, Sailors, Airmen and Families' Association (SSAFA) Forces Help".

The United Kingdom is blessed by many service and regimental charities and associations. This is mainly due to Britain's heavy involvement in the two World Wars and many other conflicts around the world up to the present day. For most Operation Corporate personnel involved in the Falklands War, the latter was probably the most notable life-changing experience they had endured. It even eclipsed the experiences held by the many Northern Ireland veterans who were deployed to the South Atlantic.

By 1995, other than retaining a few close personal friends, most veterans were losing contact with one and other, and this increased the feeling of isolation that many of them felt. To this end, Denzil decided he would investigate the need for and feasibility of establishing a members' association for British Veterans of the Falklands War that would also include Falkland Islanders and the families of those who lost their lives in 1982. Following meetings with several leading military personalities of the war such as Lieutenant-General Sir Hew Pike (former Commanding Officer of 3rd Battalion, the Parachute Regiment), Surgeon-Captain Rick Jolly (Commander of the Surgical Team at Ajax Bay), Lieutenant-Colonel Tony Davies (former Regimental Sergeant-Major of 1st Battalion, the Welsh Guards), Major-General Julian Thompson (former Commander of 3 Commando Brigade), and also Lieutenant-Colonel Simon Brewis (Army Benevolent Fund), it was identified that there was indeed such a need for a special association. The South Atlantic Medal Association 1982 (SAMA 82) was therefore inaugurated at the London Falkland Islands Government Office in April 1997 on the fifteenth anniversary of the war.

My involvement and the future

In 1982 I was the Chief Officer of the cruise liner SS *Canberra* returning from a world voyage. Instead of setting out on a Mediterranean cruise, within three days, on 9 April we had become a STUFT ship (Ship Taken Up From Trade) and were sailing to the South Atlantic without civilian passengers, but as part of the British Task Force with troops of 40 and

42 Commando (Royal Marines), and 3rd Battalion, the Parachute Regiment, together with their arms, ammunition, equipment, and stores. One of the young Paras on board was Denzil Connick. Also with us were the 3 Commando Brigade Medical Squadron, two Surgical Support Teams, Field Ambulance personnel, a full Royal Marine Band, and many other units. Where our large passenger swimming pool had once been, a fully operational flight deck was constructed over it and, by removing a lifeboat and inserting piping, we were made capable of re-fuelling at sea. We were so heavily laden that our ship's load line was raised by 13.5 inches.

Ninety-four days and 27,187 nautical miles later we returned to Southampton on 11 July. We had experienced being in the multiple roles of troop carrier, landing ship, multiple helicopter deck, casualty receiving ship, prisoner of war camp, water producer, and provider of food and comfort wherever and whenever we could. We had been in port only once, at Freetown, Sierra Leone, for eight hours on the initial voyage south. We refuelled at sea seven times from the Royal Fleet Auxiliary, the longest fuelling being for 10.5 hours whilst steaming at twelve knots and at a distance of 125 feet from the tanker RFA *Olna*, when we received 2,695 tons of fuel oil. In total we had burned 15,421 tons of fuel, produced 39,522 tons of fresh water and served 646,847 meals. Of those 27,848 were eaten by our 4,144 Argentine prisoners of war whom we repatriated to Argentina in one lift. We had treated 172 casualties, of whom eighty-two were British and ninety were Argentine, and had drawn 1,310 pints of blood. Anything less like a regular passenger voyage for a ship that became known to the British Task Force as "the Great White Whale" could not be imagined.

We had buried at sea four of those who died on D-Day of 21 May, that day of the decisive and highly successful San Carlos amphibious landings on East Falkland. I had helped the wounded, both British and Argentine, in our hospital unit and saw in close-up the horrors of modern warfare. I had also put many of the units of 5 Infantry Brigade ashore during our second landing at San Carlos on 2 June, where I found the temporary grave of Marine "Mac" MacAndrews of 40 Commando, who had been killed in an Argentine Skyhawk air attack near the San Carlos settlement. He was one of the men who had lived with us on board *Canberra* for forty-two days prior to the initial landings. I made him a promise there and then that I would see him properly buried. However I do not know what made me say that nor did I know how my promise would be fulfilled.

Two years later I returned to the Falkland Islands as the Executive Officer of SS *Uganda*, an ageing passenger liner which was being used as a troop transport. During the conflict she had been the British Task Force Naval Ocean-going Surgical Hospital Ship and her medical personnel had provided great service to both British and Argentine wounded. My voyages in her brought back many memories, both good and bad, of the conflict in 1982, and I began to realise how deep the impressions had been. At one stage we anchored at a location in San Carlos Water close by the British Falklands War Cemetery, and near to the place where I had found Mac's temporary grave. I realised then that, emotionally, I was totally unable to go ashore and look, either at the new Cemetery or for the old grave. I sent my young officers instead.

In 1997 one of my colleagues who had been serving aboard *Uganda* in 1982 told me about an Association that was being set up for holders of the South Atlantic Medal. I joined SAMA 82 with member number 379. Since then the total membership has increased steadily, so that now there are more than 2,500 persons who belong to the Association. It organised a Pilgrimage to the Falkland Islands for 200 members on the twentieth anniversary of the war in November 2002, and I was privileged to be one of the organising committee. As an advance party of one, I reached the Islands three days before the main party. My first immediate obvious task was to cross the Islands to San Carlos and check on Mac's grave, which I managed to accomplish. The site is now graced with a rock and plaque; he has been given a decent burial and, in a way, I have kept my graveside promise made in 1982. Afterwards I visited the San Carlos Falklands War Cemetery where, at last, I found peace.

In 2003 I was elected Chairman of SAMA 82. Since than I have been working to strengthen the Association, and we are about to register with the Charity Commission. Following the forthcoming twenty-fifth anniversary commemorations of the war, we expect our membership to increase with a concurrent subsequent increase in workload. Consequently our organisation will have to expand. However, the Association will remain dedicated to keeping holders of the South Atlantic Medal in touch with each other, in promoting pride and comradeship, involving us with those organisations caring for ex-servicemen, supporting our members in need and, finally, continuing our links with the people of the Falkland Islands. We are a member of the Confederation of British Service and Ex-Service Organisations, where our voice is heard and respected by the veterans' community and the Ministry of Defence, particularly in the realms of care and welfare.

I conclude with an extract from the final broadcast made on 10 July 1982 to the ship's company from our Senior Naval Officer on board *Canberra*, the day before we reached our home port at Southampton:

The Gods were kind. We did survive and now this family is on its way, nearly home, every one of us grateful to be alive. Not one of us will forget this thirteen weeks – it has scarred us all.

Enemies in War, Friends in Peace

María Isabel Clausen de Bruno

Throughout this colloquium I have learned many things and have understood that human beings commit many blunders. On occasions we believe we own a non-existent truth and are mistaken. When I met Vietnam War veteran Mark Sandman, he asked me why was it that I did this "thing" that I do – worrying about the Malvinas veterans? I told him that it was my duty as an Argentine woman and teacher. Now, after experiencing these past days, I feel able to clarify this answer further.

Once the war ended, the Armed Forces had to analyse the tactics applied and the consequences the conflict had for the country. It was necessary to keep on moving. Historians had to write "the history" and from their research, hundreds of stories about that epic event came to light. The few of us who do not fear the results of our actions dedicate our thoughts to the one who performed those deeds, and therefore wrote "the only true history": that is the one of the the soldier who lies abandoned in some corner of the land and who should, at the time, have been the most important issue for all of us. I was one of those who chose this attitude.

My name is María Isabel. As I grew up, my friends began calling me "Marisa", two names for the same woman. Malvinas, Falklands. Falklands, Malvinas: two names for the same territory. Our names may have been changed, but not our nationality. Both are Argentine.

I have come from far away to speak about those young people in my country who had to face a war without having been psychologically prepared for it, and about a people that was not prepared for it either. The Malvinas War was very strange and I will not debate whether it was, or was not, right. I believe no war is, for men, women and children get mutilated along with countries, and in the latter's name man violates the right to live. A supreme being put us on this planet so that we would build, maintain and improve this world which was destined to us for that using our intelligence and love we could turn it into a beautiful, fertile and benign place for generations to follow. For that reason He created it whole, without borders or languages. But men divided it up into pieces where to impose their power, and used different languages to lay down codes so that they could hide their intentions and attitudes from each other. And when a man wants to show his superiority over one of those parcels we call countries, he uses a great part of his talent to destroy not only mankind, but the universe at large.

Nobody but God owns the earth, the sky and the sea, and there will never be a human being able to change this, not even those who decide upon wars. Meanwhile, those who fight wars can only leave behind their testimonies of post-traumatic stress which still, after nearly twenty-five years, are attached to their souls as illustrated below:

Testimony 1

"The war killed my mother, for when I returned from the Malvinas I tried to commit suicide twice. I would lock myself in and would not eat, speak, or sleep. I would only curl myself around the memories of horror. None of us who went there ever did come back, in a sense we are still there. My mother's son did not come back, so three years later she died of sorrow."

"Twenty-four years went by; memories continue striking and forgetfulness does not arrive."

Conclusion: Not only they are losers in the war, but also on their return.

Testimony 2

"I did not go to the Malvinas, but lived the war in the south, on the mainland. I cannot stop blaming myself for not having followed my companions to the Islands so as to help them out, and for this I live alone. There are moments in which I cannot stand having anybody around."

Conclusion: Post-traumatic stress affects not only those who have seen combat.

Testimony 3

"I do not want to go into the subject of the Malvinas, because even though I was on the Islands, I did not go into combat. People ask me if I saw companions die, if I killed any English or saw how the Gurkhas killed, and I have nothing to tell them. How do I explain to them that I was in the Malvinas and did not fight? How do I make them understand that the only thing one hopes for when one is eighteen and in a war, is not to kill, but to live and not be called a coward?"

Conclusion: The lack of understanding shows no mercy.

Testimony 4

"They sent us to war without asking us, or telling us where we were going, like punished prisoners. When we returned the punishment was worse, they abandoned us and neglected us for a long time. Today they are starting to value us, but the damage is already done, we carry it inside and nothing can erase it."

"First we were heroes, later cowards and finally martyrs. They forgot we were common human beings, not warriors. There were cases in which our own parents did not want to mention that we had been in the Malvinas. They would not employ us; we did not know whether we inspired pity or shame. We were lost inside a blind alley; and some of us are still there."

Conclusion: There are only failures.

Testimony 5

"I had a military career ahead of me, a solid family with two sons. I went as a whole being into war. I knew what I was going to and why I was doing it, but lost my right foot and the shrapnel rendered my arm useless. We in the military know that these are risks we take to defend our country. My career was finished as of that moment. My younger son could not get over it. Having a disabled father who is also a loser gave him serious psychological problems. I blamed it on myself and felt inefficient. I had to fight with my burden and could not find the strength. My family's struggle for life did not end with the Malvinas. We have to fight it day by day, and it is now more than twenty years since it has been going on, I do not know if it will ever end."

Conclusion: Post-traumatic stress settles in the homes affecting the familiar environment.

Testimony 6

"Sometimes when I am alone at night in my job I watch the sky, waiting to see the flashes and hear the explosions breaking the silence of the fields. Then I cry in my loneliness without telling anybody, so that they don't suffer. But there are moments when everything revives and memories hurt so much that you would wish to die. I am fortunately fond of writing, which soothes it all for me."

Conclusion: They live looking for a way to escape.

Testimony 7

"I remember the hunger, the shouts of pain, the desperate running, the falls in the dark, the wounded, the limbs scattered over the peat, the stench of death, the bombs, the bullets, the cold, the wind, the weariness, the fear ... because the war is fear. But I also remember the good advice from my commander, but for which I would not be here today. It helped me to survive. I learned to value my family. I found God and learned true friendship. I did bring some good things out of the war, it is only a pity that I had to pay so high a price to learn them."

Conclusion: In limited situations we identify true values which help our survival.

Testimony 8

"When I came back I left everything: family, sweetheart, friends and studies, and I left the country. The return from the Islands was unfair and cruel; I believe that we did not deserve it. We had done everything we could and in the best possible way, but people did not seem to understand it."

"To live in Argentina became difficult, they treated us like crazy people from the war, traitors and losers."

"After several years I understood that I had to return, live in my country, get my compatriots to understand what we had lived through in the Malvinas, both for those we left buried there as for those who returned."

Conclusion: A desire for success can turn itself into cruelty.

Testimony 9

"I am proud that my legs were left behind in the Malvinas, so that in a way I am still there." (A year ago he died of pulmonary cancer in the middle of the bush, in the north of my country, with neither medical nor social aid. In a stained and wrinkled paper he wrote his last message: "Viva la Patria! Viva las Malvinas!" He was a Pilagá Indian, a soldier, an unknown hero of the Islands.)

Conclusion: So do we Argentines love the Malvinas

There are many testimonies which are comparable or similar to those presented above. For that reason, and in the name of mankind, I ask the professionals in this subject, especially Lars Weisæth, Mark Sandman and Eduardo Gerding not to abandon their attitude of solidarity, to bring their knowledge together and gather more professionals to perfect the understanding of this subject, to set up an international institution and to continue supporting those who have undergone the lashing of a war, no matter which flag, language or religion they stand for. Be just as the saviours of life, especially for the soldiers from the Malvinas, men affected today by post-traumatic stress and who, almost twenty-five years after the fighting, are still looking for a refuge in suicide. For as I wrote: "Why die when life begins and finishes constantly? It is only necessary to accept this with faith in God and ourselves."

And one man did. For the safe, optimistic, successful Mike Seear standing here in front of you is not the same of our first letters. That Mike was one of the survivors with post-traumatic stress from a war that made him say, "It would have been better to die in the Falklands than to return."

These expressions were identical to several uttered by some of the ex combatants in my country. I forgot his nationality, he entered my heart as one more of "mine" and I led myself to rescue the man, because of that "something" that feelings dictate to us without giving or requesting explanation. Or, perhaps, in gratitude for what many Argentine conscripts had told me: "The English treated us well when we surrendered."

I thank those English military who are present here today and helped our wounded when the war was over. I do so as an Argentine citizen and in the name of all the parents whose children returned. From Hiroshima onwards, science took care of fighting against the monster of radiation because its effects can be seen on the skin. Post-traumatic stress is more dangerous, because it kills from the skin inwards and is usually not detected with enough promptness to allow to fight it successfully.

From Mike's first letters I understood that the enemy was not celebrating. Well dug in, as he was, in his psychological trench, his words curled around memories. We had both lost: he had lost his inner peace, I had lost my Islas Malvinas, the only part of my country that I have not visited. A hidden pain hurt my reason and, branded with fire, made for so irrational an attitude. How can men kill to live? What about peace? What about reconciliation?

In 1997, an Argentine newspaper ran the story of an English soldier who was looking for one of mine. A furious impulse came to my hand and made me write on white pages words of reproach and resentment. Miraculously, after five years in which letters travelled northbound and southbound with words that tried to bring together two survivors of different nationalities who had both been to the same war and through suffering post-traumatic stress so they could support each other, those feelings turned into affection. The enemy became a friend, the lines turned into hugs and into winning against the suffering. An English soldier, an Argentine soldier and a woman who loves her country, united their hands to seed hopes on their dreams that someday peace will wake up out of its lethargy and be fertilized in the world for the love of life. We could plough the furrows for it to germinate, become ears of corn and let the wind scatter its seed to different countries, turning it into bread of subsistence for mankind. Nothing was easy in this story, neither the letters, nor the encounters, which were three:

• 29 March 2002: Mike travelled to Argentina and we embraced for the first time in Plaza de Mayo in Buenos Aires, the federal capital. There was no resentment there, only the emotion of friendship.

• 24 March 2003: I travelled to Río Gallegos, in Santa Cruz province, looking for Nicolás Urbieta, and hoping to make him break his silence. He was the hardest one.

• 20 September 2003: At 08.00 hours in General Roca, Córdoba province, Mike and Nicolás met each other in their first ever meeting after twenty-one years of searching. Hugs and tears sealed part of the past. No, it was not easy. There was much anguish troubling the blood and shaking the skin. The eyes would not be empty holes, and salty cascades bathed the faces, wiping aside the past, directing them to the future through tears of happiness and understanding, for friends do not have to think the same. This situation allowed the three of us to build a British-Argentine bridge of brotherhood, even through our dissent over the Argentine sovereignty of the Malvinas.

Mike carries the Malvinas as prisoners of his mind and heart in order to recover from the pain so that strength and optimism will help him build a new life. Nicolás and many Argentine veterans will have to do the same. I take the islands as prisoners in my mind and heart to love them and recover them as national possessions by means of peace and dialogue. In addition, since 1982, we are evened out and united by the most horrible monument to life: a military cemetery, its white crosses seeding the South American sored peat, whose lacerations may heal when the war memorial is inaugurated on the Islands. Mike, Nicolás and I might be present, holding hands and winning over the pain from a past that still bleeds in and under our skins, and the miracle of peace begins to germinate in the southern end of the world. For that reason, that day, we embraced each other in Argentina, like three brothers who have just found each other:

I looked backwards
I saw sky clearness
and darkness of abysses
I looked in the corners
and life appeared
I lingered at its eyes
In awe I saw that with the one
it cried and with the other it laughed
but its light of ignited hope
was so beautiful
That I turned my face
I affirmed my steps
and kept on forward.

I pray the survivors of wars may achieve this.

Adjustment to a "Non-Warring" Lifestyle: Veteran Peer Support

Mark Sandman

Background

From around the world, through informal exchanges and gatherings at various conferences and colloquia, mental health and other professionals serving in unofficial and official programmes have found several common factors in dealing with their combat veteran clients, including overwhelming work loads, insufficient staff who labour over-extended work hours, and the necessity of spacing out visits with existing combat veteran clients. Although it is generally understood to be bad policy to "wait-list" combat veteran clients, many treatment programmes simply have had to find creative ways to delay appointments. There are too many clients for the number of professional counsellors. What makes this situation more difficult is the fact that only the bow-wave of returning combat veterans from the war in Iraq and Afghanistan has hit treatment programmes thus far.

In the United Kingdom and Argentina, programmes for combat veterans attempting to come to grips with the personal horrors of the long-ago battles of the Falklands-Malvinas War are squeezed into competing for time and space with other veterans – if they can get support services of any kind to help them. In short, all reasonable expectation is that the existing treatment programmes and their combat veteran caseload will be stretched much further in the coming months and years. Viable alternatives must be sought and found, alternatives that will not "break the bank" of limited financial resources currently available, whilst being safe and effective in their use .

Implementation of the Veteran Peer Support model would solve a number of existing problems in one co-ordinated move. Importantly, the current manpower dilemma facing most combat veteran programmes would be solved. Credibility of the programme staff would be enhanced for returning soldiers. Older combat veteran clientele would find their combat experience useful in a new way during their retirement years. The new help would be partly volunteer, and partly more economical, so any budgetary drain would be constrained. Finally, this model would ensure that younger individuals begin to find their way onto the clinical team rosters of existing official and unofficial programmes alike.

Psychological bonding in combat

In combat when the time came to function whilst under fire, the action was done for each other, our squad or team members, and our fellow soldiers. For many in this situation, the idea of fighting for romantic notions of liberty and independence are not considered as motivating factors. Nobody in their right mind really wants combat. Initially, functioning under fire was difficult and a leader who chose to lead from the front would get up with rounds impacting all around him and scream at the rest of his unit to "Get moving and cover your team so they don't die!" This was an effective way to move along a reluctant or hesitant soldier. Later, the "reluctant soldier" who functioned as an "old hand" could move others along in the same manner. This style would simultaneously accomplish two things. First, it demonstrated that one could actually live through the feared combat and, secondly, that one did not want to be the only person to let down his brothers and fail to act.

The bond formed by successfully overcoming this fearful hesitation or paralysis together becomes woven into the very fabric and essence of one's being, seared into one's heart and soul. To be able to depend on each other enables individuals in a team to continue for a little bit longer. You rarely hear anyone say they are an ex-combat veteran or a former combat veteran. It is not likely, because the bonds formed are too strong and not so easy to break. Indeed it is much like the old stories that suggest there are no ex-Catholics or ex-cops. There is similarly no such being as an ex-combat veteran. Often combat veterans feel trapped in a purgatory of continuous transition. Somehow they are always working on trying to improve their situation, but never quite gain complete recovery.

I know my fellow combat veterans in Portugal as Colonial War veterans, in Argentina as Malvinas War veterans, in the United Kingdom as Falklands, Gulf and Iraq War veterans, in Azerbaijan as the Soviet Occupation veterans, in Kuwait as Gulf War I veterans, in the USA and other countries as Vietnam, Gulf War I and Iraq War veterans. Combat veterans can be loud and obnoxious, quiet and reclusive, angry and calm, rich and poor, black, white and brown, respected and despised. I know them all as myself and believe no matter what our cultural background or socio-economic status happens to be, that combat is the great human equalizer.

Together in combat with each other, we feel alert, strong, and exhilarated. We experience a physiological "high" caused by the rigours of the combat experience and, when all is working just right as it should do, then it feels exceptionally good. We hear people describe it with words such as thrilling, exhilarating, an adrenaline rush, and a "high". We experience it as a focussed alertness, a heightened strength and fantastic endurance, an overwhelming feeling of competence ready for instant response. It is not unusual for us to experience time moving so quickly that it appears to stand still. We see everything before our mind's eye moving slowly frame by frame. We are on a hair-trigger. We experience a timeless euphoria in our lives. We look back and remember specific missions with eventual combat action as the most exciting and meaningful time in our lives. It is the highest of peaks in our lifetime journey compared to which later civilian life might seem utterly flat and dull.

With joy we return from operational action to our loving families and supportive communities, but with a vague hollow feeling inside of us. This is an experience not unlike a drug withdrawal, of feeling bored, apathetic and, perhaps even depressed. We feel shoved along by life from behind with no control, and are attracted many times to dangerous thrills, excitement and, oh God, something with meaning and the feeling of being alive. We try to re-adjust to a "non-warring" lifestyle. Some of us can do this successfully on our own, but many need assistance with this readjustment process, such as in official government programmes set up to provide this support. Nonetheless many will not trust these structured mechanisms to help them in their greatest time of need. So where is there to go if this situation prevails?

Veteran Peer Support

One supportive option is to establish a programme of veterans helping veterans, a Veteran Peer Support programme, ideally suited to make the best possible civilian use of the insights, skills, and experience gained from the psychological bond that has been formed in combat. A Peer Support programme supports and encourages veterans to overcome their problems including those service-related medical misdiagnoses, or Personality Disorder, Substance Abuse Disorder and, perhaps, administrative military discharge issues.

As well as having a positive effect on morale, reducing work absenteeism, and providing support and direction for veterans who are feeling hopeless and contemplating suicide as the ultimate option, the Peer Support team helps to identify problems early. The development of trust between the team and the vulnerable combat veterans enables referrals to experienced and interested mental health professionals where necessary.

Screening

It is important to find the best possible Peer Supporters who possess a "clean" desire that is neither uncritical nor represents a dream to be a "world reformer". The ideal is a veteran who, in most cases, has some type of combat experience in his background to use as a guide or reference. Someone who has an understanding of veterans and veteran families and the unique, complex problems and stresses that can occur. Well-qualified veteran candidates will have enough assertiveness to counter the habit some veterans possess of acting in an intimidating way, but also with a demeanour that is warm, caring, and compassionate. Moreover this Peer Support veteran should have enough flexibility to work in uncomfortable locations, and at odd hours of the day and night, whilst maintaining and practising excellent social and communication skills and, preferably, in addition, a degree of political sophistication.

It is important to note that, as Peer Supporters, female veterans appear to be as effective as male veterans, equally having as much credibility. This includes their providing support to those individuals who are perceived as difficult cases.

Training

Through three days of difficult and focussed training, Veteran Peer candidates will learn, and develop a fluency in perhaps the most important component of being a Peer – that of active listening skills. The course teaches Peers how to recognize and assess veterans' problems, when referral to professionals is required and how to select the proper and most qualified professional resource. Veteran Peer candidates learn how to develop problem-solving techniques and skills, how to communicate effectively, deal with death and dying issues, and how to respond to relationship problems. Peer Support candidates learn the keys and techniques of basic and advanced communications skills, including the use of verbal and non-verbal skills, how to recognize and manage feelings and emotions, and about perspective, or one's point of view.

The Veteran Peer Support training course helps each candidate to become acquainted with crisis and trauma events and the theories of intervention at various response levels. The focus is on the history and background of crisis and trauma reactions, and on psychological survival. Peer Supporters also learn about the benefits of intervention during times of grief and bereavement. In addition, they learn how to recognize substance abuse issues, the visible signs of abuse, about enabling behaviours, as well as related marriage and family issues.

During these days of training, Peer Supporters also find out about the qualities of effective mental health professionals, building trust, and how to co-operate and work effectively with them in issues of family support, stress management, substance abuse and traumatic stress.

Benefits
Peers can develop a trust and rapport, as well as an ability to empathize with other veterans that often leads to instant credibility and a connection bond. This credibility allows Peers to assist fellow veterans in developing social skills, which are especially important for those who are reluctant to talk with official mental health professionals or become involved in official programmes. For those of us returning to so-called high-risk occupations such as fire-fighter, police, and those of us in highly skilled public occupations, for example teachers and nurses, there is especially a fear that our records will be used against us for premature termination or unwarranted disciplinary purposes.

Can our current employer obtain our medical records? We also worry that talking about our experiences will open the feared "can of worms" that simply cannot be closed afterwards. There is a fear of the stigma of mental illness, and this pervading feeling prevails for many of us. We worry about the possible negative limitations applied to our career if we wish to have access to official mental health services.

Many of us believe that the transition to a "non-warring" lifestyle is virtually impossible for some traumatized veterans, because of the internal conflict created by some painful war-zone events that often boil inside ourselves. This internal conflict is unsettling and disturbing, and can prevent many veterans from gaining access to the help and support they need and deserve. Many have been "burned" by the system during their military service in one form or another and, struggling with mixed feelings, are reluctant to access official programmes. There are unanswered questions that increase our reticence to seek help. Will we be labelled "crazy"?

Veteran Peer Supporters have the necessary training, motivation and skill to fill this obvious void for all those combat veterans who do not trust anything official or those who do not participate fully in the system. One final strong point for the Veteran Peer Support concept is that it builds upon, and further enhances, the military system of "buddies", thus extending and re-defining this military strategy into a highly effective and efficient civilian application.

The guiding principle of the Veteran Peer Support programme is that "nobody is better equipped to do for you than what you can do for each other".

Operational Mental Health in Modern Defence Forces

Lars Weisæth

Introduction

In the following meditations I shall argue that the time has come to review not only the old doctrine of "forward military psychiatry" but probably that a change of focus in military operational mental health also be made. New conditions of warfare challenge us to change from a one-sided focus in providing and maintaining manpower to a more balanced doctrine so as to preserve combat strength, whilst doing the utmost to protect the mental health of personnel at risk. Furthermore the reluctance of combat-stressed soldiers in urgent need of preventative or therapeutic intervention to seek such help calls for a change in the organization of military psychiatry in the field.

If killed in battle, soldiers should be honoured and commemorated. Soldiers who have been psychologically injured by combat stress, prisoner-of-war experiences or other war-related stressors, should be offered high quality health services comprising early preventative interventions, early adequate treatments and, if needed, rehabilitation services. If physical or psychological injuries become of a more permanent nature, restitution and compensation should also be offered to them.

In addition to the primary tasks of fostering pride and friendship among combat veterans, veteran organizations also have an important role to play in securing appropriate health services for its members. Combat veterans and veteran organizations can also, because of their experience of the true reality of war, contribute in a unique way towards reconciliation between former enemies and provide support to those who have been exposed to and suffer from war's traumatic stresses.

Historical background/context

The scientific history of psychic trauma is outlined in my chapter in *Reconstructing Early Intervention after Trauma* as part of combat stress studies (Weisæth, 2003). The existence of psychic trauma and ensuing health consequences is, to some extent, acknowledged by society and severe stress is identified in, for example, sexual and violent abuse of children. In this understanding, therefore, it is more difficult to deny war trauma as a type of severe stress, although it had been "forgotten" for a century until the 1970s when this painful fact of life was "re-discovered". History shows that even the psychological and psychiatric insights gained during wartime possess an episodic nature, tending rapidly to be forgotten after the war. A contemporary historian (Shephard, 2000) has succinctly described the apparently recurrent cycle in respect of war neurosis: "At first denied, then exaggerated, then understood and finally forgotten."

Definitions and constructions of combat stress reactions (CSR)

Definitions of CSR have not only included descriptions of symptoms, but also implied assumptions about cause-effect relationships. Such assumptions may be decisive for conceptualizations of CSR, diagnosis and treatment. In spite of his lasting interest in traumatic neuroses and his view that they differed from ordinary neuroses, Sigmund Freud stated that every war neurosis had a purpose and was a flight into illness by subconscious intentions. He also stated that war neurosis would disappear in the aftermath of the war. History was to prove him wrong on all counts (Eissler, 1986).

US Army General George Patton, whose views on this subject are thought to be extreme, stated that "any man who says he has battle fatigue is avoiding danger". This traditional equating of CSR with cowardice is still sometimes encountered even in modern armies. Courage is not absence of fear, but the mastery of, and ability to overcome, fear. This prejudicial attitude probably has contributed to the lack of psycho-education of officers and their men in how to cope with the natural fear evoked by the vastly underrated and little discussed huge "fight in the mind" of the "fear of the unknown" prior to combat, in both the long and short-term; the danger in combat, and how it affects one's perceptions, cognitive functions, emotional and behavioural control (Seear, 2003). Negligence of such education and training has most definitely reduced effectiveness in battle.

According to an earlier British Army definition, a psychiatric casualty was a soldier who became ineffective in battle as a direct result of his personality being unable to stand up to the stresses of combat. A more recent definition has implied causality by stating that "he is a soldier whose instincts of self-preservation (fears of death and being maimed) have temporarily overcome his loyalties to his fellow soldiers and his military mission" (Jones, 1994).

Definitions such as those quoted probably have sought to prevent CSR by scaring soldiers beforehand in the belief that fear of failure and feelings of shame and guilt and the terrible stigma attached to psychiatric breakdown in battle should have a preventative effect. It is not necessary. All soldiers fear they will not be able to cope with the ultimate experience of coming under live enemy fire. Of all soldiers from western cultures half waiting to go into battle fear the failure to perform as much as they fear being wounded or killed. Amongst officers the fear of failure, because of their heavy professional and personal responsibility in making life or death decisions, is felt by most of them as the major cause of stress.

Cultural factors may, however, greatly modify the meaning of fatality. The author found in the study of bravery in Gurkha soldiers facing grave danger that their belief in reincarnation, if killed in battle, and their fatalistic attitudes about a pre-determined fate, accounted for this phenomenon (Weisæth and Sund, 1982). Any apparent lack of compassion for incapacitated soldiers can be understood in relation to the overriding goal of the military Medical Corps, which is to "preserve manpower".

In modern NATO terminology CSR is used to describe acute reactions, of any severity and nature, which do not comprise a recognized mental disorder, manifested in military personnel exposed to exceptional physical or mental stress. A CSR is seen as a reversible reaction in a previously fit soldier who is temporarily overwhelmed by combat stress and is rendered less combat-effective or combat-incapacitated. This descriptive definition, emphasizing the stress of battle as the major factor, lessens the stigma attached to CSR, and allows a significant focus to be made on stress and stress reactions, thereby dealing with them in an effective and efficient manner.

Prediction of CSR in conventional warfare
It is expected that the ratio between the various categories of casualties in conventional warfare are as follows: Killed in Action (KIA) 1: Wounded in Action (WIA) 4: CSR: 1. If unconventional weapons are employed the proportion of combat stress reactions in relation to KIA and WIA is expected to rise. However, in peacekeeping missions where the soldier's ability to control the situation by the use of force is much more limited, it has been apparent that the proportion of psychological problems is higher than expected from the numbers of killed or wounded on actual operations (Weisæth and Sund, 1982, Weisæth *et al.* 1993).

In the first Gulf War it was realized that the potentially toxic effects of many modern environmental hazards, or the threat caused by them, could lead to the development of poorly defined syndromes, such as the "Gulf War Syndrome". The current conclusion is that this may relate more closely to other unexplained environmental syndromes, known as "medically unexplained illnesses", than to disorders within the post-traumatic stress spectrum (Wessely, 2001).

It is usual that a higher proportion of psychiatric casualties materialise from some frontline units, indicating the importance of collective factors, which are characteristics of the military unit in its generation, maintenance and resolution. The realisation that combat breakdown is better predicted by collective factors than by individual or combat situational risk factors, was an extremely important finding from both a theoretical and practical perspective. It has led to a stronger focus on protective factors such as group cohesion, leadership, motivation and morale, and has also helped develop military psychiatry.

The development of forward psychiatry
The lack of a true understanding of the role of anxiety and fear in the human organism's struggle for survival had, until the First World War, prevented the development of an effective intervention for soldiers who suffered psychiatric breakdown in battle. Before the First World War the theoretical model invoked to account for the combat stress reactions had varied from the purely somatic, organic cerebral to the moral, social and psychological. The one-sided bio-medical focus, for example, on the human heart, had initiated and maintained the idea that the cardiovascular symptoms, reported by soldiers in combat (palpitations, chest pain, rapid pulse and respiratory problems), were attributed to over-stimulation of special nerve centres at the base of the heart. Such an analysis gave rise to a long-running tradition of diagnoses focussing on the heart, and the condition became known as "Da Costa's

Syndrome" (Da Costa, 1871), "irritable heart", and "soldier's heart", to be re-named neuro-circulatory asthenia or "disorderly action of the heart" and, finally, in 1917, "effort syndrome" – the third most frequently quoted cause for discharge from the British Army. No wonder when it was stated that once a soldier had been told he had "soldier's heart", it was extremely difficult for doctors to persuade the soldier concerned that his heart could ever again become normal and therefore impossible to persuade him to return to his military duty.

The British psychiatrist, Charles Samuel Myers, had introduced the term "shell-shock" in 1915. The early intervention programmes that followed involved evacuation away from frontlines for hospital treatment and eventual discharge, based on an understanding of shell-shock as an "organic molecular commotion" in the brain, an organic brain injury. Ahrenfeldt (1958) attempted to explain why an organic interpretation of shell-shock was held for so long: the biased trends of "modern" medical science of the time; the belief that British soldiers who were "heroes" could not possibly show mental symptoms; that a condition construed as an injury with an organic basis offered a solution of sorts for all parties. These explanations led to the soldier saving his self-respect, the doctors did not have to diagnose personal failure or desertion, and the Generals avoided critical questions about the morale among their troops and in the meaning of the war.

That combat stress reactions could be a consequence of a mental conflict arising from a sense of duty being matched by an unconscious wish to survive, was first adapted to battle psychiatry by the psychoanalyst David Eder (1916) whilst working with soldiers evacuated from Gallipoli. "Flight into illness" and "illness gains" were the first analytic concepts accepted by the military psychiatric community. Myers and others introduced a series of intervention principles that became known as "forward psychiatry" or "Salmon's principles" (Salmon, 1917) after the American psychiatrist. In August 1916, the British Army was ordered not to evacuate shell-shock cases. Not only had Myers decided that the diagnosis of shell-shock was undesirable, it has been concluded from British and French, and later from German, studies that at least eighty percent of shell-shock cases had an emotional etiology. From July to December 1916, more than 16,000 cases of shell-shock were recorded amongst British battle casualties and a disproportionate number had fought in the first Battle of the Somme. Over time, some improved understanding was achieved about the relative roles played by individual vulnerability, battle stress and collective factors, in the genesis of CSR (War Office, 1922).

The intervention principles of forward psychiatry
Those insights were instrumental in developing an intervention model that enables the great majority of battle-stressed soldiers to return to duty within a day or two. However, this particular set of principles had to be re-discovered during both the Second World War and the Korean War:

Protection and reduction of stress. Because the condition is caused by stress it is necessary to reduce the stress exposure by removing the soldier from the most dangerous battlefield area.

Avoid evacuation to the rear if possible. Evacuation out of the combat area can worsen the soldier's condition and prevent his recovery, primarily by the three following factors:

- Evacuation may make the soldier feel a personal failure in terms of his own ego ideal, and that he has let down his comrades, his unit, the Army and his nation.
- Evacuation will remove the soldier from his comrades, his primary group, which is in fact the best recovery environment. The new and deeper understanding of group dynamics emerged from the accumulated experiences of psychiatrists who worked within the Armed Forces during the Second World War (Main, 1989). A main point of progress was a more considered view of that existential ideal which makes soldiers prepared to risk their lives in war: 'Men do not fight for a cause but because they do not want to let their comrades down' (Marshall, 1947).
- Evacuation away from frontlines, whilst damaging the soldier's self-respect, may spare his physical life. This primary gain is very difficult to give up, but is a pre-condition for return to duty.

Immediacy. Time is of the essence, early intervention achieving a faster and more complete reversal of combatants' reactions than if the intervention is postponed.

Role of the soldier versus patient or civilian role. The combat-stressed soldier should wear his uniform, retain his kit and personal weapon. The psychological risks involved in a soldier reverting to a patient or civilian identity, thereby giving up his soldier identity, should be thoroughly understood and appreciated.

Restore. Rest and sleep is often necessary since fatigue is frequently an underlying cause of the breakdown.

Psychological support. Explanations and acceptance of the stress reactions and underlining their normalcy and adaptive value, rebuild the soldier's belief in himself and his unit.

Recovery and rehabilitation through activity. If not a full return to duty, relevant restricted military service may be necessary as part of the recovery process. Ergotherapy (occupational therapy) had been introduced already in the First World War, underpinned by the principle of 'cure by functioning' (Brock, 1918).

Positive expectancy of recovery and return to duty. A curative element in the role of positive expectancy is that this attitude expresses a strong trust in the soldier's resources, that he is regarded as strong and healthy, and that his stress reactions are reversible and temporary (Solomon *et al*. 1986).

The advantages of retaining combat casualties near the front and in the military environment was obvious to senior officers, as was the all-important creation of the proper atmosphere of cure, reassurance and rest. Furthermore, the personality of the medical officer and quality of the patient-doctor relationship influenced outcomes. Gradually the principles of forward psychiatry came to be practised by military personnel other than the Medical Corps, including combat officers and, indeed, by the men themselves.

Today's challenge

In February 2006, a few days after it had become known that a Norwegian religious periodical had published caricatures of the Prophet Mohammed, a unit of the major Norwegian contingent with the international force in Afghanistan was attacked by hundreds of local civilians, many of them armed. The confrontation, which developed into a regular battle with heavy exchange of fire, raged for hours and several soldiers were wounded. At one point a critical development occurred when it was observed that two of the rioters approached the compound with petrol drums, obviously with the intention to set the compound ablaze. A Norwegian sniper was ordered to kill them, which he did. The isolated military unit was saved when after some hours it was reinforced by a British Army Quick Reaction Force. When the sniper with his identity still hidden, was interviewed on Norwegian television, months later, he was in tears.

This episode illustrates the dramatic changes that have taken place in the past decade with new geopolitical situations, new threats, and new enemies. This situation is probably most dramatic for the smaller Western nations that for a generation during the so-called Cold War have possessed a military defence geared to protecting their own countries, whilst expecting to receive reinforcements from other NATO countries in the event of a major European war. In a war to defend national independence against an invading military force, a "citizen soldier in uniform" is able to be mobilised. With national military conscription service as his trained background, and his nation's very survival at stake, it would be most meaningful for him to risk his life and, indeed, make the ultimate sacrifice in fighting for his country.

However, currently and probably for the foreseeable future, military operations will be conducted far away from home in foreign cultures under primitive conditions fighting asymmetrical threats. The local environment can be hostile due to environmental hazards, diseases and maybe dangerous animals. The media will be active with real-time reporting from the field which could negatively affect morale and support on the home front, as well as morale and "the will to fight" with military in-theatre personnel. Furthermore, web video has proved to be the perfect medium for watching war and counter-insurgency operations in extreme close-ups through soldiers' own personal video blog diaries. Thus potential viewers of YouTube Broadcast Yourself, an Internet media outlet at YouTube.com, can be provided with the absolutely realistic and brutal chaos of war much better than TV could, or would, record and broadcast. There is also a risk that some future antagonists might not adhere to the "rules of war" as proscribed by the Geneva Conventions. Fanatical enemies will not surrender, but will fight to the end. Troops may be challenged by child soldiers and civilian "combatants". Constant attacks by the detonating of improvised explosive devices will make transportation one of the most vulnerable operations, whilst defence against suicide bomber attacks has already proved to be a major challenge to implement.

Conclusion

In groups characterized by high cohesion, the soldier would, even in military operations as those described, be willing to risk his life for his fellow soldier. But it would be both for the soldier and his nation much less acceptable and meaningful to suffer high numbers of psychiatric or physically disabled combat veterans, and tolerance to losses by death would not be as high as in a defensive national war. Accordingly, it has been even more important than in the two World Wars to operate in such a manner that losses are kept to the absolute minimum. Furthermore, it has, not surprisingly, become a goal for the antagonists to maim, torture and kill as many soldiers as possible. Such methods are not likely to achieve their aim in attrition warfare by gradually wearing down the military, but rather are directed towards affecting military families in the home country in addition to negative general public opinion. The intention here is to make the war, or in the current cases of Iraq and Afghanistan, counter-insurgency operations, unpopular – thereby leading to an increase in political costs that will finally generate an unwillingness to continue the deployment. Indeed, studies we have conducted in Iraq confirmed that the tabloid newspaper method of media reporting on such issues will compound the stresses on the family at home, which, in turn, fuels a vicious circle as it then becomes a further mental burden on the soldier in the field (Tønnessen *et al.* 2006).

In a war to defend their homeland, soldiers at the front will accept that medical services are restricted because of their likely use for the whole nation during such a difficult time. There is, however, no reason to accept that military medical services in modern international operations should not have the same high standards as civilian health care. Unfortunately, this does not appear to be the case. For example, there have been reports from recent wars or counter-insurgency operations that some soldiers were sent home for psychosocial reasons or, conversely, have been returned to military duty without being evaluated by mental health personnel. This practice highlights the risk with "forward psychiatry" that personnel who participate in military operations and suffer from mental disorders will not receive the standards of care that are medically and qualitatively acceptable.

We have therefore proposed (Weisæth *et al*, 2006) that, when a reasonable number of troops of five hundred to one thousand or more are being deployed, a Mental Health Unit (MHU) should be attached. The way "forward psychiatry" has been practised in the past is that the first priority always goes to providing and maintaining manpower. However, we believe "forward psychiatry" should be practised in a more balanced way by combining both the need to preserve combat strength, as well as protecting the mental health of personnel at risk. Highly qualified mental health professionals taking advantage of the significant developments that have been seen in the traumatic stress field and general psychiatry will guarantee that the need of the individual is met satisfactorily.

Finally, as shown by Hoge and his colleagues (Hoge, 2006), a very high proportion of US troops who needed psychological care did not seek such treatment during their deployment to Iraq. The reason for this phenomenon is that a soldier utilising psychiatric services in the field will be in effect asking for a "career kiss of death". This stark fact is illustrated in that most of those who had sought such help were discharged from the Armed Forces the following year. To reverse this unfortunate situation, it is important that both the military system and individual soldier understand that most cases of combat stress-related problems can be treated successfully and a full recovery achieved.

Another recommendation is to integrate the military psychiatric service more fully into the general military medical service. The MHU personnel should operate in close co-operation with medical care units in the field. Because combat stress reactions are very basic bio-psychological responses to extreme stress, and many of the symptoms are of a physical nature, it is not necessary to single out the psychological response and make it into a separate "mental health problem" with a mental health service that has unnecessarily, and also inefficiently, been regarded as "different" from other professional spheres of the Medical Corps.

References

Ahrenfeldt, R.H. (1958) *Psychiatry in the British Army in the Second World War*, New York, Columbia University Press.

Brock, A.J. (1918) "The re-education of the adult: the neurasthenic in war and peace" *Sociology Review*, 10, pp. 25-40.

Da Costa, J.M. (1871) "On irritable heart: a clinical study of a form of functional cardiac disorder and its consequences", *American Journal of Medical Science*, 61, pp. 17-52.

Eder, D. (1916) "The psychopathology of the war neurosis", *The Lancet*, ii, pp. 264-8.

Eissler, K.R. (1986) *Freud as an Expert Witness: the discussion of war neuroses between Freud and Wagner-Jauregg*, Madison, International University Press.

Hoge, C.W., Auchterlonte J.L., Milliken C.S. (2006) "Mental Health Problems, Use of Mental Health Services, and Attrition From Military Service After Returning From Deployment to Iraq or Afghanistan", *Journal of the American Medical Association*, 295, pp. 9, 1023-1032.

Jones, F.D. (1994) "From combat to community psychiatry": In Zajtchuk, R. (eds), *Textbook of Military Medicine, Military Psychiatry: preparing in peace for war, Part 1*, pp. 227-237, Washington DC, Department of the Army.

Main, T. (1989) *The Ailment and other Psychoanalytic Essays*, London, Free Association Press.

Marshall, S.L.A. (1975) *Men Against Fire: the problem of battle command in future war*, Gloucester, Peter Smith.

Myers, C.S. (1915) "A contribution to the study of shell shock", *The Lancet*, pp. 316-320.

Myers, C.S. (1940) *Shell Shock in France 1914-18*, Cambridge, Cambridge University Press.

Salmon, T.W. (1917) "The care and treatment of mental diseases and war neuroses ('shell shock') in the British Army", *Mental Hygiene 1*, pp. 509-47.

Seear, M. H. (2003) *With the Gurkhas in the Falklands: A War Journal*, Barnsley, Pen and Sword Books.

Shephard, B. (2000) *A War of Nerves, soldiers and psychiatrists*, London, Jonathan Cape.

Solomon, Z., Benbenishti, R. (1986) "The role of proximity, immediacy and expectancy in frontline treatment of combat stress reaction among Israeli CSR casualties", *American Journal of Psychiatry* 143, pp. 613-17.

Tønnessen, A., Rød, T.O., Weisæth, L. (2006) "Norske soldaters mestring av tjenesten i Irak" (Norwegian soldiers' mastery of service in Iraq). *Norsk militært tidsskrift*, 176, pp. 4-8.

War Office Committee of Enquiry into Shell Shock (1922) Report of the Committee, Cmd 1737, London, HMSO.

Weisæth, L. (2003) "Historical background of early intervention in military settings": In Ørner, R., Schnyder, U. (eds) *Reconstructing Early Intervention after Trauma*, Oxford, Oxford University Press, pp. 3-13.

Weisæth, L., Sund, A., (1982) "Psychiatric problems", *International Review Army, Navy Air Force Medical Services*, 55, pp. 109-16.

Weisæth, L., Aarhaug, P., Mehlour, L. (1993) "*The UNIFIL Study: Report – Part 1, Research and recommendations*, Headquarters Defence Command, Norway, The Joint Medical Service, Oslo, Norway.

Wessely, S. (2001) "*Psychological injury. Fact and fiction.*" In Braidwood, A. (eds). *Psychological Injury. Understanding and Supporting.* pp 33-44. London: Department of Social Security, HMSO.

Weisæth, L., Michel, P.-O., (2006) *Operational Mental Health – A NATO Programme Adopted for the 21st Century.* Presented to the NATO Comeds Panel on Military Psychiatry (January 2006).

The Land Theatre of Operations, 2 April -14 June 1982.

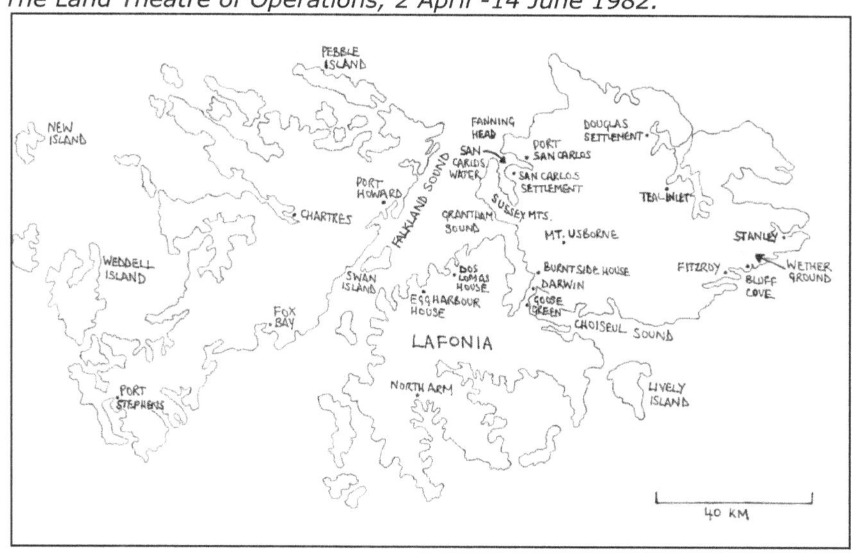

Nearly twenty-five years later, debriefing the Battle of Tumbledown in the Ye Olde Trip to Jerusalem pub in Nottingham. From left to right (foreground): Eduardo Gerding and Mike Seear, (in the background) Jorge Pérez Grandi (obscured), Carlos Hugo Robacio (obscured), Eduardo Villarraza, and Nicolás Urbieta (standing).

Prior to the colloquium dinner, Falklands-Malvinas War veterans and others. From left to right (rear): Toby Elliot, Jorge Pérez Grandi, David Morgan, Carlos Hugo Robacio, Mike Scott, Alan Warsap, Nicolás Urbieta, and (front) Eduardo Gerding, Eduardo Villarraza, Angus Smith, Diego García Quiroga, and Jeremy McTeague.

The Commanding Officers make their presentations. From left to right at the top table: Mike Scott, David Morgan, Carlos Hugo Robacio, (interpreter), and Eduardo Villarraza.

The Battle of Tumbledown, 13-14 June 1982.

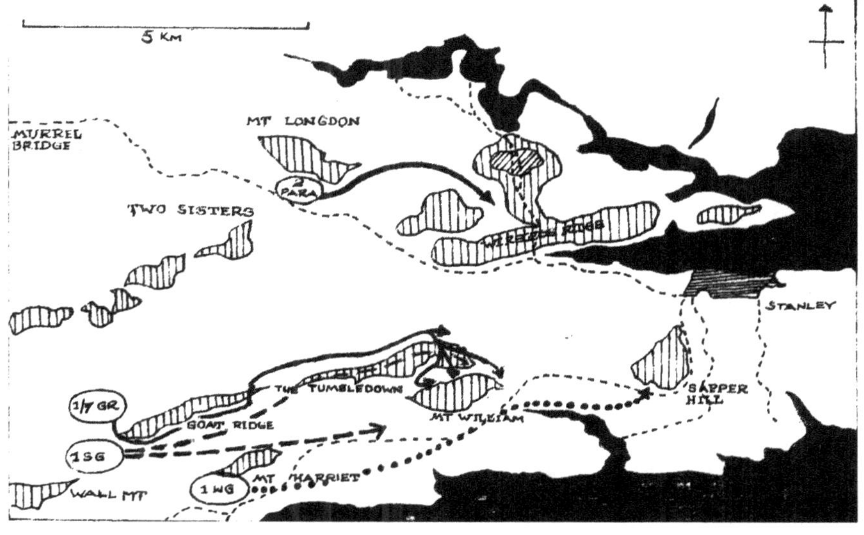

The two former main adversaries of the Battle of Tumbledown: Carlos Hugo Robacio (left) and Mike Scott.

The Tumbledown Commanding Officers and the Officers Commanding. From left to right: Mike Scott, Carlos Hugo Robacio, David Morgan, Eduardo Villarraza and Simon Price.

*Part 2
Reflection and Analysis*

Argentine Media in the Malvinas-Falklands Conflict

Lucrecia Escudero Chauvel

Introduction

One morning in Argentina, we all awoke to newspapers and morning news programmes telling us that we had invaded the Malvinas and, as such, were now at war with Great Britain. At midday, 2 April 1982, I went with a friend to the Plaza de Mayo. Many of the city's apartment windows were already decorated with the national flag. All sorts of people were there, spontaneously gathering. Some carried small flags and others wore ribbons in the national colours. During the war, my family had not escaped the contradictions that beset many Argentine households. My cousin, who was studying political sciences, signed up for the Army under the disapproving glare of my grandfather, who came from a long and steadfast democratic tradition, and for whom this whole war was just a "nationalist circus".

My father, a retired Naval officer who had had an important position in the 1955 revolution that unseated General Juan Domingo Perón from power, was in incessant meetings at the Naval Centre and meticulously followed the military communiqués about our Navy's movements. When Argentina surrendered, he was completely overcome and took to his bed for days. I associate the whole period with a background tune of León Gieco. His song Sólo le pido a Dios que la guerra no me sea indiferente became a sort of hymn. It played a crucial role in channeling the feelings of a generation towards war, and marked the resurgence of national rock music, which would become one of the forms of cultural protest against the military government.

We were all suffering from the same syndrome: we read all the national newspapers and weekly news magazines about the war, we listened to every radio programme about it and, because we could neither separate nor unglue ourselves from the topic, we maintained on-going telephone contact about it too. The conflict deeply affected us. We were active opponents of the military regime and convinced that an Argentine victory would guarantee, as my grandfather said, "a military empire for the next 150 years". At the same time, though, we could not let go of a cause that seemed to us to be a just one; our generation – like the one before it – had grown up with the conviction that "las Malvinas son Argentinas" (the Malvinas are Argentine). The war's paradox and huge emotional force was composed of two simple but deep passions: our childhood schoolbooks, in which we had coloured the Islands in blue and white, and the rationalisation of an absurd conflict victory in which would perpetuate the cruelty of the Military Government.

We also listened to foreign radio programmes, and my foreign friends told me that maybe we were losing. I can admit without guilt that we were aware of other versions of the war's progress. I cannot say that we voluntarily kept ourselves "misinformed" or that we indiscriminately believed in the triumphs reported by the national media. It was simply that these "other" versions of the war did not form part of the Argentine media world which we consumed, and accepting them would have put our own daily referential universe into extreme crisis. This issue constituted the war's second paradox: "inside" news, the "true" one that we believed in as our own, versus "outside" news. Could not that "outside" news form part of a world counter-plot of misinformation against our country? But only one year after the invasion of the Islands, the Argentines began to understand that the "outside" news, which everyone knew, but which no one wanted to accept, was sadly true: there were Argentines who had disappeared and there had been concentration camps in the centre of our main cities.

The Malvinas War contributed, as no other contemporary political event, to the disarmament of a complex system made up of basic certainties and "objective truths" with which some Argentines had comfortably consoled themselves. If war is a bloody form of conversation between two adversaries, then what were the mechanisms used to develop a mass news strategy that generates public consensus and political legitimacy?

Protagonism versus neutrality – the first days of the conflict
Among the interpretative hypotheses that can be formulated about the unleashing of the Argentine-British war with the landing of Argentine troops on 2 April, the one that appears to be the most exhaustive and probable is the close link between the economic crisis and the political institution. According to this hypothesis, the Argentine Military Junta – which was strongly divided – decided to find a subject that would galvanize public opinion so as to shed itself of internal pressures. And the subject was Argentina's claim to sovereignty over the Malvinas-Falklands (Hastings and Jenkins 1983; Cardozo et al. 1983; Verbistky 1984). In fact, the effect produced by the landing on not only the British and Argentine but on the entire international press was a surprise.

The Argentine newspapers registered the political-diplomatic escalation that would culminate with the Military Government's decision to recover the Islands through military action, but in the days that immediately preceded the landing, the media agenda was devoted to the General Strike of 31 March. Organised by the General Labour Confederation (CGT), it was the first labour strike after the 1976 military takeover which overthrew the democratic but weak government of General Juan Domingo Perón's widow and initiated the bloodiest period in Argentina's history with its high level of assassinations and disappearances. But on 31 March 1982, the popular slogans resounding in the Plaza de Mayo during the huge demonstration that took place rejecting military economic policy, already contained some indicators of the imminent military conflict. "Peace, bread and work", was the slogan that rallied the CGT organisers. The demonstration ended with the arrest of over a thousand people, among whom were the entire staff of the CGT. "In the Plaza de Mayo," – *Clarín* wrote – "the crowd shouted 'Argentina! Argentina!', 'They must go!', 'We want jobs!' and 'Down with the military dictatorship!', but the following eloquent slogan could already be heard: 'If they're so brave (the military) let them go and fight the British and the Chileans!'" (*Clarín*, 31 March 1982.).

How did the media present itself during the conflict? As of 31 March, *Clarín* placed the British press's view of the repercussions of the political-diplomatic escalation on its front-page agenda, and the rumour was already circulating that British nuclear powered submarines were being sent to the Argentine coast. This key position of the press – Argentine and British – whose prime function was to inform about the imminent invasion, became determinant in the narration of the backdrop to the Argentine landing:

> The episodes that took place during the strained vigil indicate that, in unofficial circles, the situation between the Argentine and British Governments after the events that occurred on 19 March[1] in the Malvinas, is reaching a point of maximum tension. *Clarín* was able to verify that at 19.15 hours yesterday, Vice-Admiral Juan Lombardo, Commander of Naval Operations, travelled to the naval base at Puerto Belgrano. (*Clarín*, 1 April 1982)

It is illuminating to observe the account that the Argentine press gave of the commentaries of the British newspaper The Financial Times, according to which the danger existed that the Argentine Government could "fall prisoner to its own rhetoric" because, for the first time in seven years of silence, a strong opposition against the military government had appeared, or because the Military Junta was using the conflict as a "dissuasive tactic" against internal pressures. The press's activity was marked with precision – identifying times, places and events – along with different modes of newspaper routine:

> As this edition is going to press, the landing at Port Stanley, capital of the Malvinas, by Argentine troops is considered imminent. The action's objective is to recover the Southern territory occupied by Great Britain since 1833. (*Clarín*, 2 April 1982)

The media's stress reached its apex at 10.00 am on 2 April when radio and television transmitted the first communiqué by the Argentine Military Junta.[2] It stated that a combined action by the three services of the Armed Forces had carried out a landing and initial combat to recover the Malvinas, Georgias, and Southern Sandwich Islands:

> It was 7.30 am when an emergency meeting of the Presidential Cabinet was called together by General Leopoldo Fortunato Galtieri. Present at the meeting were General Benjamín Menéndez, commander of the operation and the Armed Forces, and the Military Governor of the Malvinas. With a categorical "Good morning, Argentines" Galtieri began the meeting. Chancellor Nicanor Costa

1 The South Georgia episode.
2 Television and radio, which were owned by private companies, were taken over by the Military Junta during 1976 and strong censorship applied to the reporting of issues and to journalists.

> Méndez gave his report about the important measures that had been taken. (*Clarín*, 3 April 1982)

The treatment of information in these first reports about the Argentine landing was radically different in the other national newspaper, *La Nación*. In an opposition that we can call "protagonism versus neutrality", *La Nación* produced a complementary effect. The tone was impersonal and neutral. The journalist entered the scene only with a stylistic and narrative effect. Unlike the operation of "live transmission" produced when reading *Clarín*, *La Nación* chose to use the strategy of simultaneously presenting all the actors involved in the events. Let us see how this enunciative strategy of neutrality works:

> Argentina and Great Britain broke diplomatic relations yesterday and Chancellor Costa Méndez travelled last night to New York to defend our country's position in front of the United Nations Security Council, whose deliberations were being reinstated as the edition went to press. After the re-conquest of the Island territory that was consolidated yesterday at dawn, the Government of the Armed Forces is now ready to fight an international diplomatic battle (*La Nación*, 3 April 1982).

In this brief narration, attention is focused on the two collective principal actors: the Governments of Argentina and Great Britain, while Chancellor Costa Méndez, who would find in the future a large amount of reporting on his actions in this particular newspaper, is clearly delineated. Later, the differences between *Clarín* and *La Nación* become more accentuated. Here is an example of how Britain's response to the Argentine Government was handled:

> British Chancellor Lord Carrington announced today in a press conference that, given the situation in the Malvinas, his Government had ordered the severing of diplomatic relations with Argentina (*Clarín*, 3 April 1982).

> From Her Majesty's Foreign and Commonwealth Office, the Secretary of State greets the Argentine Embassy's Business Minister and informs him that, given the Argentine invasion of the Falkland Islands and the dependent British territories, Her Majesty's Government is breaking diplomatic relations with the Government of the Argentine Republic (*La Nación*, 3 April 1982).

Asked about his own version of the events narrated by both newspapers, the then business Minister Atilio Molteni told what he experienced on 2 April in London:

> I was in London, charged with running the Argentine Embassy, when, on 2 April, Chancellor Costa Méndez telephoned me. He told me that at the very moment he was calling (09.00 London time) Argentine forces were landing on the Malvinas. There had been indicators that the situation was about to reach breaking point. I had

received instructions from the Chancery – as shown in the Franks Report – to attempt to obtain a response from the British Government to the treaty proposal that Argentina had presented in New York during February of 1982. In my conversation with the British Foreign Office representative Mr Ferns, who was responsible for Latin American relations, it did not appear to me that the British had any intention of changing their attitude. I interrupted negotiations at the order of the Chancellor. I thought that what would happen at that point was what was supposed to have happened, in other words a confrontation on the Georgia Islands and an escalation in the conflict. Instead, what occurred was an invasion of the Malvinas and this let Great Britain declare Argentina as the aggressor! On the Georgia Islands the situation would have been different since we were authorized to be there. The Argentine landing changed the rules of the game and, in my opinion, was a mistake. On the morning of 2 April I was called by the Foreign Office and given an official appointment for 5 pm I had no idea what would happen. They handed me an official letter severing diplomatic relations. It gave me until Thursday to leave London. In a meeting with the Chancellor I gave him my opinion which was that the English would fight us down to the last man.[3]

From the very beginning, the United States' intervention in the matter signalled enunciative differences between the press "protagonism versus neutrality" strategies which characterized the beginning of the narration about the Argentine landing. While *La Nación* always maintained an impersonal and distant register, presenting the story under the headline,"The United States asks Argentina to withdraw its forces", *Clarín* presented it on its first page with its characteristic direct reporting style: "Reagan: 'I didn't think they'd do it'".

The News Malvinisation Syndrome
In 1982 78% of Britons read at least one national newspaper daily. This percentage, one of the highest in Europe, rose to 85% if one includes those Britons who also purchased at least one regional newspaper. Argentine data from the same period show similar trends.

IPSA found that 77% of the population read a national newspaper and 60% read weekly news magazines during the war. BBC1 and BBC2's television and radio news programmes had the largest audience, followed by ITN's (Independent Television News) and IRN's (Independent Radio News) during the conflict. Beyond these stations' general programming, those broadcasts specifically focussed on the war which had the highest number of viewers were ITN's News at Ten, with 17 million viewers the day that the Argentines surrendered on South Georgia, followed by BBC1's Nine O'Clock News. The most controversial programme broadcast during the period of the war was undoubtedly the BBC's *Panorama*.

During the month of March 1982 the Argentine viewing public

3 Testimony of Ambassador Atilio Molteni quoted in Escudero, 1996, 87.

preferred to watch football (28.4 rating) and two soap operas (27.2 and 24.5 rating). According to IPSA during April, however, the viewing choices completely changed as the public focussed its attention on the state channel ATC news programmes, with the magazine *60 Minutes* and *Good Evening Argentina*, giving nationalistic and triumphal coverage. From Saturday 20 May to Sunday 21 May ATC broadcast 24 hours for the Malvinas, a telethon that included the country's principal television stars, dedicated to Argentine soldiers in the Malvinas as a demonstration of solidarity (31.2 rating). The state channel also presented *To England with Humour*, which satirized the British Secret Service in prime time (28.3 rating). The month's programming closed with Channel 11's weekly Saturday night tribute to examples of Latin American solidarity *Argentina, You Aren't Alone*. In the month of June, practically on the eve of the Argentine surrender, Pope John Paul II's visit reached the second rating place with a 42.3 rating (12 June). In the month of July, with the war now over, news broadcasts fell to ninth place and sitcoms occupied the first three place rating levels (almost a 35 rating). News broadcasts on Radio Belgrano, Radio Continental, Radio Mitre, Radio Splendid and Radio Nacional reached average ratings of 16 to 18 during the same period.

I label this phenomenon "the News Malvinisation Syndrome" due to the fact that the quasi-totality of the news media in Argentina was directly related to the conflict. From the beginning of the war, the audience could not find a "neutral" space in those media that did not discuss the event. An immediate effect of this syndrome was a dissemination of the conflict throughout the whole of the news sector as presented by the newspapers and audio-visual programmes in such a way that the audience found itself practically "imprisoned" by the discourse about the war. This syndrome was constant in Argentina's two principal daily newspapers, *Clarín* and *La Nación*, and on the national TV channel ATC. When compared to their British press counterparts, the following is evident:

Both Argentine and British newspapers published special editions about the Argentine forces' 2 April landings.

The Argentine newspapers did not modify their internal structure with special sections concerning the war. This means that, from the conflict's beginning *Clarín* and *La Nación* refused to sever textually their traditional news presentation system in order to cover the war. In contrast, the majority of British papers immediately constructed a specific section dedicated to the conflict.

The Argentine newspapers' choice was a diffused news strategy for the war which longitudinally and transversally crossed all sections, thereby producing the effect of an "imprisoned reader" and the News Malvinisation Syndrome. The British papers, as a result of their strong sections, clearly produced a contrary effect in which the reader was free to circulate within general news and pause – if desired – at news items concerning the war.

To conclude this rapid panorama of the general news system during the war, unlike the two major Argentine national newspapers whose internal and external organisation did not change during the war, the weekly magazines such as *Gente*, *La Semana* and *Revista Diez* presented special issues of the conflict and pubished external and internal logos indicating the different items of the war such as "In State of War", "The Georgia Battle", "We win", etc. (*Gente*); national flags with Malvinas Islands in *Revista Diez*, and a section "Semana" at the front lines of victory for *La Semana*. Weekly news magazines were transformed into actual devices that graphically focused on and set a scene for the war. This was done as an attempt to compete with the television information, and above all to offer the reader something that the news rarely presented in the two enemy countries: images, making the difference in post-modern war visibility.

Objectivity, censorship and press agencies

Censorship made images a rare product of information. In fact almost two hundred war correspondents had to leave the Islands during the conflict.[4] In terms of the military's control of the Argentine media during the conflict, it can be argued that initially, during the first two weeks, the Military Junta sought to achieve a "participatory" position with the principal newspapers in order to construct favourable public opinion.[5] With the worsening of the conflict towards the end of April, the unfruitful negotiations by the US Foreign Secretary of State Alexander Haig, and the re-conquering of South Georgia by the British, the Armed Forces had total control of all information about the war.[6] As was to be revealed later, Argentine journalists suffered from a news black-out during the conflict's final month. Journalist Oscar Raúl Cardozo, from *Clarín*, told of the practices of journalists and his perception of the era's censorship and auto-censorship:

> I covered all the information coming from the United States. I remember particularly being in New York – it was a key moment in the negotiations – I went back to my hotel, turned on the TV and saw CBS News, the first thing they showed was some BBC footage. I called Buenos Aires. The Editor's office answered and euphorically they said, "We sunk the Invincible!" I was seeing something else, live, at that moment. I said to them, "Look, I'm seeing something to the contrary," and they answered, "That's all just a psychological plot." I used to dine with British journalists. They also distorted information. I was with the News Director of the BBC during his conflict with Mrs Thatcher when he stated: "The BBC doesn't need Mrs Thatcher to give it lessons in patriotism". This type of attitude was absent in Argentina at the time. I think that the news expressed two clear objectives: a) gestating military thinking about the war, e.g. the fact that the USA was supporting us and that Russia was going to help us by intervening; and b) when this turned out to be impossible, we had to deny the fact. What the Military Government did was not so much to sustain a lie as to prevent the rest of the world's reports about the war from penetrating into Argentina. This

4 *Clarín*, 8 April 1982.
5 *Clarín*, 3 April 1982; La Nación, 3 April 1982.
6 The resolution was published in its totality on the first page of *La Nación*'s 30 April 1982 edition.

was already clear with the issue of the disappeared people. The response was "I did not know anything about it". There was also the complicity of the public: the public wanted to believe that they did not know anything. I arrived in Buenos Aires from New York two days before the defeat and I remember that there was no awareness of what was happening; people still thought we were winning. The press was clearly responsible in the construction of this image: the press lied by omission more than by action. It abandoned its role as a watchdog; when we were at war, the press did not question. And when reality did not fit, it was censored. It was an internal auto-censorship.[7]

Performing a quantitative classification based on the frequency and amount of information expressed in news about Malvinas-Falklands conflict during the totality of the war by the two principal Argentine newspapers, the following can be seen:

	La Nación	*Clarín*
Total news items (2 April to 16 June)	7,325	8,510
Malvinas-Falklands news items	2,161	4,529
% Malvinas-Falklands news items	29.5%	53.2%

Apart from being eloquent, these figures indicate the Argentine press's effort to cover the event in an exhaustive manner despite the restrictions they were under in terms of information sources and military censorship. The data indicates that a third of all information published by *La Nación* and more than half of that published by *Clarín* made reference to the war. In the weekly news magazines analysed, no differences were found between them, and the Malvinas-Falklands conflict made up 90% of the material published.[8]

This profusion of information from first to last page of the press and magazines confirms, at least from a quantitative viewpoint, the News Malvinisation Syndrome. It also raises a question: just who or what were the information sources within this considerable information flux?

Sources in war information
It seems evident that the issue of information sources' use during a war is a recurrent problem in the study of press-production routines. It forms part of the debate about the objectivity of information. Even if statistical indices reveal that most of the information expressed through the written press uses national and international agency sources, Argentina's *Clarín* and *La Nación* inverted this tendency during the war.[9]

7 Testimony of *Clarín*'s journalist and war correspondent Oscar Raúl Cardozo, quoted in Escudero, 1996, 73-74.
8 Research carried out in the Faculty of Political Sciences, University of Rosario (Argentina), under my direction in 1987.
9 Testimony of Richard Kirschbaum, quoted in Escudero, 1996, 69.

	La Nación	Clarín
Percentage of use of agency information	28.9%	42.88%
AFP (France)	3.6%	7.66%
EFE (Spain)	3.7%	7.35%
ANSA (Italy)	5.4%	7.17%
AP (USA)	6.4%	6.53%
UPI (USA)	4.7%	5.54%
Latin Reuters (UK)	1.8%	5.21%
DYN (Argentina)	1.7%	2.45%
TÉLAM (Argentine Government Agency)	1.6%	0.97%
Institutional/official and unofficial sources	71.1%	57.12%

Although *La Nación* and *Clarín* had correspondents in London, Washington and New York, itinerant reporters in Paris, Madrid and Havana, and special envoys in the Malvinas-Falklands, because of the upcoming British invasion, all Argentine journalists had to leave the Islands in April by order of the Military Junta. The use of institutional and unofficial sources can be explained by the fluidity of their contacts with the Government. A cover-up by these papers is indicated through their use of stable information sources in diverse political lobbies, which found resonance in both newspapers. Seen from this viewpoint, the two newspapers do not escape Tuchman and Gan's characterization of the relationship between sources and the power pyramid (Tuchman, 1978, 38, 1988; Gans 1979, 116-145).

Interviewed about the way in which *Clarín* used information sources, Ricardo Kirschbaum, *Clarín*'s editorialist during the conflict, and now Editor in Chief of the newspaper, affirmed that: "You had to decide between either military information or agency cables. There was no other alternative. It was a war where there was no independent press, just an official one. *Clarín*, for example, did not have a journalist stationed on the Islands, neither did any other Argentine media. The TÉLAM agency, though, was there throughout the whole war".[10]

In a written interview Bartolomé Mitre, director and owner of *La Nación* at the time of the war, lists the information sources used by his newspaper. His statements coincide with those of Kirschbaum about the legitimacy of the Argentine Minister of Foreign Affairs' information sources:

La Nación's sources were the Argentine Chancery, the Armed Forces, political parties, Argentine specialists on foreign politics, and naturally, members of the Executive wing. Adding to these national sources were national and diplomatic ones, ONU and OEA officials, foreign newspaper correspondents, etc. In Argentina, our information

10 Testimony of Richard Kirschbaum, quoted in Escudero, 1996, 69.

was received by *La Nación* journalists covering official, private and diplomatic organizations. Outside Argentina, the information came through our correspondents in Europe and America, as well as those covering international organizations. Foreign news cables were always used, including those that came from Great Britain.[11]

DYN and TÉLAM were Argentina's national and governmental news agencies. They made up an extremely low percentage of the sources used and cited by both papers. This percentage never went beyond three percent of all the information presented in these journals. It is possible that the journals considered DYN's and TÉLAM's information to be biased as opposed to the information received from international sources. Whatever were the reasons that led *La Nación* and *Clarín* not to use information from these agencies, at the very least, these agencies revealed a weak capacity for interpretation and adaptation to the construction of the newspaper's agendas.

In a series of qualitative interviews with twenty-four to fifty year-old middle-class Argentines about the press's credibility and consumption during the war, the suspicion of their having been presented with "distorted information" is strong and current:

It was drivel given by Galtieri. They falsified information, they were liars. But Argentina is generally like that. The press is like that, there isn't a culture of criticizing, or of informing. The media has total impunity (male, 46, businessman).

I believed them (the press) all equally. I didn't believe one more than another. I also didn't trust any of them because deep down I knew that they were lying to us, but it was a lie and illusion. I wanted to believe the media illusion. I knew that playing with information was part of war [...] in any case, I enjoyed all the Argentine exploits. But I think that it was false information. In terms of the result, up until two days before the defeat we were going to win and suddenly they had to admit that we'd lost! (male, 37, architect).

You had to see that the press was controlled by the government like the television, that they falsified information. The written press tried to adjust its search for the truth. The magazines in general were orientated to sensationalism and didn't have much to do with news. In general, the media based itself on official sources that were very popular, but weren't objective about the conflict. I believed in *Clarín*'s political analysis and in *La Nación*'s foreign information sources (male, 35, businessman).

I had good information because I had friends in the Navy. I never trusted the press because they steer and distort the news. An example? The Navy's decisions. The internal power struggles in the military were very complex and there wasn't ever any real access to

11 Testimony of Bartolomé Mitre quoted in Escudero, 1996, 70.

what was actually happening in other military ranks (male, 35, union leader).

In the end, no one dared to say that we'd lost! (male, student, 24).

Many years later

The Malvinas-Falklands conflict – which has entered into the modern mythology of media wars – was an example of coverage in a period when globalised media had yet not arrived, if we compare it with the coverage of the first Gulf War by CNN. It was played out far from the Theatre of Operations of all the political actors involved – including the Argentines – and for the large-scale public it only acquired visibility through pictures and words. It was a narrative war, as CNN was a televised war. As in all global events that shake a society, intensity and duration do not matter (e.g. 11 September 2001). In wars, terrorist attacks, earthquakes, etc. the media is there to report and to construct the event. In the case of Argentina's coverage, it suffered the contradictions between internal political pressures and journalism's ethics, between how to tell and what to say, in the context of a brutal censorship.

However, the force and power of the story managed practically to contaminate all of the reporting world and, in this way, the audience cannot escape the fascination that the conflict produced. I believe that a complementary hypothesis must be added to "the News Malvinisation Syndrome": namely that the Malvinas-Falklands conflict was possibly the last war of the twentieth century attributable to the colonial values at stake, the monopoly of power and censorship, the attempt to place a single rationalization – brute force – over the plasticity of diplomatic negotiations, and finally its enactment as a given naval conflict, with its particular time-flow. These long waits – waiting with an expectation of the conflict's outcome – had to be filled by media stories. After the Malvinas-Falklands conflict, war was to be covered in different modes.

References

Cardozo, R.O., Van der Kooy, E., Kirschbaum, R. (1983) *Malvinas: La trama secreta*, Buenos Aires, Sudamericana.

Escudero Chauvel, L. (1996) *Malvinas, el gran relato. Fuentes y rumores en la informacion de guerra*, Barcelona, Gedisa.

Escudero Chauvel, L. (1996) *Media Truth: fiction and rumors in war news in the Malvinas-Falklands conflict*, Toronto, Monograph Series of the Toronto Semiotic Circle, No. 18, University of Toronto Press, Victoria College.

Gans, H. (1979) *Deciding what's news*, New York, Random House.

Hastings, M., Jenkins, S. (1983) *The Battle of the Falklands*, London, Pan Books.

Tuchman, G. (1978) *Making the news*, New York, Free Press.

Verbitsky, H. (1984) *La ultima batalla de la Tercera Guerra Mundial*, Buenos Aires, Sudamericana.

"Saving the Nation":
Post-Conflict from the Point of View of the "Guilty"

Sophie Thonon-Wesfreid

On 24 March 1976, a Military Junta composed of the Army, the Navy and the Air Force took power in Argentina and suspended the constitutional organs for seven years up to the elections of October 1983. Its first leader was the General of the Army, Jorge Rafael Videla, who dominated the country from 29 March 1976 to 29 March 1981. The repression led by the military and police forces was the cruellest ever imposed on Argentina and probably in Latin American history. Savage tortures were systematically applied to the people arrested and 30,000 persons "disappeared", the bodies of whom have never been found.[1] During the trial undertaken in 1985 against the different members of the four successive Juntas, the prosecutor, Julio Strasera, qualified the repression as being "ferocious, clandestine and cowardly".

The first task undertaken by the dictatorship was to justify the coup perpetrated against an elected government, the one led by Juan Domingo Perón's widow and third wife, Isabel Perón, and then to justify the repression. The Armed Forces denounced the civil government as totally unable to assume its mission and therefore responsible for all the national disasters, such as anarchy, corruption, lack of productivity, financial speculation, etc. which were supposed to have gangrened all state institutions. On the contrary, the military power, supposedly uncontaminated by these vices by being endowed with moral and ethical principles, presented itself as the only one able to restore order, strength and faith to the Argentine nation and as being in charge of a divine mission: the search for the common good and national restoration.

In order to justify the bloody and clandestine repression exercised by the military forces, a concept was created called the National Security Doctrine, an expression of a new plan of domination by the United States over Latin America. This doctrine, elaborated by President Richard Nixon's administration, consisted in the reinforcement of Latin American armies for the destruction of the enemy, from inside or outside of the country, in order to assure the protection of North America's interests, both in strategic and economic fields.

In a famous open letter written a year after the coup on 24 March 1977, a journalist and writer, Rodolfo Walsh, drew up a balance sheet of the dictatorship: 15,000 people had "disappeared" – double that number by 1983 – through the systematic use of torture, and 400 illegal centres of detention were scattered throughout the whole country; there had been widespread destruction of productive forces and political and trade union structures; poverty had increased – in a year the purchasing power of the worker had been reduced by forty

---

1 One of the methods used to eliminate people and then "disappear" their bodies, was to throw them, alive but drugged with pentothal, from aircraft down into the sea of the famous Río de la Plata.

110

percent; unemployment had reached ten percent of the working population – and would be more than doubled by 1983; and financial speculation had replaced productivity. The external national debt of eight million dollars in 1976 had grown – and would equal forty-five million dollars by 1983. Rodolfo Walsh "disappeared" because he wrote this letter.

The combined effects of the repression and disastrous application of uncontrolled liberal economic principles[2] generated a deep frustration among the population. Marches and demonstrations were organized all over the country. On 7 November 1981, the day of the famous saint, San Cayetano, about 50,000 Argentine workers gathered to protest against the military regime, its repression, and unemployment. Five months later, on 30 March 1982, more workers' demonstrations took place all over the country on the basis of the same slogan: "The military dictatorship is ending". There was a march in Buenos Aires to the Plaza de Mayo, that is to say directly under the windows of the military power.

Three days afterwards, 1,000 Argentine troops from the Army, Marines and Air Force disembarked in Puerto Argentino on the Malvinas Islands, Argentine territory occupied by Great Britain since 1833 under the name of the Falkland Islands. The next day, the new leader of the Military Junta who had assumed power on 22 December 1981, General Leopoldo Fortunato Galtieri, announced in public the recovery of the Malvinas Islands on the basis of the legitimate right of Argentina with its national patrimony, in the name of "all and each of the Argentines without distinction of groups or flags", adding that "the place taken had been decided without any political consideration". Such a remark implied, indeed, an obvious political motivation which has been revealed by the very reaction of the Argentine population.

The recovery of this Argentine territory occupied by a colonial nation was, in fact, an old claim on the part of Argentina. The aim decided on by the dictatorship was to remain at the head of the nation, gathering the population under the same banner and making it forget the bloody repression and the disastrous economic situation through a glorious campaign for liberation.[3] The reaction of the Argentine population was enthusiastic, along with that of several Latin American countries, for this campaign was considered a defence of national sovereignty against colonialism and a new war for independence. The Military Junta had been so devoted to the United States and its demands that it was certain of American support.

On the day of the landings, President Reagan asked Argentina to

2 In a speech delivered on 30 October 1980, before the Argentine Chamber of Commerce, General Jorge Rafael Videla rejected state intervention in the economy as being the germ of social and economic disorder.
3 In 1985, in the trial of the Junta by the newly elected government of Raúl Alfonsín, a voluntarily retired Argentine officer, José Luis García, being an opponent of the same Junta from the first day of the coup, denounced the sacrifice of young soldiers and officers in order to save the dictatorship from infamy.

withdraw its troops immediately and, as a second step, he turned his back on the Argentine dictatorship and provided help to British Prime Minister Margaret Thatcher. The Chilean dictatorship, led by Augusto Pinochet, also provided help to the British Government and its troops, support that Margaret Thatcher would remember when the ex-dictator was arrested in London sixteen years afterwards on the basis of an arrest warrant issued by the Spanish judge, Baltazar Garzón.

Galtieri explained later that he had been indeed "expecting a reaction" from Great Britain "but had never contemplated such a mobilization for the Malvinas". He added: "I have to say that I feel a great bitterness because the North Americans know very well that, as the Supreme Head of the Army, that is to say, before being the President of the Nation, I always tried to be close to them and their Administration and to renew the mutual understanding weakened by the former Administration. I was very disappointed when Haig backed the English".

The war was short and intense. Its start was marked by two main events.[4] The first took place on 2 May when a British Royal Navy nuclear submarine detected the Argentine cruiser ARA *General Belgrano* outside the Total Exclusion Zone determined by the British Government. Without warning HMS *Conqueror* torpedoed the ship, which sank in a remarkably short time. Three hundred and twenty-one Argentine sailors died. The second event occurred two days later when the British Royal Navy destroyer, HMS *Sheffield*, was hit by an Exocet missile launched by a Super-Étendard fighter aircraft flown from its base at Río Grande. In this attack twenty of the ship's company died. On 14 June, Brigadier-General Marío Benjamín Menéndez surrendered to the Commander of the British Land Forces, Major-General Jeremy Moore. The war was over after seventy-four days and nine hundred and four fatalities. The remaining days of the Argentine dictatorship were numbered.

In December 1982, the Junta established a commission to hold an enquiry into the responsibility for this shameful war. This was commonly known as the Rattenbach Commission, "as was demanded by national sovereignty and the dignity of the Armed Forces". It concluded that "the method adopted by the Junta to prepare the nation for this

---

4 A specific event has to be mentioned: on 25 April, as part of Operation Paraquet, Royal Marine Commandos landed at Grytviken on the small island of South Georgia where the Argentine naval officer Alfredo Astiz had been in command of the Argentine contingent for three weeks. He immediately "surrendered to the enemy, without due resistance" (according to paragraphs 837g, Ch. XII and 850p, Ch. XIII of the Rattenbach Commission). His picture appeared on a national television programme which would permit his being recognised by several mothers of the famous Argentine "Madres de la Plaza de Mayo" as an infiltrator of this group in Buenos Aires and Paris, who gathered information from group members whilst pretending, under the false identity of Gustavo Nino, that he was looking for his supposedly disappeared brother just as the mothers were looking for their disappeared children. Alfredo Astiz has never been convicted by Argentine justice but by a French criminal court, which sentenced him to life imprisonment on 16 March 1992. However Argentina has never extradited him.

war has neglected the most elementary rules of organization to be implemented within the military forces. This explains that fundamental errors have been committed in political orientation and military strategy with which the conflict has been initiated and concluded".

On 15 March 1986, the three Generals, Anaya, Galtieri and Lami Dozo, were sentenced to fourteen, twelve and eight years in jail by the Supreme Council of the Armed Forces. In October 1983 the Military Junta was obliged to organize elections, which were won by the Radical Party of Raúl Alfonsín. A civil trial took place in 1985 against the Military Junta, led by the Argentine Federal Court of Justice, which sentenced to life in prison the main leaders of the dictatorship for the atrocities they had perpetrated. Very few nations have committed to trial their dictators, who are more often, even if though very rarely, judged by international courts of justice or *ad hoc* jurisdictions.

Hundreds of criminal enquiries were opened in the country by judges to allow the imputation and the condemnation of military soldiers or officials responsible for torture, murders, rapes, illegal detentions, disappearances and robberies. In spite of this exceptional victory in the difficult fight for human rights, in 1986 and 1987, under military pressure,[5] two laws called "Final Point" and "Due Obedience" were passed by the Argentine National Congress, granting impunity to the murderers. Later, in 1992, a decree of pardon was handed by Alfonsín's successor, the Peronist Carlos Menem, to the previously condemned Generals, who were then freed. A long night of impunity fell on Argentina, impunity from which it has still not emerged despite the progress made.[6]

In 1992 trials were held on the basis of the only exception allowed in the two previously mentioned laws, which dealt with the illegal appropriation of new born babies whose mothers had been arrested, kept alive until the delivery and then disappeared. The generals previously condemned were arrested and committed to house arrest as they were older than seventy years of age. They have not yet been judged.

But the main fight led the victims, their families, the Human Rights Associations and their lawyers, a few judges and prosecutors, and left-wing progressive parties to demand annullment by the National Congress of the "Final Point" and "Due Obedience" Laws. Success was achieved in 2004. Hundred of cases that had been closed in 1987 were then re-opened and investigated. The first conviction was made on 17 September 2006 against a police officer, Miguel Etchecolatz, for "crimes against humanity committed within genocide": this was the first

---

5 Two officers who had fought in the Malvinas War, Aldo Rico and Mohamed Alí Seneildín, formed a rebel group of soldiers called "Carapintadas", which demanded the cessation of the criminal investigation.
6 A culture of impunity developed not only in the domain of crimes against humanity perpetrated by the dictatorship, but also in public and private finances, a great favourite through auctions of public properties and services. Financial crimes, such as embezzlement of money, bribery of civil servants, illegal royalties, white-washing of black money, and tax evasion were neither tried in a court of justice nor were they really condemned.

condemnation ever pronounced in Argentina on this criminal ground and, as such, it recognized the very nature of the crimes perpetrated by the dictatorship. That is to say, criminal acts, committed on a massive scale, according to a systematic plan of elimination of people because of their beliefs, and whose horror violates human consciousness.

However, the cases are numerous (one thousand and four), scattered all over the country (in fifty-two cities), and the financial means provided do not make allowance for the importance of the task. For example, a key witness in the Etchecolatz case, Julio López, recently disappeared. Neither the political leaders, with the exception of a few, nor the police seriously considered the criminal dimension of such an event and what it implied in a democracy. The criminal investigation then took on a tragic and fatal delay. Witness protection, along with a thorough cleaning-up of the police, is required, because the fight for justice in Argentina is still a dubious battle.

Without doubt the Malvinas War hastened the fall of the dictatorship, but did not cause it. On the contrary, what the Junta achieved was the destruction of a country in which a political generation disappeared and the external debt of eight million dollars rose to forty-five million. What the four Juntas actually caused were the plagues of Argentina which survive even today: namely unemployment and poverty, lack of state control, corruption and a difficult justice.

Post-war, the problem of the Malvinas remains and, indeed, it is even worse than before, with the United Kingdom still reaffirming its refusal to decolonize the Islands. The Malvinas continue to be, even in the twenty-first century, one of the last vestiges of colonial times.

The Malvinas War and the Genesis of Aggression

María Fra Amador

The bloody and aggressive origins of the human species belie the supposition that in nature there is harmony. Aggressiveness appears in the search for food, space, or mating opportunities. Among predator beasts, victims are chosen to satisfy biological and survival needs. If purportedly culture has a predominant role in the behaviour of individuals, what is the reason for the ostensible pervasiveness of blood-thirstiness, aggression and death among human beings? Scientists and thinkers from different disciplines have analysed the evolution of the species and have found that there is no single answer to the question of war and peace.

According to Robert Sapolsky, of world-wide notoriety for his thirty-year-long studies of the baboons in the savannahs of Serengueti, "the human species has more in common with violent primates than with pacific ones, but it is not the only species that organizes violence collectively". He also asserts that [...] "combat is not the only way for selection in the evolution of the species" (Sapolsky in Bassets, 2005, p. 2). Of course, we are not unique in waging war, but neither are we alone in reconciliation nor in co-operation. Perhaps our specific origins should be traced back to the time of hunter collectors; in the ways in which they distributed food and the notions they had on how to share it. It may be said, as Lee indicates, observing the *!kung* tribe in Africa, that there exists a fundamental contradiction in the transition between sharing – which is a central element in the hunter-gatherer civilization – and saving (or controlling) resources, which is the central element of the agricultural and animal-rearing form of life (Lee in Leakey, 2005. p. 171).

One of the most gruesome indicators of human history, as Sahlins points out, is "the death-toll left by wars which become increasingly violent" (Sahlin in Leakey, 2005. p. 171). Sigmund Freud said that men are not good-natured and friendly beings wanting love for, in his mind, he thought men have a basic instinct for aggression which repeatedly becomes apparent on the battlefield. To Freud "wars will not end as long as people live in such different conditions, as long as the value of individual life is so different among them and the hatred that separates them represents such overpowering instinctive forces" (Freud, 1984, p. 97).

When, for instance, observing Andean architecture and the constructions and monuments of the ancient world, we can perceive an iconography of power, a show of military force, an unmistakeable display of blood and aggression. But is this constant aspect of our recent history enough of an indicator to say that human beings are by nature aggressive and that war is in our genes? Looking back on the so-called "agricultural revolution" of 10,000 years ago, a period in which population growth began, and of concentrated population centres, we find the traceable beginnings of aggression in humans. Leakey believes that, as villages became cities and cities, in turn, became organized into states, human beings gradually became a source of conflict and confrontation (Leakey, 2005, p. 18).

In a scenario where population increases and capital are more and more concentrated, the Malvinas conflict appears as a clear-cut episode of aggression, in the sense of the behaviour and use of an arbitrary resource by the Junta (the Military) and Mrs Thatcher's Government (the Nation), as the chosen expression in the face of respective loss of power as a popular and citizen's mediation. An aggression the English carried out in 1833 is repeated on 2 April 1982, by the Argentine Government, for the sake of recovering lost territory.

This case of the recovery of Argentine territory, called the Malvinas War, has deep origins in the identity of a people and it gives us an opportunity to analyse the motives that impel men towards conflict. It is possible to present the hypothesis that what changed with the shift from nomadic hunting and harvesting to the sedentary practice of agriculture was the nature of society, not man's nature, since men are essentially cultural beings able to answer in different ways to similar dominant situations. It is also possible to infer that what takes men to war and aggression are exogenous causes or, rather, war could be viewed as the political and social answer to a change in economic circumstances; to ambition and power as the *leitmotif* of aggression in men.

Sapolsky indicates in his study of baboons that the dominant males are rarely particularly aggressive, and when they use violence it is because they are beginning to lose their dominant position. His observation is correct because holding the dominant position requires social intelligence and control of the impulses, the ability to make sensible coalitions, show tolerance towards subordinates and ignore most provocations (Sapolsky in Bassets, 2005, p. 2). Concomitantly it might be said that the Generals of the so-called *Proceso* had not only lost the political and institutional control of the country but also used the vindication of the Malvinas to perpetuate their power, as the Malvinas had come to be the result of the symbolic representation of the national cause and identity.

The Malvinas were the only entity that could unite a country with such political-institutional discontinuity. As Guber indicates, "in a political process plagued with untimely ruptures, constant losses of legitimacy and persecution for political reasons, [...] the diffusion and welcome of the Malvinas by the most varied audiences and their representation as a popular cause took place in the context of denunciation of oppression and injustice towards the humble rural folk, those in cities, the popular political movements and youth" (Guber, 2001, p. 102-103).

The context in which the war of the Malvinas occurred was one in which internal aggression existed already. There was a war between Argentinians, there were Argentinians who had disappeared. Until 1982, the ideologies that dominated the political spectrum in Argentina were, on the one hand, that of the military along with the elite of landowners and, on the other hand, the one of Perón and the working masses. The Malvinas "represented the political and social exclusion of Argentinians"

(Guber, 2001, p. 103); this status can translate into the Islands being conceived more as an object of desire than as being loved. They were represented as despoiled, forlorn and left aside, miserable Islands where not even savages wanted to live but, at the same time, in the Argentine being there exists a desire to be born again from constant defeat, whence the value of the Malvinas as symbol in the historical context of the internal political fight for control of the nation (Fra Amador, 2005, p. 291). We may infer that the Malvinas cause transcended the political scene and its contexts of oppression or questions about the legitimacy of sectors of the State, as Guber indicates (2001, p. 105). The assertion used in all these cases that "The Malvinas are Argentine" has meant "to recover the nation that was always and in a renewed way is still represented as lost" (Guber, 2001, p. 106).

Bleichmar indicates that she finds in the feelings and behaviour of Argentine society a country that has been defeated and constantly revives: "what moves us is the fall of the hero and his recovery, his capacity not to let himself be defeated" (in reference to Diego Maradona as a symbol of national identity) (Bleichmar, 2006, p. 11). Argentines and Argentine history, indicates this author, are like the history of Gatica, Gardel or Maradona, "a man who falls and rises, who falls again and rises again. We Argentines are Diego: we are capable of making sublime and frightful things, we defeat ourselves and rise again, and we fight creatively against all our traumas" (Bleichmar, 2006, p. 11).

Argentina appears throughout history as full of institutional ruptures, to a great extent due to the fact that "the ideologies that dominated the Argentine political spectrum were imbued by the military and therefore also by Perón, presenting politics as synonymous with internal division, and the nation as a synonym of national unity" (Guber, 2001, p. 108). That is to say that the Malvinas appear as the dichotomy of the internal political division of the country, like "the language of the nation, and as the continuity of its being with a contrasting logic against political discontinuity", indicates Guber (2001, p. 107). In other words, continuity is represented by the nation and discontinuity by politics.

Malvinas for the Argentines, Falklands for the British. Falklands-Malvinas were taken away from the authority of the River Plate, at that time under the Government of Buenos Aires, and occupied from 1833 by the British. Since then, successive Argentine governments have – without exception – stated their claim for repossession of the usurped territory by means of various diplomatic mechanisms, raising, indicates Freedman, the prospect of "its return in the name of territorial integrity" (2006, p. 122). All Governments since 1833 have agreed in continuing the fight for the recovery of the Islands. It could be inferred that this is the only state issue that does not have political colour, yet has continuity as the nation's foreign policy. But, in the eyes of all Argentines, the results had scarcely been satisfactory and would continue to be an issue of national identity and international prestige.

Thus throughout the centuries, Argentines, first from their schooling and then from their particular experience of citizenship, have constructed different pictures of the Islands which, alongside the historical narrative, the one felt by each Argentine, and the one appropriated by successive Governments in turn, conformed to an identity of "Argentine being" built around the notion of the Malvinas past and present, their fall and their resurgence. It seems then that the Malvinas represent a focal point in the recovery of the Father of the Nation who will finally guide Argentines towards a true political and national unity that has been lost. Argentine society is permanently in pursuit of the recuperation of its nation and its society (Bleichmar, 2006, p. 11). "Instead of searching for the essences of being Argentine," says Guber, "and placing among these the Malvinas Islands and their recovery, we have chosen to understand the nation as a constructed symbol of community speaking to us about the relations between the state and its subjects and other states" (Guber, 2001, p. 160).

In this sense, the Malvinas become the representation of a country that "is lived not as much as a progressive conquest, but as a constant loss. The invocation of the loss is called upon like the restoration of a past golden age; the recovery of the Islands becomes thus a metaphor of the final recovery of Argentina" (Guber, 2001, p. 163). All that has been lost and is still pending becomes mixed up in a timeless ambiguity over the loss or waiting involved in respect of the disappeared, the rising financial market and the battle of the big economic groups, the military *coups d'état* performed with the acquiescence of rural-exporting elites, and the economic blows to democracy along with the great economic groups, the political devastation, the corruption and embezzlement of ideas, and the overall political and social divisions.

For this reason, Guber wonders "what is it that is lost and what is it that is still pending?" According to Guber "the ambiguity of the Malvinas symbol [...] alludes simultaneously and successively to territorial loss; to the loss of the hierarchic republic; to the social and political exclusion of workers, of the masses, of Peronism, of Perón; to the surrender of the nation by the exporting oligarchy; to the fall of Argentina's position in the worldwide concert of nations; to the loss of political and civil rights, and to the loss of popular sovereignty" (Guber, 2001, p. 164).

The graffiti reading "The Malvinas are Argentine, so are the disappeared" incarnate a metaphoric power not only in the sense of the Islands having been occupied by the British imperial usurper; in addition, and fundamentally, it sinks deep into the bitter depths of the so-called "dirty war" and in a feeling of living in a permanent state of despoliation, of social, economic and political loss. The graffiti incarnate everything the Argentine people has lost, and at the same time, represent the inability to realize the role it has played throughout history, or the responsibility it bears as a society. The graffiti evoke the fall of the hero and its resurgence.

Why the disappeared? Why the improbable conflict used as an excuse for the recovery of the identity of a nation in such an internally and externally complex historical moment, also handled in such an untimely fashion? Why the Malvinas as a unique symbol of national identity? Maybe because the Malvinas allow Argentines to situate the individual biography in some notional shared place: a place where

Argentines represent their crises, their breakages and downfalls, their ways of thinking, of acting, and of imagining themselves as a nation and vis à vis the world. Malvinas is a myth, the symbolic element representing the constant and repeated loss throughout the centuries (Lombardozzi, 2006, p. 186).

Perhaps the projection that Argentine society makes through the eyes of the Malvinas shows the incapacity of a people for self-administration and self-government. This social and political imbalance is reflected throughout Argentine history and, even more clearly, in successive economic and institutional crises, in corruption and vandalism, all collective actions that have sunk the country into the present marginalization and overcrowding in which more than half of Argentines are immersed; in the hopelessness and the concealed aggression of a people which does not manage to position itself in space, nor in time, and repeats its behaviours *ad infinitum*.

Yet human beings are something more than merely aggressive and bloodthirsty. Leakey writes that "the human being is, without a doubt, a very adaptable creature and can respond to changes with appropriate technological solutions. Our possibilities for survival would seem, certainly, very large" (Leakey, 2005, p. 18). Nevertheless, a glance at human history might dim this note of optimism. In fact, indicates Ardrey, "man is man, and not a chimpanzee, because through millions and millions of years we have killed to live" (Ardrey in Leakey, 2005, p. 68).

Freud recognizes that civilized men have lost the ethical sensitivity of the primitive man that returns as the winner of the fight, "to whom it is not allowed to walk in his town or to approach his woman until having purged his war homicides through eventually very long and laborious penances" (Freud, 1984, p. 118-122). Argentine society is so criss-crossed by an impenetrable shadow of corruption and impunity that it becomes very difficult to reverse the situation and punish or condemn those who have behaved illegally because I believe there is a certain acceptance of the fact that, already, nobody is able to throw the first stone. And this is very serious because it prevents building a "re-citizenship-ness" (Bleichmar, 2006, p. 11).

Yet I am not pessimistic, I believe in the art of living, as Kant said: through mistakes and through repeating our mistakes we will learn from others. I believe in cultural diversity as a daily task through which we must build the present and the future by sharing values with others. I believe in the art of dialogue and in commitment, not in war. I also believe that the Malvinas have made it possible to re-build the identity of a people that was adrift.

References

Bassets, L. "La paz de los babuinos", *El País*, 29 December 2005.
Bleichamr, S. (2006) *"Somos una extraña mezcla de talento, brillantez y derrota"* Buenos Aires: diario *La Nación*.
Fra Amador, M. C. (2005) "Malvinas-Falklands Revisited: Prelude, War and Aftermath": In Demaria, C. and Wright, C. *Post-Conflict Cultures: Rituals of Representation*, London, Zoilus Press.

Freedman, L. (July-September 2006) "La relación especial, entonces y ahora": In *De Foreign Affaires en Español*.
Freud, S. (1984). *El Malestar en la cultura.* Madrid: Alianza Editorial S.A.
Guber, R. (2001). *¿Por qué Malvinas? De la causa nacional a la guerra absurda.* Buenos Aires, Fondo de Cultura Económica, S.A.
Leakey, R. E·. (2005). *La Formación de la humanidad.* Barcelona, Ediciones del Aguazul.
Lombardozzi, A. (2006) *Figure del Dialogo*, Rome, Edizioni Borla s.r.l.

Transcendental Echoes or the Snares of Intra-Colonialism
Falklands-Malvinas and the Poetry of War[1]

Bernard McGuirk

The first poem by an author of renown to deal with the Malvinas-Falklands conflict was "Juan López y John Ward", published in Buenos Aires in *Clarín* on 26 August and, in a by no means unproblematic translation, in *The Times* of London, on 18 September 1982.[2] The poem has been dissected variously and multiply, as part of the Jorge Luis Borges critical industry, but it is still pertinent to situate it in the context of the genre of war poetry:

Juan López y John Ward

Les tocó en suerte una época extraña
El planeta había sido parcelado en distintos países, cada uno provisto
de lealtades, de queridas memorias, de un pasado sin duda heroico,
de derechos, de agravios, de una mitología peculiar, de próceres de
   bronce,

---

1 [Editors' Note] The closing address of *Conflict and Post-Conflict in Latin America: The Falkland-Malvinas Conflict 25 Years On* was delivered by Bernard McGuirk, holder of the Chair of Romance Literatures and Literary Theory at the University of Nottingham, where he is also Director of the Centre for the Study of Post-Conflict Cultures. The editors of the present volume wish to thank Professor McGuirk and the publishers of his recent book, *Falklands-Malvinas An Unfinished Business* (New Ventures, Seattle, 2007), for the permission granted to them to reproduce here, from that monograph, the adapted extract which formed the basis of the address made to the veterans and academic colleagues who took part in the unique event of 17-19 November 2006. The twenty-fifth anniversary of the Falklands-Malvinas conflict produced a high degree of public interest in the topic, and readers will discover in McGuirk's study how a literary critic has explored a rich archive of creative works, on many of which virtually nothing has been written. His audience will be not only specialists in war studies and war literature, in international cultural politics and in Latin America studies, but also all those intrigued by the ever-topical legacy of the war itself and of its still resonant post-Galtieri and post-Thatcher effects. The book analyses fiction, poetry, song, drama, and film that deal directly with the conflict. In Argentina and in the United Kingdom, over the last quarter of a century, cultural historians and literary critics have occasionally addressed and sought to account for the impact of the 1982 war on the creative imaginative and artistic output of their respective cultures. Habitually, they have done so in isolation or, at best, with cursory cross-referencing to "the other side". McGuirk looks beyond national frontiers to consider not just the so-called Falklands-Malvinas factor in politics, but the conflict's multiple effects in literature and the arts worldwide. He reveals how writers and artists have continued to draw on a complex and, ostensibly, still ill-comprehended war not only in terms of political history or failed diplomacy, of conflicting ideologies or the sheer waste of lives and national resources, but also of other more markedly symbolic investments and imaginaries.
2 The poem was later published in *Los conjurados, Obras completas* (Buenos Aires, Emecé, 1989), vol. 2, 500.

de aniversarios, de demagogos y de símbolos.
Esa división, cara a los cartógrafos, auspiciaba las guerras.

López había nacido en la ciudad junto al río inmóvil.
Ward, en las afueras de la ciudad por la que caminó Father Brown.
Había estudiado castellano para leer el Quijote.
El otro profesaba el amor de Conrad, que le había sido revelado
en un aula de la calle Viamonte.
Hubieran sido amigos, pero se vieron una sola vez cara a cara, en unas
islas demasiado famosas, y cada uno de los dos fue Caín, y cada uno,
    Abel.
Los enterraron juntos. La nieve y la corrupción los conocen.

El hecho que refiero pasó en un tiempo que no podemos entender.

Juan López and John Ward

It was their fate to live in a strange time.
The planet had been carved into different countries,
each one provided with loyalties, with loved memories,
with a past which doubtless had been heroic, with
ancient and recent traditions, with rights, with grievances,
with its own mythology, with
forebears in bronze, with anniversaries, with demagogues and
with symbols. Such an arbitrary division was favourable to war.

López had been born in the city next to the motionless
river; Ward in the outskirts of the city
through which
Father Brown had walked. He had studied Spanish
so as to read the *Quixote*.
The other professed a love of Conrad, revealed
to him in a class in Viamonte Street.
They might have been friends, but they saw each other just once,
face to face, in islands only too well known, and each one was Cain and
    each one, Abel.
They buried them together. Snow and corruption
know them.

The story I tell happened in a time we cannot understand.

(Translation by Rodolfo Terragno)

So be it? Amen? The construction of an opening gambit of Olympian
distance, impersonality, objectivity, disinterest, a refusal to take sides, a
mere "naming of parts"; thus might the word "fate" be seen to operate,
reiterating a classical trope of juxtaposing destiny with the "strangeness"
of time, as if history were always in excess not only of its writing but also
of our understanding of it. The apparent pre-determination implicit in the

division of the planet into potentially martial factions would make it appear that, not for the first time, here is a Borges going transcendental; opting for the difference between countries as pre-destined, unavoidable point of departure on a road to cyclically repeated wars. According to the terms of such an irresistible binary, the only predictable construct would be that of Nationalisms, Histories writ large, official versions, "loyalties" to be tested, and attested, by check-lists of "past", "heroic", "cherished memories", "anniversaries". The writing-implements of such a polarized reading of history are meticulously mapped: "rights" and "wrongs".

Thereby a mythology has been produced and, in Borges's representation of it, is shown to be inseparable from proprietary rights and ownership. The reality effects of such strong myths are the hammered bronze echoes of anniversaries, the resonance of demagoguery and the unequivocality of symbols. Only once in the opening sequence of the poem has a "doubtless" crept in, near-casual prefiguration, its ironizing frame easily missable, of an overt, a sententious and, thus far, it might seem, a dangerously unopposed, omniscient voicing: "Esa división [...] auspiciaba las guerras" (less meticulously mapped – without, indeed, any cartographers at all – in Terragno's "Such an arbitrary division was favourable to war").

As in the case of all closed meanings, the planet-wide carve-up into differing Nationalisms, into different signifieds, might indeed have been for too long read as ordained by fate and agreed by men ... agreed but arbitrary, and with no positive terms. Read retrospectively, however, the "different countries" of the opening sequence might be said to require a re-writing of their respective histories in excess of the confining terminology, the straitjacket of those nationalizing ideologies which endow countries with auguries, auspicious or ill, both of, and for, war. It is in this light, therefore, that the wording "was favourable" might be said to point to an over-dominant metaphysics, the supposedly unavoidable (and historically repeated) resolution of conflicting mythologies of nation through military confrontation.

As the Juan López and John Ward of Borges's text are schooled in the respective cities of their differential fates, the private and public strands of their lives (their perusal of Conrad or Cervantes, their perambulations along the River Plate or through Chesterton's suburbs) are interwoven only to lead them to the particular circumstance of their signifying encounter. This particularity is not just constructed on difference. The specificity of the brief attributions to Buenos Aires (displaced inheritor of an *hidalgo* tilter at dreams) and London (misplaced scene of a bumbling detective theology), is complemented by a prolonged disclosure of, and an openness to, reciprocity and its potential. An encountering without othering is tentatively approached via Juan and John as *literati*, through their readerly preparing for, their conceiving of, the translatability of a mediated other – that Other filtered through literatures, through traditions, through societies, and which consists of cultural difference. The hypothetical status of such *un*reality effects is however confined, consigned, to but a short sentence, "They might have been friends", before the onset, the onrush, of a more divisive outcome... the interbayonetry of that form of cultural transfer which will always set its face against negotiated settlement (of differences). War-war, not jaw-jaw. Mistah-Missus Kurtz; s/he *not* dead... Non-negotiable. Art of darkness. Literatures in conflict.[3]

In a "just once", in sheer instantaneity, the Borges text confronts the meeting of faces though not of eyes. In the borrowed terms of narrative analysis, the only available sphere of action is the double actant space where each is Cain and each is Abel. For the absolute narrative, transcendent History, can cope with, and will apportion, no blame, no fault, no right, no wrong. In such an ironized story, the Juan/John "fate" is, inevitably, both to live and to die in "a strange time", buried together under the cover not of darkness but of a more pervasive, chilling, snowy blankness, and the corruption of a shared, a *same* death, which, macabre aspiration, abolishes the difference of self and other, self in other. A same death which permits no story, no history of their difference, their common particularity, resolved or dissolved in the illusory coming together of the time and its telling. But is "a time we cannot understand" merely a conclusive note of resignation to fate, to strangeness, to incomprehensibility? Or an invitation to read back through the poem, attempting to listen not to what "*we*" cannot understand but rather to the fact "*I*" tell?

The excessive relation of the individual's voicing to simultaneous histories-become-History constitutes an invitation to listen again, whether to the Borges poem or to the official spokesmen of the Thatcher Government, the Ian MacDonalds, the John Notts. What we are asked to hear is a counterpoint to the clipped, flat, matter-of-fact intoning cultivatedly understating the course, and the discourse, of a history of the excessively famous, the notorious. Thus the Borges poem subverts, even as it broaches, the construction of dangerous *clichés* of *in*difference; will not allow Juan and John an infamous loss of particular identities whereby they are turned into "The Unknown Soldier", become transfused by, confused with, a sentimentalizing *dulce et decorum est pro patria mori* ... Particular differences between Juan and John should be no less legible now than is that instance of differences at play within *Juan López* and John *Ward*; the projected inscription of Jorge Luis's own initials into a (warred) relationship with the (linguistic) Other overtly inscribed by both trace and excess of intratextual conflicts.

Counterpoint and excess also serve to characterize the relation of the Borges poem to its Wilfred Owen precursor, "Strange Meeting". Direct echoes are muted but an overt interpellation in Borges's opening line, "strange", convokes both title and the ghosts from Owen's face-to-face encounter in Hell in order to pre-figure his own protagonists' entrenched inseparability in an all too similar "profound dull tunnel". Owen's first-person – "out of battle escaped" only to confront his also dead adversary of but yesterday's jab and parry – is allowed a point of view:

"Strange friend", I said, "here is no cause to mourn."

2 Governorship of "an island" is promised, in Volume 1 of Cervantes' novel, to Sancho Panza when Don Quijote becomes an emperor or wins honours and awards for some great deed. In Volume 2, the Duke and Duchess create a mock island and governorship for Sancho. D and D? Dictatorship and its other (half).

"None", said that other, "save the undone years,
The hopelessness. Whatever hope is yours,
Was my life also".

(Owen, 1918: in Silkin, 1982, 196-8)

Borges, however, ethically refraining from any identifying relation with the combatant Owen's option for eerie dramatic dialogue, borrows only the hypothetical. "They might have been friends" performs the defamiliarization necessary to his own respectful visit to the grave of the predecessor's poem, and his strategic retreat from it. If Borges' Juan and John are not permitted to enter such an exchange as "I am the enemy you killed, my friend. I know you in this dark", it is because of an *excess*. In appropriating but requiring to go beyond Wilfred Owen's "Strange Meeting", the later poem reminds us too that it is written after the era of *La Grande Illusion*: "but they saw each other just once, face to face". Concomitantly, Owen's "Let us sleep now..." finds in Borges's "Los enterraron juntos" a counterpart but without hint of consolation. "My hands were loath and cold" derives from a personal voice not available in the Argentine's bleaker rendering of the icy effect of war: "Snow and corruption know them". Thus is the final line of the Borges poem calculatedly prepared for. Facts? History? Such events as have rendered *too* famous mere outcrops of the South Atlantic must exceed understanding; must confound nationalistic apportionings of roles of right and wrong; must allow for no making capital out of *History*; must refuse the writing of *Myth*.[4]

The "Falklands Conflict" came to represent a particularly dominant metaphysics of presence in the strife-torn early 'eighties. Amongst the scandalously repressed absences of that period of burning UK inner-cities, of strikes and counter-strikes – Brit versus grit – was the term *Malvinas,* itself repressing another by now faint imperial echo, less of Britain's "naming of parts" than of Britanny's parting with names – St. Malo, whence *Les Iles Maloïnes*. Now, out of France, in a late twentieth-century rivalry of post-imperial but never post-economic colonizing powers, was cast the shadow not of Breton exiles but of bolt-on Exocets. The creation of a meta-geography (and a metal market) favourable to war suggests that the ever bullish economy of Nationalism emerged, in April 1982, as a fragmentary narrative of half-locatable places where, with stunning rapidity, all too recognizable visages of power *chose* to come face-to-face. Perhaps not apocryphally, the Galtieri-Thatcher struggle over southern (dis)comfort on the rocks is said to have been described by Jorge Luis Borges as that of "two bald men fighting over a comb".

A powerful representation of history as repetition yet of translation as betrayal occurs in a poem from her 1987 collection *Ova completa* by the Argentine writer Susana Thénon. If the somewhat less than celebratory pre-quincentenary gift of Prime Minister Thatcher to the Galtieri regime

---

3 The Borges strategy, here, as I read it, confirms Simon Featherstone's view that: "To treat wartime as a parenthesis of history is to depoliticize it, blur the social and cultural complexities of its literature and thought and ultimately make it mythical rather than historical" (Featherstone, 1995, 23).

Hors de Combat: the Falklands-Malvinas Conflict in Retrospect

came ten years too early, at least the unseemly rush across the South Atlantic, again to see and sack new worlds, allowed Thénon the time (she died in 1990) to situate the translatability of inseparably monarchic, ecclesiastical and military post-colonialism as not only a commonplace North-South, English-Spanish, relation but also as an effect shown to be operative between Spanish and Spanish, between Spanish American and Spanish Americans. Here, Thénon shows up the virtual taboo-subject of *intra*-colonialism. Within the political-ideological frontiers of Spanish America, there would appear to be a need not (only) for translation of the message of resistance against cyclical colonizing aggression into the language (English) of its latest perpetrators but (also) for its repetition, in difference, to the often indifferent (Spanish American) other:

Poema con traducción simultánea Español-Español	Poem with Simultaneous Translation Spanish to Spanish

Para ir hacia lo venidero
 para hacer, si no el paraíso,
 la casa feliz del obrero
 en la plenitud ciudadana,
 vínculo íntimo eslabona
 e ímpetu exterior hermana
 a la raza anglosajona
 con la latinoamericana.

To move towards what is still to come,
to construct, if not paradise,
the happy house of the worker
in the plenitude of the city,
intimate bond ties
and outer strength unites in brotherhood
the Anglo-Saxon race
with the Latin American.

Rubén Darío, *Canto a la Argentina*   Rubén Darío, *Song to the Argentine*

Cristóforo	Cristóforo
(el Portador de Cristo)	(the Bearer of Christ)
hijo de un humilde cardador de lana	son of a humble carder of wool
(hijo de uno que iba por lana sin cardar)	(son of one who got wool without carding)
zarpó del puerto de Palos	cast anchor from the port of Palos
(palo en zarpa dejó el puerto)	(stick in his grasp he left the port)
no sin antes persuadir	not without first persuading
a Su Majestad la Reina	Her Majesty the Queen
Isabel la Católica de las bondades de la empresa	Isabel the Catholic of the bounties of the enterprise
por él concebida	by him conceived
(no sin antes persuadir	(not without first persuading
a Her Royal Highness	Her Royal Highness
die Königen Chabela la Logística	die Königen Chabela of the Logistics
de empeñar	of pawning the
la corona en el figón de Blumenthal	crown in the eating-house of Blumenthal
con-verso)	con-vert)
así se vertiesen litros y litros de	even if spilling litres and litres of
genuina sangre vieja factor RH negativo	genuine old blood factor RH negative
(así costase sangre sudor y lágrimas	(even if they cost blood sweat and tears
antípodas)	antipodean)
se hicieron a la mar	they made out to sea
(se hicieron alamares)	(they made decorative fastenings)
y tras meses y meses de yantar solo	and after months and months of vitt'ling alone
oxímoron en busca de la esquiva redondez	oxymoron in search of the elusive roundness
(y tras días y días de mascar	(after days on end of chewing
Yorkshire pudding	Yorkshire pudding
y un pingüino de añadidura los domingos)	and a penguin in addition on Sundays)
alguno exclamó tierra	one of them cried land

(ninguno exclamó thálassa)

(none of them cried thálassa)

desembarcaron
en 1492 a. D.
  (pisaron
   en 1982 a.D
jefes esperaban
en pelota
genuflexos
  (mandamases aguardaban
  desnudos
  de rodillas)
Cristóforo gatilló el misal
  (Christopher disparó el misil)
dijo a sus pares
  (murmuró a sus secuaces)
coño
  (fuck)
ved aquí nuevos mundos
  (ved aquí estos inmundos)
quedáoslos
  (saqueadlos)
por Dios y Nuestra Reina
  (por Dios y Nuestra Reina)
AMÉN
 (OMEN)

they disembarked
in 1492 AD
  (they trod
   in 1982 AD)
chiefs were waiting
stark naked
genuflecting
  (bosses waited
  stripped
  kneeling)
Cristóforo triggered the missal
  (Christopher fired the missile)
said to his peers
  (whispered to his followers)
coño
  (fuck)
see here new worlds
  (see here these unwashed)
keep them
  (sack them)
for God and our Queen
  (for God and our Queen)
AMEN
 (OMEN)

(Thénon, 1987, 28)

The very title of Thénon's poem broaches humorously the problematic issue of difference *within* as opposed to the more conventional difference *between* languages. However many millions the United Nations might spend on the provision of simultaneous translation, its peace-making or peace-keeping services will always founder amidst the kind of pious idealism or melting-pot Utopianism encapsulated by, but not restricted to, the Rubén Darío epigraph. Seldom will a rhyme be so ironized as when *eslabona/anglosajona [links/Anglo-Saxon]*, read retrospectively and *after* Thénon's text, rattle out, in (un)chained melodrama, the bond(age) of brotherhood links. Here, the South-to-North "chain" metaphor is no less prone to a solution-cum-pollution, cure-cum-poison reading than is any *pharmakon.* For Thénon's poem undoes many a familiar metaphysics. Not least a time-honoured adoptive practice whereby Darío is appropriated as honorary Argentine; whereby over-awareness of cultural difference struggles with under-bewareness of dependency; wherein a high-serious tradition of Buenos Aires *literati* resistance to the condescendingly deemed "facile" word-play of such as *Ova completa* is contestatorily pastiched by Thénon's intervention.[5] The sacrosanct territory of Borges's own meditation on *non*-simultaneous Spanish-to-Spanish translation, in "Pierre Menard, Author of the Quixote", is revisited. Here, in what effectively operates as "Margaret Thatcher, Author of The Conquest", the precursor Columbus cannot be (agonically) engaged with ... without excess. An excess of history and an excess of language. The official version will ever

---

4 *Ova completa* is Thénon's spoof on the necessary incompleteness of any and all *Obra completa* or *Complete Works.* Or of any and all translation.

be shadowed by the parenthetic (trace of) supplementarity.

A *traduttore/traditore* view of translating as traducing need not be confined to language; the question of history as repetition, as action replay, is posed only to be deposed; "source" is mined only to be undermined; "target" will be gauged by missal *and* missile... intertextuality cum infra-red brutality. Playing the translation game, Thénon's poem indulges an illusory binary of past versus present, 1492 versus 1982, (West-seeking) aetiology versus (heat-seeking) teleology. It is as if the brackets which represent, visually, the simultaneous translator's version were, auditively, ear-phones conveying the message of a constant, and sardonic, interference.

"Cristóforo", linguistically and culturally foreign to the Spanish ear – Genoese commoner in spite of the Greek grandeur of his name's etymology – might be retrospectively interpreted as the Bearer of Christ to the New World though, to the pretentious contemporaries of the court of Ferdinand and Isabel, the *Reyes Católicos*, he was but the importunately supplicant son of a wool-weaver... only much later to be Agnus-deified. (Crackling through the earphones come the interfering obscenities: on the make via "lana"/lucre; but not scoring via "sin cardar"/without *screwing*?) The historic casting of the anchor of Discovery from the southern Spanish port of Palos de Moguer echoes excessively (clenched in the fist is the sword-cross staff of the Conquistador). Lest we forget Enterprise Culture, the bonds no less of 1492 than of 1982, and should the near-equivalent Isabeline/Elizabethan (II) coincidences not suffice, the Christ-bearer impressario must serve Her Catholic Majesty with both goodness and bounty... never forgetting a courtier's syntax. (The *logos* of persuasion in the Windsor-once-Saxe-Coburg Gothic transference is multiply scrambled. HRH the Princess Lilibet is infantilized, in echo of the Infanta Chabela [=diminutive of Isabel], persuaded to pledge the seal of Royal Appointment, the Crown-pawned conversion of HM fleet at the dictat of the all-consuming military Logistics of the Falklands War Effort. A monetarist's bargain struck over a cheap me(t)al in a "figón"/"eating-house"? By smooth tonguing [con-verso/with-verse]? Conversely, background noise might be un-jammed... Blumenthal, persecuted, exterminated by fifteenth-century Spaniards and twentieth-century Germans (or Argentines) alike, but never wholly expellable, or silenced. Is *con-verso* the Jew trans-ported, rather than integrally converted?... And, by the way, was Colombus himself a New Christian? The propaganda "pure blooded" line(age) of *limpieza de sangre* – genuine dynasty or not – intermingles RHesus/Royal Highness with the negative factor guaranteed to spill New World blood or, in a Churchillian rhetoric revamped for the Task Force of Albion's Expedition to the South Atlantic, the "blood, sweat and tears" of an Antipodean adventurism. Shall "we" always fight them on the beaches... whatever the cost?

And so to sea (and sew to see the officers' braid? Press-studded by the press-ganged?). Old time-spans of months on board and the archaism "yantar", "to dine", recall the first voyage of Colombus, months of unrelenting flat(Earth)ness with nothing to ingest but solitude and air. The proximity of oxymoron to oxygen – in echo of the expression "comer aire"/"to starve"– encapsulates the sharp-dull ache of the epic (but, for the near mutinous hungry sailors, the unrelenting) failure to reach the Indies by sailing West. For the "Brits", nearly five centuries on, the speedier expeditionary rhythm cannot disguise the chewing monotony. For them, separation from home means no (trace of) Sunday roast with the Yorkshire pudding, let alone the (difference of) beefing about Mrs Thatcher's "enemy within", the Yorkshire miners – only *The Sun*-style (supplement of) penguin-stereotyping ... "10 Things You Didn't Know About The Argies".

The operation of worrying linguistic excess, up to this point in Thénon's poem, has made any repeat-call "to get back to history" but a reminder that the discourse of history, too, comes laden with between-the-lines reading possibilities. For the textualizing of the climactic event of the *annus mirabilis* is framed thus: "one of them cried land/(none of them cried thálassa)". What access can there be to tone, other than through the supplementarity of a saturated translation? The dry relief of arrival at the *terra incognita* of the Other finds expression always against the intertext of linguistic and, here, of historico-literary difference. Before the encounter with, fear of, the Other can turn into xenophobia, Xenophon-through-ear-phone intrudes in a (quasi-) simultaneous translation. *Thálassa*! – cry of blissful return homewards, from Mesopotamia to "civilization" of war-weary Greeks – is the crafty classicist Susana Thénon's own oxymoronic landfall-seaview reminiscence of *Anabasis* (401 BC) – inverted prefiguration of the poem's doubled "a.D." basis.

Written dates now perform in excessive relation one to the other, highlighting the limitations of the frame of history. *Un*repeatability, *un*translatability allow particular perceptions of political events to resist such blanket rallying calls to imperial adventurism as that of a Churchill-echoing Iron Lady of 1982. The "a.D." repetition has acquired, via the covert classical B.C. precursor text, not only a historical comparison but also, with renewed emphasis, a religious difference. An Athenian nationalism under reconstruction was the backcloth to the expedition of Xenophon, "one of the "Ten Thousand Greeks" who went to Asia to seek their fortune, unaware till it was too late to withdraw that Cyrus meant to win the Persian empire by a blow directed deep into its heart".[6] Any "unawareness" on the part of the *conquistadores* is no less open to interrogation as "disembarked" becomes "trod". Four hundred and ninety years on, the effect of historical accuracy and objectivity in the representation of Discovery is undermined by the echoing tread of Christendom's inseparably colonizing-proselytizing mission. For lurking in the background is "la Católica"/ "la Logística", the Church Militant, ever crushing underfoot the serpent of an eternally sinful Edenic barbarism. Thénon's poem also feeds on oxymoron.

The archetypal primal scene of North-South/East-West encounter is re-enacted in rapid-fire rhythms as the tread-mark of post-Freudian as well as of post-colonial imprinting is trans-scribed. Christopher Colombus,

5 Thénon held a Chair of Classics at the University of Buenos Aires. For a fuller understanding of her play with Anabasis, see Encyclopaedia Britannica (London, 1963), vol. 23, 836.

Hors de Combat: the Falklands-Malvinas Conflict in Retrospect

Bernal Díaz del Castillo, Pero Vaz da Caminha, scriptors all, shadow the official résumé: hierarchy in suspense, raw nakedness, religious submission (belatedly: Argentine guv'nors on tenterhooks, stripped, on their knees). And the phantom-scribes in the translation from Santo Domingo to Port Stanley? "Our" own correspondents. Un-author-ized versions. An excess of history, too, is revealed in the surplus moral (re-)armament of the missal (missile). Christ is borne on the trace(r)-bullet-points of binary bearers, preached (hissed) to peers (or followers)... apostles all. And who are these disciples to punish? The expletive, somewhat unusually in the documenting of history, remains *un*deleted in official and unofficial versions. Translation intervenes only as an intensifier. Force, contempt, sex, obscenity... transgression. Behold new worlds/Go forth and multiply possession. (Behold these unwashed "Argies"/*Gotcha*!).

The intonation would appear to be univocal as the text approaches its Vespers. For the only time, the ear-phone parentheses apparently contain the self-same locution in the translation as in the original: "for God and Our Queen" (encore). Faithful? Where linguistic and historical differences disappear is in *cliché*, language emptied of particularity, the imprecation which carries us once more onto the breach of all nations at war. Fateful? Or avoidable as soon as differential reading is allowed? For the boomed imperative of faith-*full* resignation "AMÉN" faces faith-*less* future when translated with the inclusion of a supplementarity borrowed, perhaps, from the opening line of the epigraph: "to move towards what is still to come". If the *question* of history, if the *question* of language, if all *questions* of representation are, indeed, always already excessive with respect to histories, languages and representations, then the "So be it" of Church and State conformity will always be the least digestible of imperatives. The slippage from "AMÉN" to "(OMEN)" supplements South-to-North vassalage with a warning of resistance to all unquestioned assumptions regarding translation and translatability. In the politicization of reading practices, the necessary supplementarities, in any case, are to be traced not only between the lines and between the cultures, but also *within*. The claim that Susana Thénon's poem confronts *intra*-colonialism inseparably from its uncompounded progenitor needs be re-addressed now only by re-posing the *question* of the repeatability of "AMÉN" within *Latin America*. So be it?

To any and every Latin American who has said, since 1982, "What *we* need is a Margaret Thatcher", the poem pleads *"coño"* (and only in brackets "(fuck)" for the Anglo-Saxons who never listen until it suits them). For in the wings, always opportunist, are the listeners – on the inside as well as on the outside – who will (mis)interpret the plea, hear differently the same words. For those Latin Americans who still regard their own history and language as subordinate to their *empresa* – Cristóforos? – prayer will easily be (mis)read as imprecation, invitation... "(see here these unwashed)" [...] "(sack them)"[...] "(OMEN)". From *within*, too, comes the subversion, the ominous call for outside intervention by those who have always (ever ready) been poised to pounce, and to sack – "(fuck)".

A discredited counterpoint of West-East effects will now have already been represented by scenes chosen from that England conceived of as "back home" in the roast-beef-and-Yorkshire-pudding imaginary of the 1982 British Task Force. For the wounded deprived of a place in the front ranks of triumphalism at the October Falklands Victory Parade held in central London, being hidden away as the "negative factor" surplus to representation of the Nation, here was perhaps an unintended opportunity. A chance to ponder their exclusion from the (national) front-row as being strangely in keeping with the relegated role of millions of other Britons? One function of this coda might be to extend a belated but open invitation to all, to reflect again, if not always, on the internal differences at work *within* the "United" Kingdom just before and, after, intensified, the so-called external Malvinas conflict was over.

As I conclude, the national presses on both sides of the Atlantic are gearing themselves and their variously vested and invested interests for anniversary scratchings of illusorily healed-over scars. "A new history book" just "distributed to every secondary school pupil in Argentina", that tells a wholly familiar and hardly novel version of the status of the Islas Malvinas, is reported in the following terms: "Sovereignty of the islands remains a popular cause in Argentina, something President Kirschner clearly wants to tap into before national elections next year" (*The Guardian*, 27 September 2006, 18). The next day, a hardly coincidental counterpoint is trumpeted – recounting the possible first "disappearance" of the peace, albeit the real and very troubling case of Jorge Julio López, under the headline, "'Dirty War' torture witness goes missing" and followed by "Former members of the military and their sympathisers claim that the Dirty War was a necessity to prevent the take-over of the country by communist guerrilla movements" (*The Times*, 28 September 2006, 39).

Like the news reporting, the literary and cinematographic representation of the 1982 war, conflictually, politically, differently and differentially, will never avoid controversies. That writing goes on; untroubled by anniversaries, it has never stopped. It only awaits informed readers. The inexcusable insularity of any non-comparative assessment of a struggle that perhaps in the literary re-representation of it can be viewed in the light of not just, say, Theodor Adorno's celebrated general proposal for understanding the effects of war: "It is now virtually in art alone that suffering can still find its own voice, consolation, without immediately being betrayed by it [...] it is to works of art that has fallen the burden of wordlessly asserting what is barred from politics" (Adorno, 1985, 313).

For the notion that art and politics must somehow stand speechlessly, infantilely, apart from each other is contradicted not only by the poetry of Jorge Luis Borges and Susana Thénon analyzed here but also by the works of the many artists whose writings I have analyzed in my *Falklands-Malvinas An Unfinished Business*. The Borges and Thénon poems have been chosen here, as I address the ex-combatant veterans and the academic colleagues from Argentina, from the United Kingdom, and from the many other nations represented in this first such encounter in nearly a quarter of a century, emblematically to evoke the epic logos of a little war and its undiminished resonance, to demonstrate that powerful writing draws on and demands, inseparably, discursive *and* ideological effects.

Adventurisms of hubris are never restricted or confinable to any one side. If the art of war has anything to gain from the literature written on it, the strategist must look beyond even the classic militarist's most basic insight that the "The military is a great matter of the state. It is the ground of death and life, the Tao of survival or extinction. One cannot but examine it" (Sun-tzu, 2002, 3). The challenge posed by the depiction of war and its effects in imaginative literature is to recognize that to examine is but to reveal that there is nothing which is not already and always, and inseparably, conflictual *and* textual.

References

Adorno, T. (1985) "Commitment", In *The Essential Frankfurt School Reader*,
Eds. Arato, A., Gebhardt, E., New York, Continuum, pp. 313.
Borges, J. L. (1989) *Los conjurados, Obras completas*, Buenos Aires, Emecé, Volume 2, pp. 500.
Featherstone, S. (1995) *War Poetry: An Introductory Reader*, London and New York, Routledge, p. 23.
McGuirk, B. (2007) *Falklands-Malvinas: An Unfinished Business*, Seattle, New Ventures
Owen, W. (1918) In Silkin, Jon, ed., (1982) *The Penguin Book of First World War Poetry*, London, Penguin Books, pp. 96-8.
Thénon, S. (1987) *Ova completa*, Buenos Aires, Editorial Sudamericana, p. 28.
Tzu, Sun, (6th Century BC) *The Art of War*, trans. The Denma Translation Group (2002), Shambhala Publications, Boston and London, p. 3.

Part 3
Retrospectives

Malvinas-Falklands Suite

Jean Andrews

Diego García, an island and a man.
With the right R.P. accent,
echoing the surname of another,
Mike Seear, once enemy, now friend.

Señor García and Mr Seear,
compatriots in the fjordic north
through conjugality.
Polar bears dancing in the eternal midnight
of the frozen streets,
pursued by the price they did not pay,
armour-clad in endless night
beset by faceless ghosts
which turn all certainty to treacherous,
shape-changing mud.

No love, no reconciliation of the past,
no therapy nor pills has yet de-mined
this honour-gifted, guilted path.

*

Two men apologised
for not having suffered more.

One with three bullet-holes,
in his arm, his groin, his thigh.
The other with his burden of lost years,
nightmares and elusive sleep,
occasioned by the management of war.
Each man was once the enemy.
But, enmity now spent,
the foe these days is time
with its constant embassy of pain
even as it fades into oblivion
their cold and brutal
South Atlantic campaign.

The mask of one severe, often irascible.
The other voluble, a big man
built around a core of tears,
his friend then melting, caressing steel.
This one dressed for dinner,
a last and hurried communal meal,

Hors de Combat: the Falklands-Malvinas Conflict in Retrospect

the other, seventy-two hours standing,
with chalk-dust on his navy blazer
and eyes too dry and sore to weep.

*

If flashes of fire had hit me
before I'd seen them,
torn holes in my flesh
before I'd felt them,
if I'd been wounded in battle
with only one foot on the disputed ground,
the other still alighting
from my armoured car,
if I'd trained and sweated
and stared down the anvil of fear
only to be the first casualty spirited out,
how could I face
those shadows of my past,
those others who had stayed
and paid a price
in sentient pain?
All this, when
half a millennium before
my family had been
one of the great names
to come as conquistador
to these South Atlantic shores.

*

My friend Mike cannot pronounce my name.

His people are politicians.

He himself is a fluent communicator,
once the voice of war,
now the howl of the pity of war.

And still he cannot pronounce my name,
perhaps because he could never forgive himself
for what was done to me
in the name of war.

Maintaining the Momentum

Mike Seear

> *The rush of water, to the point of tossing rocks*
> *about. This is shih*
> *The strike of a hawk, at the killing snap. This is*
> *the node.*
> *Shih is like drawing the crossbow.*
> *The node is like pulling the trigger.*
>
> Sun-tzu, 6th Century BC

The Chinese word *shih* means the power inherent in a configuration. As a student of Sun-tzu, I was acutely aware of the potential of this phenomenon during those five months of work in assisting to plan the international colloquium. Pulling the trigger to start the event did indeed release that gradually accumulated energy all at once in those two unique November days at Nottingham in 2006. This was the node: that abrupt moment at which something occurs – the present, between past and future. And this is the power of *shih*, with the energy released all at once, in one spot. Afterwards I decided on a personal attempt to maintain the momentum caused by that particular *shih* for the ensuing twenty-fifth anniversary year of the war and beyond. This began by working with Diego into the first few months of 2007 on the production of a manuscript for this book's eventual publication; whilst concurrently I continued in a military consultant capacity to generate amendments and comments for Bernard McGuirk's unique book *Falklands-Malvinas: An Unfinished Business*, as well as working on a text revision for the paperback version of my first book *With the Gurkhas in the Falklands: A War Journal*.

After these initial tasks were completed, Bernard invited Diego and me to attend the University of London's March colloquium *Remembering the Malvinas in Argentine literature and film*. Attempting to camouflage personal irritation, I heard my voice many times during that interesting day correcting some presenters' distorted facts and errant assumptions about the war. The cause of my interventions was existential authority – after all, I had been there, those lecturing had not. Those targeted were, no doubt, equally irritated by my oblique invitations to confront reality.

Concurrently throughout that first quarter of 2007, Eduardo Gerding in Buenos Aires and I in Oslo were furiously exchanging e-mails in order to formulate our detailed plan for a visit that Lars Weisæth and I would make to Argentina one week after the University of London event. This would be our second joint visit to that country, the first being in December 2002. We were also indirectly promoting "the Nottingham spirit" begun by those participants in the colloquium five months before and for whom Eduardo had coined the title "the *Nottingham-Malvinas Group*". Similarly, our thirteen days in Argentina had an underlying theme of reconciliation. On arrival at Buenos Aires on 23 March we met up as planned with Cliff Caswell, Assistant Editor of the British Army's

Soldier magazine, and his photographer Steve Dock prior to an impressive dinner that evening hosted by Jorge Pérez Grandi in the magnificent Military Circle building. The twenty-six guests included retired Brigadier-General Mario Benjamín Menéndez who had been the Governor of the Malvinas Islands in 1982, and Carlos Hugo Robacio.

Heavily dependent on Eduardo's Spanish interpreter skills in Buenos Aires, Cliff and I carried out a series of interviews in the next two days with veterans of "the other" side. The last was the most memorable. This was my two-hour post-war "reconciliation" meeting with nine of the Argentine 5th Marine Infantry Battalion Malvinas War veterans, including six from that unit's 81mm Mortar Platoon which had fired six hundred mortar bombs at the Scots Guards and Gurkhas during the war's final battle. Cliff's stunning series of *Soldier* articles (for a magazine that has a monthly circulation of ninety thousand copies) on the Falklands-Malvinas War and the work he did from Argentina won the British Association of Communications in Business best event report. Before the award ceremony on 23 May 2008, he referred to the short-listing of his work for the award in a series of e-mails sent to me (and Eduardo):

> … if we win the award at *Soldier*, it will be an award for you, Eduardo and Bernard too. The stories we covered simply would not have been possible without your help. That Sunday afternoon in the lobby of the Hotel Anexo del Centro Naval was one of the most extraordinary assignments I have ever covered, especially seeing the way the Argentine veterans reacted to you. The images Steve Dock took, I think, summed up the emotionally charged mood so well. I'm really proud of the way it all worked out, particularly representing both sides of a story of twenty-five years ago that continues to resonate into our present. I feel as if I'm a part of the story. For some, the war has never fully ended, and those men deserve to be looked after in the knowledge that they have our full understanding and respect. I will keep you posted, but the judges were very interested in the fact that both sides of the conflict were represented in the story. The work you, and the *Nottingham-Malvinas Group* has done in reconciling veterans has been nothing short of amazing, and the collected memories in *Hors de Combat* make it one of the best and most-rounded books on the conflict ever produced. It is a story of men in battle, a tale of the consequences of conflict in their later lives and an uplifting journey of veteran reconciliation in one volume. A unique collection of viewpoints from both sides, this is a compelling account of war in the South Atlantic.

Lars and I had also planned a semi-formal platform to our mission by providing four lectures on the aftermath of the war and traumatic stress. Our first was given to the JFK University: this also being Cliff's final event before flying back to the UK. However the media baton was then passed to BBC Radio 4's Jack Izzard who began recording a series of reports on this reconciliation theme throughout all the following day which would be compiled into an eventual broadcast from Argentina to the UK. His work started at our second lecture held in the lunch meeting of one hundred ladies of the Buenos Aires Womens' Forum, with Carlos Hugo Robacio enhancing our efforts there by his interesting presentation on the war.

Next day we travelled by bus north through the Pampas and into Córdoba province where Lars and I provided a double reprise of our act in another two towns. Supported by the wonderful planning and hospitality of Marisa Clausen de Bruno, there was a presentation to more than one hundred war veterans and inhabitants of General Roca and, the following day, to two hundred schoolchildren in Oliva. We returned to Buenos Aires so I could witness the twenty-fifth year war anniversary commemoration ceremony on 2 April at the Malvinas War Monbumnet to *Los Caidos* (the Argentine fallen) in Plaza San Martín, and then spend a pleasant final evening with Eduardo Villarraza and his charming family in their apartment. Jack's six-minute news report on our activities was also broadcast late that evening. Bernard was listening, and afterwards I received his immediate anxiety-relieving mobile phone text message of "Authentic, true, lasting" before flying back to Oslo.

Receiving the proof of my paperback in May, I completed yet another detailed text revision before travelling to London for the opening of the Falklands War Exhibition at the Imperial War Museum. Diego was there too, and his presence was of significance to many. In a way this also gave the event an underlying sense of reconciliation, best personified in the caring attitude of Baroness Margaret Thatcher towards Diego, and best remembered by her laconic "I wouldn't repeat it if I were you. Please don't do it again" request to him.

However I was racking up the flying hours. There were four more events on my calendar the following month. The first was attendance in Southampton at a Falklands War Commemoration Lunch on board RMS *Queen Elizabeth 2*, the Cunard liner that had transported us to the South Atlantic. I met briefly Robert Lawrence, a Scots Guards subaltern who had been severely wounded in the head by an Argentine sniper's bullet during the war's final day. My attempt to invite him to the Nottingham colloquium had failed, so I felt guilt when told by him that he would have liked to have participated.

The next week I gave illustrated presentations on *The Gurkhas in the Falklands War* at the National Army Museum in London on 14 June, Falklands Liberation Day, and the following day at The Gurkha Museum, Winchester. Forty-eight hours later I went on parade for probably the last time in my life at the Falklands War Commemoration event that incorporated a drumhead service on Horseguards Parade, Whitehall, London. For many veterans the formalities' highlight was the beautiful singing of *Somewhere Along the Road* by the thirty-year old daughter of Major Roger Nutbeem, killed in the Argentine air strike on RFA *Sir Galahad* anchored in Port Pleasant. I thought of my daughters Victoria and Emily who were only slightly younger than Kathryn Nutbeem in 1982. This parade was sandwiched between a remarkable Gurkha Falklands War veterans' reunion in a hired boat plying up and down the

River Thames during the morning and early afternoon, whilst the party devoured a wonderful Gurkha *bhat* lunch and – afterwards – the yarning about our war experiences and post-war lives over an evening glass of beer on a floating Thames pub. I have never felt more relaxed for years in the convivial company of those that had gone to war with me.

However my personal climax of this special year arrived in November when I became a pilgrim on the South Atlantic Medal Association 82 and Combat Stress organisation's Pilgrimage to the Falkland Islands with many other war veterans. After the long flight via Rio de Janeiro, our ensuing week spent on East Falkland was, at times, an emotive – but always therapeutic – experience. Four of my precious days were spent tramping around the Goat Ridge-Tumbledown-Mount William battlefield in a personal confrontation with trauma's reality. Half of my time was spent on the battlefield. The organisors had worked hard on a highly detailed programme which imposed time limits to exploring the still highly visible British and Argentine forces' defensive positions. Nonetheless my digital camera was in overdrive snapping one image after another. These would be needed for designing an imminent presentation on the Pilgrimage because, thirty-six hours after arriving back in Oslo, I was airborne again to the UK and University of Nottingham's follow-up colloquium *Hors de Combat: Falklands-Malvinas Anniversary Retrospective* to mark the *Hors de Combat* book launch. At this event I met my co-editor Diego again who, that summer, had moved to Geneva. Our presentation titles had been neatly devised by Bernard: mine was *Look back (not) in anger*, and Diego's *Look what a year can bring*. It was also a clairvoyant choice. My friend's performance was a relaxed strategic offering, whilst mine was driven by a combat veteran's raw emotions of having just returned from a close-up exploration of his former battlefield.

Three weeks later I was on the move again, this time to re-join *QE2* at Southampton as a guest lecturer on the eight-day "Christmas Markets" North Sea cruise that included Oslo as one of the four ports of call. I had prepared five lectures on *The Gurkhas in the Falklands War* which included one about the recent Pilgrimage. My task escalated as a Force 10 storm prevented us from calling at Hamburg and I volunteered to create yet another Falklands War "enrichment" lecture to assist in alleviating the stressed Cruise Director's entertainment crisis and his need to compile a subsequent new programme for the extra day at sea. The new offering focused on reconciliation and my individual total of four visits to Argentina in the past five years essentially to meet, talk with and get to know those I had once fought against. These PowerPoint presentations that included DVD-video clips of the war and its aftermath, led to on-board sales of forty-seven copies of my first book as well as some copies of *Hors de Combat* and Bernard's book.

There was a natural spill-over of activity into 2008. On the twenty-sixth anniversary of the 2 April 1982 Argentine landings on the Islands, I made back-to-back presentations on the war to officer cadets at the Swedish Military Academy in Stockholm (1 April) and Danish Military Academy in Copenhagen (2 April), as well as "opposing" cadets in their war-gaming and presentations on various aspects of the war. Since Diego wrote in his *Hors de Combat* contribution that the initial Argentine Special Forces' landing "... happened, contrary to several books on the war, with the use of rubber boats and shortly before midnight on 1 April", it was appropriate that my two tasks straddled both days. Instructing to a younger generation of officers about a veteran's experiences gained, mistakes made and lessons learnt was a hugely satisfying affair. This feeling was enhanced by two Danish Army officers who had been my guests at the international colloquium and their assertion that they had been witnesses to a truly historical event. The power of its *shih* also gave them a motivation of their own to visit the Islands four months later.

My penultimate event of these eighteen months had a degree of symbolism. Later in that same month as my Scandinavian military academy presentations, I attended the inaugural British Task Force Hospital Ship HMHS *Uganda* Reunion at Southampton. Since *Uganda* was a P&O ship which had been wrecked off Taiwan by a typhoon in the South China Sea in 1986, the reunion took place on board P&O's cruise ship SS *Aurora*. There were one hundred and seventy-five people present, including Royal Navy surgeons, anaesthetists, nurses, Marine band stretcher bearers, crew, casualties and next of kin. My qualification to participate was provided by the ship's conversion into a troop transport after the war and transporting the Gurkha battalion I was serving in back to Southampton. It was humbling to meet or see some of those casualties of the war at the *Aurora* gourmet lunch, and also inspiring to hear a few talking about their "second life".

Like our 1982 return voyage on SS *Uganda*, this could have provided an appropriate end to maintaining the momentum of this tale. However another task remains. I had already signed a contract with a publisher before the international colloquium to write a manuscript for the sequel to my first book. *After the Falklands and Gurkhas: A Post-War Journal* will not only ensure the detailed documentation of my journey through these past eighteen months, but also provide many more personal Gurkha, British and Argentine soldier's accounts of the war and their return to a "normal" life. If all goes according to plan, it will be published at the end of 2010. Completion of the manuscript will also mark the end of a long personal cathartic process.

Oslo, May 2008

Interviewer: Veterans of the Falklands War from both Britain and Argentina are meeting in Nottingham this weekend to mark twenty-five years since the invasion. The actual anniversary is next spring but the University of Nottingham is hosting an event on the conflict which is believed to be the first time that high ranking officers from both sides have discussed what happened. Diego García Quiroga was an officer with Argentina's Naval Special Forces and was one of the first Argentinians to land on the Island. Mike Seear was with the First Battalion of the 7th Gurkha Rifles and they're both in Nottingham now. Good morning to you both. Diego García Quiroga tell us how you felt about the invasion at the time when you had been ordered to land on the Island.

DGQ: I learned about the invasion while I was at sea, already deployed, and I had no particular feelings about it happening when it happened. I was a professional officer at the time so I was just doing my job and it felt quite alright to do it.

Interviewer: And in terms of the way it was carried out. How did you feel about that?

DGQ: Well I was a member of the Special Forces at the time so I felt we were very well prepared, we were very well briefed. For what I can speak about, I felt it was quite alright.

Interviewer: Mike Seear, how is it now so many years later to be in Nottingham meeting people who were on the other side at the time?

MS: An absolutely fabulous experience.

Interviewer: In what way?

MS: To meet the other within the University of Nottingham and to meet others you were fighting against and be able to discuss and debate with them what they felt like being on the battlefield of the Falkland-Malvinas Islands, and then what they were going through in the quarter of a century afterwards, all their thoughts and their feelings on what the fighting was all about... and we find continuously that we are meeting together with the same thoughts. It's quite remarkable. I've been to Argentina three times so I've got a very good network of people in Argentina whom I have invited to this particular colloquium. There are in fact a total of fifteen veterans at this colloquium. Ten British and five Argentines.

Interviewer: But the same thoughts being what?

MS: Fear on the battlefield; that you are a professional soldier; that you have to do your job to the best of your ability and do it efficiently, fast and effectively so that, at the end of the day, the fighting can come to an end and you can return home to your families… and that is the same type of thoughts that the opposition had as the British had.

Interviewer: It seems a remarkable coincidence that both of you now, as I understand it, live in Norway?

DGQ: That's curious.

Interviewer: Curious because in a similar sense you both felt let down about how you were subsequently treated?

MS: No.

DGQ: No.

MS: No. That's wrong and that is one of the major issues that we wish to debate.

Interviewer: Forgive me but I forgot that.

DGQ: That's right. It's been commonly understood like that at least on the Argentine side but, as I said, even though we had some experiences of which I'm not able to tell you because I did not experience them personally, I do know that there are a lot of soldiers that came back and, with reason, felt that they did not have the welcome they were, supposedly, awarded – and that is true. I don't know about the British side; I don't know, Mike, if you can say.

MS: We had the old issue that pops up, again and again, of the suicides and, yes, the suicides occur and what have you… and we do have people talking about Post-Traumatic Stress Disorder and, yes, many people do have that but we never hear about the other side of the coin; we never hear about how you can grow on, and from, this particular experience and how you can put into practice in your later life all the lessons that you have learned from such a stress situation. We never hear about that. There is another side of the coin and I wish that we could debate this at the colloquium today and tomorrow.

Interviewer: I'm sure it's a conversation that will go on there. Mike and Diego thank you both.

Interviewer: So it was twenty-five years ago today that British forces liberated Port Stanley to reclaim the Falkland Islands. It ended an eleven week war with Argentina. Not so long ago Nottingham though played host to a special event which saw British and Argentine veterans of the conflict meeting for the first time and we were there to record the veterans experiences.

MS: My name is Mike Seear. I am a Falklands war veteran. I was an officer with the Gurkhas. I have still locked into my mind the early morning of the 14th of June advancing along the northern slopes to Tumbledown to attack and we get half way up and suddenly all hell lets loose and we are caught in a bombardment of shells and we were very lucky because two of those shells landed fifteen metres away from us but they were duds. Responsibility weighs very heavily on your shoulders as an officer and I had never appreciated it in peacetime. Because at the end of the day you are going to be taking life or death decisions and I think I was very, very affected by fear and anxiety and that affected my performance in the Falklands. I don't think I performed optimally as I should have done and I will feel guilty until I go to my grave.

JPG: My name is Jorge Pérez Grandi. I was leading the regiment force from "Monte Caseros", Argentina. I was fighting in Two Sisters and then I was "hurt" in the same place. For me to be here is a strange experience because I think that the British people, or England as a country, is not my enemy. I think we have another enemy today. But I have to comply with orders. I am happy to be here because I am closing one circle in my life.

Interviewer: Interesting, really, to hear those memories and those thoughts... Well, with us is the man who helped to organise that reunion, Professor Bernard McGuirk, from the University of Nottingham. Good morning to you. What are your thoughts on on the anniversary?

BM: It's been a very hectic period. Not only here with the numerous celebrations and commemorations but also of course in Argentina. You wouldn't use the terms celebrations and commemorations of victory in the case of the Argentine but, as I said in my recent book, *Falklands-Malvinas: An Unfinished Business*, we might think about the seventy-four days that shook the world in terms of bringing us a continued Thatcher government, a shift from being the least to the most popular Prime Minister within a very few short months of the war but also to restoring what is now called a Falklands-style capability in military terms. Shook the world... Margaret Thatcher observed that, when she went to Russia, they said "we didn't think you'd do it" and, at the Conservative Party Conference the following year, she claimed that

Britain was again able to be seen to rule the waves. As for Argentines, when I say that the seventy-four days shook their world-view it is because they lost a war but gained 'democracy' overnight.

Interviewer: Yes, and there were big changes after the war, weren't there, in the dictatorship?

BM: Within forty-eight hours. But when we speak about the war, of ten and a half weeks, one of the problems we have when we look at Argentina from Britain, and from Europe, and from Washington, for example, is that many of us don't understand that this 'little war' was part of a greater war for them. From 1976 onwards, to 1982, they had a vast dirty war, internal war, repression, military dictatorship; 30,000 persons disappeared; mothers walking round the central square in front of the Presidential Palace in Buenos Aires complaining about their lost children. And that continues, a legacy continues, so on both sides of the Atlantic there is a legacy, an unfinished business. And this year particularly there has been a lot of drum-beating in Argentina because it's an election year. And without going into the rights and wrongs of sovereignty arguments today, all I can remind our listeners of is the fact that the shame of having lost a war and the sense of having re-emerged into democracy are accompanied by that absolute conviction that the Malvinas, as the Argentines call the Falklands, are theirs by right, so they believe it was a just cause. They also know that they went to war albeit for a just cause but in their view at a very ill-timed moment and impelled by a vicious military dictatorship.

Interviewer: And while we're talking about wars of course we can't really ignore what's going on in Iraq and Afghanistan at the moment and I think there will probably be a lot of people saying, well actually this is what's happening now, much bigger than the Falklands was. Do you think that's fair? Do you think we'd look at that in a few years in the same way?

BM: Well, I think it's a fair comparison. Whether we look at it in a few years in the same way is more speculative. What I can say is already, and you yourself as a journalist and our listeners themselves as alert individuals to such pressing matters as war will know already, that we have problems in terms of Post-Traumatic Stress Disorder and suicides of veterans. I can tell you just as a matter of fact that more soldiers have died from suicide on the British side as a result of the experience in the Falklands than actually during the war and similarly on the Argentine side. So we're speaking about legacies of war and therefore your question is extremely pertinent. You are asking "What are we thinking about now?" not just in terms of providing troops there in Afghanistan, in Iraq. What are we going to do with them when they come home?

Interviewer: Yes, well, we'll see won't we? Thank you, Bernard McGuirk, for joining us from the University of Nottingham.

Interviewer: Well, Argentina is now a democracy, Mrs. Thatcher has long ago left office, but the Falklands War continues to affect relations between Britain and Argentina. We can talk now to Bernard McGuirk, Director of the *Centre for the Study of Post-Conflict Cultures* at Nottingham University. His book *Falklands-Malvinas: An Unfinished Business* has just been published. Bernard McGuirk, what are relations between Britain and Argentina like?

BM: Well, I think we could pick up on some of the terms used by your own BBC reporter. Very accurately he juxtaposed the term 'celebration' and 'commemoration'. You led him very relevantly to talk about economic boom and also the question – the hanging question – of sovereignty. Now all those could be picked up on from an Argentine point of view. What I've tried to do of course is to look at both points of view and indeed other external points of view. De facto, 2007 is not only the twenty-fifth anniversary of the conflict but also an election year in Argentina and we all know that in election years across the globe the politics and nationalisms and the drum-beatings and issues of national identity always come to the fore. So flag-waving, jingoism in football terms or, more particularly in this case – and this goes right to the heart of the matter – the question of sovereign territory... this is a popular cause in Argentina still and, whether we think it is just a slogan that 'Las Malvinas son argentinas' ('the Falkland Islands are Argentine') or whether we believe it's a conviction, we still have to deal with it politically and there has been considerable raising of tension, as was pointed out by your reporter.

Interviewer: Now do *they* take a view? What view do they take? Do they see themselves as a nation defeated twenty-five years ago or not?

BM: This is a crucial question. Victory, defeat, loss and gain... Imagine that the very moment of defeat militarily brought to Argentina in 1982 the loss of a horrible dictatorship responsible for at least 30,000 disappeared persons, and that this had been going on, loosely known as the 'dirty war', since 1976. So whereas, from the point of view of the United Kingdom, a seventy-four day conflict, which might be said to have restored national pride, brought back a notion of Britannia ruling waves, if not all waves, in Argentina there was this mix, this ambivalent reaction: we have lost a dictatorship as well as a war and there was a lot of optimism about the future. However, and this goes right back to what your reporter was saying about the economy, whereas the Falkland Islands have seen a boom, Argentina in the interim, at the beginning of the twenty-first century, went into bankruptcy. I think that what has been analysed in Argentina is not only the war, the short ten-and-a-half-weeks war, but also a whole thirty-one-year legacy of defeat, abjection in many respects, and self-interrogation; curiously, culturally and politically, an infinitely more intensive self-analysis than has been the case on the British side. I summarise by saying that this year I have witnessed in many events that have been organised a certain sense of celebrations or, as was said, commemoration, yes, on the British side, but not on the Argentine side. What have they got to celebrate? What have they got to commemorate? They are still living out a painful process which began in '76 and came to a head, and exploded, in '82.

Interviewer: There are those who look at this from the British side and say that perhaps the most lasting remnant of the Falklands conflict was Thatcherism in the sense that the War saved the most unpopular Prime Minster of all time.

BM: That's irrefutable. I would add to that that if we are speaking about legacy, we should look at the veterans and what they have to say? I organised, in November last year, the first coming together of veterans from both sides and it was a fascinating opportunity for us all to look at the legacy of, for example, the suicides; the fact that more men on the British side have killed themselves after coming back from the Falklands than actually died and something similar will be said about the Argentines. More than 350 Argentine suicides when, if we leave aside those 321 who died on the Belgrano, there were 328 other fatalities so, once again, we have more suicides than deaths in war. And this is something that has been neglected, I believe, and specialists on both sides would agree with me that we've lost an opportunity to find out exactly what the legacy is because we talk too much about political myth-making.

Interviewer: Thank you very much.

On the Making of *An Ungentlemanly Act*[1]

Stuart Urban

Publicity/background notes, written in 1992

In 1982 I sat back and watched with disbelief as we went to war for a place most Britons probably could not have found on a map a few weeks before. Although I consider myself British first and foremost, I have relatives in Buenos Aires, and spent time in Venezuela for various parts of my childhood and youth (I still have dual nationality). I not only felt torn between Britain and Latin America but was also fascinated at how two developed nations supported a war over this outcrop of rock and grass or, as some would have us believe, for the principle of it all. In 1986 I wrote my first screenplay on the war set amidst the Paras. It very nearly got made on two occasions but its would-be backers ran out of funds and its time passed. But the beginning had always fascinated me, a mini-Khartoum or Dunkirk or Singapore, yet without the degree of bloodshed that would have made the war inevitable and the story too painful to watch. This beginning proves that this was a war fought on both sides for wounded honour; the Argentines at what they saw as a century and a half of usurpation, the British at the insolence of Argentine aggression.

For the first few years not enough detail came out (*The Sunday Times* "Insight" team did a very able account, but only of the British side). Then more elements started appearing in dribs and drabs and a really fascinating film began to take possible shape. To me, the outlandish shoot-out on the croquet lawns and vegetable patch of Government House provided an ideal alternative focus to everything that had come before on television about the war. No one had seemed to depict how absurd the whole thing was, few seemed to take note of the Argentine writer Borges's analogy of "two bald men fighting over a comb". I did not wish to laugh at the characters in the story – indeed, as far as I am concerned, they are very heroic. What fascinated me was the surreal sideshow in the twilight of Empire; the laughable levels of men and equipment that Britain maintained against a dictatorship that was known to be ruthless and violent; the brave Governor, whose unswerving loyalty to Mrs Thatcher never faltered and who chose to defend the indefensible Government House rather than let the wooden houses of Stanley come under fire (ironic because the Argentines, who

---

1 In the Autumn of 1992, the BBC gave a nod and a wink to the production company Union Pictures in the UK that it might wish to make the script I was developing about the extraordinary first thirty-six hours of the Falklands War to mark the tenth anniversary of the conflict. This was a tragic-comic but true tale (or should that "but" be "and") of how the Governor, Rex Hunt, and his small party of Royal Marines, received the stunning last-minute news on 1 April 1982 that an Argentine invasion force was about invade the Falkland Islands. Some thought it was an April Fool's Day prank... Here is my production diary detailing some of my experiences preparing and making the film.

presumed he would have vacated it, like any sensible bloke, blundered into an unexpectedly solid defence); the symbolic first death which occurred over a language mix-up – the leader of the Argentine Commandos was bleeding to death in the chicken run, begging to be relieved of the live grenade in his hand, while the British thought he was threatening them not to come near or he would hurl it. And in the midst of this crisis that began on April Fool's Day some Islanders understandably failed to come to terms with what was going on; one man tried to walk to work through a firefight while a lady offered tea to Marines firing over her garden fence.

In bringing this true story to the screen I rejected the usually po-faced approach of drama-documentary (even though this is technically the category *An Ungentlemanly Act* falls into), ignored the occasionally flashy thriller-genre techniques deployed particularly in pieces about Northern Ireland, and tried instead to begin the film boldly as an Ealing comedy and then descend into tragedy. This, I believe, is something like the way it was. I was flattered and delighted when Major Mike Norman, who conducted the defence by Royal Marines, agreed to be military advisor on the basis of the screenplay. I have met and talked with almost every major character in the script (both British and Argentine) and researched it to the best of my ability. Nevertheless, I try to tell the story through characters that we care for, whose fear and horror and laughter we understand. There are certain changes of time/place for dramatic convenience, a handful of minor characters get rolled into a slightly smaller handful, re-naming of a few supporting characters for legal reasons or by request of those involved. But, on the whole, in trying to be objective and using the methodology which earned me a first class history degree (I make this mention at the risk of sounding immodest but hoping to present solid credentials), I hope that what I am presenting is worthwhile. While making no apologies for the fact, I accept that presenting recent historical events as tragicomedy might be considered provocative. Some people will no doubt lambast me for concentrating on the first, highly embarrassing, chapter of this war (though my defence is that my 1986 script followed the whole course of the war and I was so keen to get it made that I even defended a High Court action to retain the copyright). But this invasion is after all the reason the war took place. Because we won, people in this country never really questioned how the war could have been allowed to happen and I think some people will be very surprised at seeing this. My purpose in the end is not merely or even primarily political. Hopefully people will conclude from these absurd, confused, and frightening events that history is not the neat arrangement of facts that some books and politicians offer us, that people can blunder into a war without stopping to think what on earth they are doing, and that in the case of a unique and fragile little community like this, force of arms is no solution because the peace and harmony of the Falklands were destroyed when the first shot was fired and as long as "Fortress Falklands" continues. But even though the minefields might never be cleared, perhaps if people can soften their attitudes after a film like this, a settlement can one day be reached.

An Ungentlemanly Act
Extracts from Stuart Urban's production diary

3 November 1991 – To Sunningdale, home of the Hunts, at 11.00 am on this last Sunday morning before I leave for the Southern Hemisphere. Fifi, the historic red Fiesta car, sits on the gravel, not indicating to any casual observer that she had survived sea voyages, gun battles and artillery bombardments. Her colour is a fine complement to His Excellency's maroon London taxi and official car, which I will see in the flesh down south.

Rex and Mavis kindly agreed to receive me at very short notice before my rushed departure. Rex is short, as I knew, but physically graceful and well-proportioned. Like Dick Baker and his wife, years of colonial service have produced an affable, friendly and engaging couple. I took Mavis at first to be a possible cook, so different did she seem, in apron strings and rolled-up sleeves, from her photographs, as she prepared the Sunday lunch. She strikes me at first as flighty and nervous, though after a few minutes' talk she actually becomes rather camp in manner and speech ("let's have a pinkie" at 12.15 pm). Rex is as helpful as he can be in his interview but, of course, I must ask myself (and him) whether what he is telling is all that he knows. Did he (as Captain Nick Barker of *Endurance* maintains) have forewarning of the invasion? If he did, I would have to change the complexion of the film's opening. Major Norman backs Rex Hunt on this, so I am inclined to discount what Captain Barker says – Mike Norman has no axe to grind.

But I question Rex closely and his disavowals seem genuine. Both Rex and Mavis are very discreet on the matter of the former Royal Marine garrison commander Garry Noott and why he was not asked to resume command as he knew the terrain much better than the incoming garrison's commander Mike Norman. I think there is something I am not being told but will I ever discover what? Mavis will not admit (indeed denies very hastily) that she told Connie Baker or Major Norman that the Falklands were not worth fighting for that night; "You see, I don't know if she told you but Connie never cared for the Falklands". Connie never gave that impression to me. I conclude that Mavis expressed those feelings in a crisis in which they all feared for their lives and that the other two (both reliable witnesses) could not have made this up. The fact is that a lot of people testify to various things about Mavis that night which I intend to show in a toned-down form. I sympathise with her greatly and she will engage the audience's sympathy but inevitably the Hunts will find some things about her portrait which they will not like and I feel apprehensive about this, because they are such pleasant people. But I feel it is my responsibility to show the truth.

To Soho via the home of Franc Roddam (executive producer of this film and director of *Quadrophenia*) and Carina and their four-day old baby Flynn, and on to Union Pictures' Marshall Street base where casting resumes. That afternoon designer Steve Hardie arrives from North Carolina, tired and jetlagged after his *Hellraiser III* but ready for the off.

Monday 4 November (extract) – Walking along Regent Street I

receive a mysterious call on the mobile from someone who introduces himself as the individual who single-handedly operated the Spanish language desk at GCHQ during the first eighty-six hours of the crisis. He was monitoring the Argentine military interception, in other words. He would not say how he knew about this film or obtained my unlisted mobile number. He provides us with fascinating information which, among other things, follows the government line on not being able to be certain that invasion was imminent until it was too late. He also confirms Rex Hunt's insistence that Nick Barker did not inform him of any imminent invasion. There was only one MI6 man in Latin America even though he was stationed in Buenos Aires. *Endurance* and Nick Barker were the main source of intercepts. But because there had been Argentine naval manoeuvres of this kind in previous years, also utilising the NATO Blue codebook, the Government did not act swiftly enough. Has Rex Hunt or someone in the Government put this "mole" up to calling me? Somebody must have.

5 November (extract – preparing to fly to the Falklands from UK) – At RAF Brize Norton, designer Steve Hardie and I are greeted at the security gate with the question is our flight "duty or indulgence?". I have to think carefully before replying. "Crab Air" destinations are billed in abbreviated form to confuse the enemy and passengers. Service is brusque in the extreme, making even El Al stewards seem courteous. A hiss from the squaddies greets the tannoy request for "officers and civilians" to go forward first and take their seats on the flight. The cargo aircraft interior is "spartan minimalist", with vast steel containers and a white rope running down starboard side in case we keel over on a forced landing or whatever. That's fine if we list to port, but what happens if we go the other way? The "cabin" is alternately freezing and roasting. There is no thermostat, only on/off (polar blizzard vs. fires of hell). I pity the "stewardess", not a conventionally attractive girl, whose safety demonstration must nevertheless be performed to a sea of leering smiles, shaved heads and ribald comments. Pork scratchings and a penguin bar (destination: Falklands, get it?) for the snack meal, a ham roll for dinner, sausages and bacon for breakfast in a package labelled "SAS partner". Good thing I'm not kosher or vegetarian. Later, the men find amusement in portable TV gameboys. The stewardess gets her revenge by barking orders and we are all finally commanded by the tannoy to sleep before being plunged into darkness (no such thing as reading lights here).

Wednesday, November 6 (extract) – On arriving in Stanley after some twenty-four hours' travelling, Steve Hardie and I cannot resist racing round to see everything we can before the sun sets. Having written about and researched this place for so long (five years when I count my first screenplay about the war) nothing quite prepares me for the Falklands, which must be one of the strangest places on earth. You step off a plane eight thousand miles down south and here you are not quite in little England but a little English colonial outpost, situated not only physically in the middle of nowhere, but also in some unspecified past. The wind, the startlingly clear air, the tame birds, the penguins on beaches, all tell you that you are well away from any civilised land mass.   Rushing round to have a quick look at the outside of Government House, it appears terribly small, so petite as to resemble a doll's house. It seems to translate on a different scale when photographed or filmed. Here, on the manicured croquet lawn at the front, and in the chicken-run and vegetable garden behind, the war began with a gun battle. Unreal.

Stanley is also very compact, almost like a model village, with its higgledy-piggledy houses with multi-coloured roofs, and in the gardens you see horses and sheep and smoking oil-drums. Almost a "toy-town", as one of my characters describes it. It has a fairytale air, despite several building monstrosities that have sprung up and ugly satellite dishes. Up to Tumbledown to catch the sunset. It is very unsettling to stand near the spot where Robert Lawrence (hero of the previous BBC drama, *Tumbledown*), whose wedding I went to, stood when he looked down at Stanley and was shot through the head in the last hour or so of the war. Birds approach us, and all around lies the fragmentary debris of war – sleeping bags, half-buried Argentine positions etc. Standing next to the memorial cross to the Scots Guards who fell here, we can see for nearly fifty miles, well past the airport. The light here is certainly most unusual and for this alone it would be worth making the film here. Steve and I decide that this is really the only place to shoot the movie because it cannot be replicated. But our mission is merely a fact-finding one, with the possibility of a second unit or reduced unit coming here after we finish the main photography in New Zealand. Back to the Upland Goose Hotel (as featured in the film!) for a surprisingly pleasant meal of steak – alas, no Upland Geese available as if you want to eat one it has to be found and executed, which requires a few days' notice.

Thursday 7 November – At breakfast I saw a man riding to work on his horse, sitting on the traditional kelper's fleece saddle. Our American waitress who is also the owner-publisher of a local paper informs us that he is called Dennis Middleton and pastures his transport outside his workplace during the day. Got to have him in the title sequence, which presents key images of Stanley. First stop is the kitsch chalet that the Argentines built for Vice-Comodoro Gilobert, boss of the military airline LADE and quite possibly a master spy, in Falklands terms. His former home is now the Falklands Museum, run by John Smith. We have brought him a fish tank from the UK for his whale embryo (a dead one). In return he gives us a lot of co-operation and assistance. Like other Islanders, he rightly boggles at the prospect of our attempting to recreate the Falklands elsewhere. A depressing call to London reveals that the New Zealand budget is looking way over and the project is now threatened, despite the tax shelter monies available there. Bollocks. There are so many people and places to see in our forty-eight hours on the Island that we are inevitably late for every single appointment, charging about on foot or in the Land Rover of our good-humoured guide, Tony Smith, the relentless wind buffeting at all times.

One surprising and depressing thing about the Islanders is their casual racism towards Latinos, calling the Argentines "wogs" and so on – even the most cultured and reasonable of them frequently emit such epithets. I feel personally insulted for, as I have said, although I count myself British I have relatives in Buenos Aires, have lived in Venezuela and still have dual nationality. But then this ambiguity of feeling is why I set about making a film on this war in the first place. I meet Pat Peck, one of the FIDF men lined up outside the Bakers' house garden wall in the mock execution scene that we will have towards the end of the film. They thought the Argentines were preparing to fire but it was just posing for the cameras. I looked at the wall, and saw the still extant bullet hole in the adjoining house, caused by an Argentine heavy machine-gun round which narrowly missed Tony Hunt during the invasion. So bizarre, the wall where men thought they were to be shot and the quaint house with its symbolic bullet hole. It would be so wonderful to recreate these extraordinary scenes where they took place. After a confusing amount of bureaucracy (Government House had lost all trace of our visit and appointment) we finally gain entry to the minuscule seat of government. A brief chat with the Governor is followed by an excellent tour conducted by chauffeur majordomo, Don Bonner, who is one of the cast of our film. He still drives the maroon taxi on certain occasions but more often the conventional Range Rover, (registration: GH1). We come across Roger Huxley, a short, Ealingesque Foreign Office man who keeps turning books over and denying us permission to photograph even the most innocuous secretary's desk for fear of unmasking some major secret of state. Don Bonner mutters oaths and mouths the letters "FO" behind Mr Huxley's back. Clearly a clash of parallel command structures as Don runs the house and Roger the diplomatic side.

Roger tells Don to "stop bullshitting" about where various bullets came through but the evidence is clear enough throughout the house, with many patched up lumps in the wall and even the odd piece of antique furniture with a part missing. In the pantry the floor is still cratered from a high explosive grenade that came through, fortunately not killing any of the defenders. I did not even know a grenade had penetrated the house so I must include this incident. Then to the chicken and sheep run where the first lethal shots of the war were fired. The mind can scarcely comprehend how Captain Giachino and his courageous Commandos simply strolled right up to the kitchen door intending to seize the Governor before they were cut down amidst chickens, geese and sheep. Giachino is a national hero with streets named after him in Buenos Aires, yet here was the spot he met his end in such a bizarre, sordid and unnecessary manner. Unnecessary, because he bled to death over a difference of language, a grenade clutched in his hand. The Marines would have rescued him, indeed tried to, but always thought he was menacing them (he was pleading to be disarmed and given medical assistance). I study the small potato shed behind which one of the wounded Argentines hid, including Diego Quiroga, and as per written testimony there are several low bullet holes which must have narrowly missed the wounded men's head.

In the same shed Argentine bodies were found at the end of the war. The chicken and sheep milling around are not descendants of the 1982 generation because they were eaten by the hungry defenders in the last days of the war. Next the London taxi in its garage, whose walls are also pitted with many bullet holes. Miraculously, the official car and its female sidekick, Fifi the Fiesta, survived the war intact and were liberated by the Paras on 14 June. We decide to ask the Governor straight out if he can assist us in the making of the film and to our surprise Mr Fullerton shows himself to be completely for it, saying that "this is the place to make the film", not New Zealand. He says he has complete authority (and indeed his authority here is second only to the Queen's) but I cannot believe he would not have to refer his decision back to the Foreign & Commonwealth Office, in which case we can kiss it goodbye. There is a definite embargo emanating from Whitehall or Downing Street on any co-operation being offered to this film, for example in the loan of men or *matériel* for filming purposes. Wouldn't it be fantastic to come here, if we could overcome the logistic and transport difficulties? To make a film with full scale action sequences thousands of miles from any film facilities or industry (except Argentina's of course – but no air travel is allowed to/from the Argies).

After dinner we meet Jim Fairfield, the ex-Royal Marine who left his two infant children and his wife to fight that night at GH, fully expecting to die. When it came to the time to surrender, Jim told the Governor to "fuck off". I struggle to understand the mentality of these "Royals" as they call themselves. But then Jim at least was fighting for his family and home, whereas others who fought were just off the boat. Jim, like most of our interviewees, remains cagey on who actually shot Giachino. Well, I've got to show someone doing it and he seems the right sort of warlike guy.

Friday 8 November – The bellicose attitude of the authorities ten years after the war means that not only is an inordinate amount of jet fuel wasted on Phantom escorts for flights across the Exclusion Zone, but travellers heading to Argentina (a forbidden air travel destination some four hundred miles away) have to endure the absurdity of a three-legged, thirty-six hour journey. It starts with a five-hour flight over the South Atlantic and Tierra del Fuego in a tiny toilet-less aircraft, staying over in Punta Arenas (Chile) whose only redeeming feature is that it is the second most southerly town in the world, then up a couple of thousand "Ks" to Santiago, change planes for the second time, and finally the one and a half-hour hop across the Andes to Buenos Aires.

Sunday 10 November – On landing, my Falklands visa is carefully bordered (but not abused or obliterated) by an Argentine entry stamp. Zooming along the freeway in one of the city's ubiquitous 1990s-built Ford Falcons with retro styling, we pass the first of many signs proclaiming the "Malvinas were, are and will be Argentine".

Buenos Aires is a delight at 1.30 am when we arrive, the streets and cafés throbbing with life and excitement and vitality. A vibrant metropolis, surely one of the unacknowledged great capitals of the world. Yet this exciting mass of people joined its dictator leaders in the escapade of the Malvinas... After a few hours' sleep I make contact with Rear-Admiral Büsser and Brigadier (as he now is) Gilobert aka the Master Spy of the Malvinas. Büsser, who insists on being called "Doctor" rather than "Contraalmirante", checks up that I am who I am by ringing me back at the Hotel Claridge. The hotel name is symbolic of the Argentine's love-hate relationship with things British, like the red letterboxes and Victorian railway stations. It is wonderful and exciting to discover that these two key Argentine characters of the script, about whom I have heard and written so much, correspond with my visions of them in the first draft. Büsser is the utterly civil caballero I expected, but his apartment is festooned with guns, militaria and photographic blow-ups of the "recovery of the Malvinas" which he commanded.

The numerous Catholic images around the place remind me of the role that religion has played in Hispanic military oligarchies – forget the military-industrial complex, this is the military-holy alliance. Büsser shows me photographs of the troops being blessed before Operation Rosario (gotta stage that scene!), and even the secret plans and logs. His recall is pretty sharp, though, like with Rex Hunt, it is presumably a well-rehearsed tale. Interestingly, he reveals that it was he who slapped the face of the Argentine NCO who was humiliating the Royal Marines and, moreover, he personally accosted and disarmed one of the enraged Commandos intending to massacre the Marines after the death of their leader Captain Giachino. What is more, he tells me that a male servant (by his description it can only be Don Bonner) came out wielding a shotgun at the flag-raising and eagle-eyed Büsser spotted him before he could do any damage. Büsser's personal snaps reveal the "spy" Gilobert in a peaked air force dress cap (his parka obscured whether he had the whole dress tunic etc. or not) which would seem to confirm he had some foreknowledge of the invasion because otherwise why would he have packed it for a short trip in which he no longer represented Argentina? Büsser also revealed (without my asking) that he had in fact shaken Rex's hand at the end of the surrender by asking "and now I hope you will do me the honour", something which Rex denies. But since Büsser also volunteered the very embarrassing information about their flag coming loose in a gust of wind I am inclined to believe Büsser on this one (note: his rather fantastic allegation about Don Bonner was also later confirmed to me by Don on the telephone). Büsser entrusts me with a photocopy of a book that will prove invaluable: eyewitness accounts by the officers and men who took part in the operation, including descriptions of Giachino dying in the chicken-run, of Norman calling to him, and the whole grenade business. One (very) sinister note: I asked Büsser whether he was frightened at coming under direct fire, presuming it was his first time. He answered "no, because I was in the war against the subversives". In other words, this man is a veteran of the Dirty War and no doubt displayed far less chivalry towards female *guerilleras* than he did to Major Norman and his Royal Marines. After spending two very stimulating hours with him, I take my leave asking whether Gilobert had been specially sent back as an undercover man for the invasion. Büsser shrugs and says "you'll have to ask him that". A very ambiguous answer. And so to the Giloberts (Hector and wife Teresa), quite the most charming people of all the characters whom I have met on the "real" cast list. A good-looking Latin couple, sportively dressed and displaying genuine warmth (rather than Büsser's punctilious civility) they offer tea, biscuits and wonderful reminiscences about the Bakers, the Hunts (especially Mavis), and a truly humanitarian view of the whole conflict. But when presented with the evidence of his spying role Gilobert just smiles and shrugs it off convincingly, on a personal level. His argument is quite sophisticated, in that he suggests perhaps the air force high command used him as a dupe, knowing full well what was going to happen when they sent him in. He suggests they just wanted a reliable bloke on the ground. Anyway, Gilobert maintains he took no uniform or items of uniform with him. No doubt he would explain away the cap (if I confront him with my having seen Büsser's snap) by saying someone gave it to him to help him be identified, since he narrowly avoided being shot during and after the surrender procedures. I must try and get to the bottom of the Gaffoglio/Gilobert uniform puzzle. (Note: in fact I never was able to do so and, in the film, I made the reasonable assumption that Gilobert had a full uniform on under the parka). I had never realised that Gilobert remained in Stanley to the bitter end and was taken prisoner. An amusing last remark from Gilobert, pointedly after I had put the cassette recorder away, concerns the moment when he took his leave of Mavis. She was highly emotional, he says, and threw her arms around him tearfully! The Giloberts, like Büsser, send regards to the Hunts and the Bakers which I shall duly transmit, along with Büsser's regards to counterparts Norman and Noott. The amazing thing is how lacking in animosity the Argentines are about it all. I encounter far less jingoism and petty feeling in Buenos Aires than in Stanley. I round the evening off by meeting my Argentine relatives who insist on taking me for yet another meaty BA meal before I say goodbye.

Monday, 2 December – (After travelling on to New Zealand to prepare the main shoot of the film, I was pulled out with Steve Hardie when co-financing through Portman Entertainment collapsed and the budget escalated. A frantic week of meetings on the way back via Los Angeles had not produced rescue finance. The production seems doomed until …). There are now two possibilities: firstly that the BBC picks up the entire cost of the film and makes it with its own crew and resources; secondly that Portman bounce back with their partner Jorge Estrada in a co-production to be made in Argentina. Bradley Adams (producer) has flown to Madrid to meet Jorge who is keen and positive. He knows the script inside out, knows Lieutenant Quiroga and Rear-Admiral Büsser very well and can secure military co-operation for the movie! The big problem would be recreating Stanley and bringing down the British cast. I am told Patagonia looks similar to Falklands terrain but it is a long way down south (opposite the Falklands, in fact). The fact is that we have not found anywhere convincing or feasible on the British Isles to shoot so many exteriors in winter (if we went down the BBC route) and the choice will be between Argentina and the Falklands if Governor Fullerton throws in his full support.

Friday 13 (!) December – Hit another major snag because BBC 2 Controller Alan Yentob feels he must consult with higher powers (John Birt, Director General of the BBC, I believe) about the controversial implications of co-producing this film with Argentina. Their offer is now a substantial one but the problem is that brokers Portman are linking the deal with selling one of their current productions to the BBC at an inflated price and Alan will not horse-trade. The situation goes through another radical change in the afternoon when we go for a crisis meeting to BBC Drama Serials boss Michael Wearing's office. This is the first time I meet the man under whose auspices (together with Alan) the film has moved forward. He is in favour of re-enacting history where it happened (i.e. the Falklands) and prefers the risk of backing the whole film and reaping all the profits (should there be any). We will shoot on Super 16 (widescreen) and the battle scenes on 35mm which still gives a fighting chance of cinema release outside this country. He is energetically working for the film, and we all know that the Falklands would be creatively the most authentic and secure option with a British cast and crew. So, from having my bags packed and ready for four months in Buenos Aires I might now be in England next week and the Falklands soon after (if we can finance the BBC Falklands route) or, should it all go up in smoke, in Zambia with my family and in-laws for a commiserating holiday. But can the BBC, having gone up from £400,000 to £750,000, really commit the entire cost of £1.4 million!?

Wednesday 21 January – (Here I was back in the Falklands again doing the recce and titles shoot with a skeleton crew. The production was now ninety percent certain, to be made in the Falklands, Ealing Studios and a few locations in the UK – e.g. HMS *Belfast*). Up at six each morning to make the best use of daylight. Nice to meet Don Bonner again and other favourites. Governor Fullerton is as relaxed, helpful and positive as ever, a source of eternal surprise when dealing with alumni of the Foreign & Commonwealth Office. We swallowed before explaining how we wanted to blow up windows, parts of the lawn, have Marines trample the flower beds etc. – a whole litany of destruction which we would of course rectify at the end of the day... Mr Fullerton took it brilliantly. The MOD are not keen to allow any co-operation because the FO seemed to have leaned on them by reason of a private understanding with Buenos Aires that we would not be dwelling on the tenth anniversary of the British victory. All the more surprising, then, that the Governor should be so happy to assist us, even using his influence to give us the reduced airfares available to service personnel and Islanders. By an extraordinary coincidence the lady of the house, Mrs Fullerton, is the namesake of "Nanny" Fullerton, the servant who is a character in our script! Must be very awkward since there seems to be a degree of upstairs/downstairs tension; one of the female staff pulls a face when Mrs "Governor" Fullerton rings impatiently for service on the old 1930s push-bell from the dining room. We film people are in the kitchen enjoying tea and coffee out of ER mugs. Fortunately for us we completed measuring and photographing in the dining room just before the Governor's wife entered for her boiled egg and toast awaiting her on the table. Perhaps we had kept her from her breakfast and thereby upset her!

Tuesday 3 March – (The first week of shooting at Ealing Studios is complete and the main unit flies down to the Falklands). Here we are merrily trooping down to make the first movie in the Falklands (and almost certainly the last!). Fortunately the aircraft is not a cargo plane like the one Steve Hardie and I flew on first but RAF catering is down to its usual standard and – typically "Crab Air" – the only hot meal is served some seventeen hours into the eighteen hour flight. Highlight of the journey is spotting none other than Air Vice-Marshall Peter Beer, who is the Commander of British Forces Falkland Islands and has turned down our requests for military co-operation. Brad seizes his chance as the Air Vice-Marshall leaves his VIP seat and queues for the toilet, casually striking up a conversation about who we are and what we are doing. We have been told (and it could be hearsay) that Beer is not pleased that the Governor virtually invited us to the Islands. In any case, he is perfectly pleasant to Brad, but does not volunteer his name or identity (no doubt for reasons of security). Brad, ever the diplomat, tactfully does not reveal that he knows perfectly well whom he is talking to – this would embarrass the Air Vice-Marshall. He merely outlines our case in a roundabout way, and the Air Vice-Marshall wished us the best of luck on the Islands, saying the project sounded most interesting. (Note: Brad never succeeded in obtaining the face-to-face official meeting with Peter Beer at which he hoped to reveal himself as the man on the aircraft, and we understand a written directive was issued preventing personnel working on our production even unofficially during leave – the subject of quite a few national press articles). We meet Mike Norman and the dozen or so members of the unit who have already been out here for some days preparing. Tonight is Mike's last night after thirty years in the Royal Marine Commandos and we lay on some champagne as a surprise. He is very touched at what must be a difficult time for him without his mates and family, back after ten years in the place he nearly died for.

Thursday 5 March – (extract). Filming the opening Stanley street scene outside a Mrs Betty Ford's house (we also have on the film's payroll A. Nutter and Ron Buckett) we ignite the flame of controversy that will grow to Kuwaiti oil-fire proportions by the end of the shoot. We had noticed in a journalistic reference that signs were put out for the butcher asking for a "Quarter Shepe Please". I thought it was either a local spelling or a mis-spelling. Either way I thought we should replicate it because I like amusing signs. It was in the background and will scarcely be visible in the film. We also had the Mrs Mozeley character in the street walking a sheep. It so happens that the woman who played her (Anne Reid, whose son was killed on the *Galahad* and who decided to settle near his grave) genuinely takes her pet sheep for walks and again this was not something invented but can be found in videos of Stanley life. Anyway, people watch us shooting a scene over and over again and although these are only two out of some 800 images in the film, conclusions are quickly reached. (The Falklanders believe from now on that the film portrays them as complete primitives. Betty Ford, who consented to the sign adorning her gate, was described by radio-station manager Patrick Watts a couple of days later as being distraught and having taken to a farm in the hills in order to get over our insult.) A Japanese TV crew who have been doing an item on the Falklands have been stranded by the (typical) non-arrival of the RAF Tristar and so decide to film us. They recount what wonderful co-operation they received from the Mount Pleasant military authorities including free air-to-air filming facilities aboard helicopters and jets. We are indignant at the way in which they are offered such assistance and we cannot even hire squaddies on their days off. But Air Vice-Marshall Beer is not obliged towards us of course, and is probably "only obeying orders". Tonight is our first action sequence with the gun battle, for beginning, for Government House: three cameras, explosions, pretty well all the local FIDF men who can turn out to re-enact the battle. The real Jim Fairfield, an ex-Marine who is featured in the film and, when he volunteers to fight with his former unit, he comes to greet us. It is the first time that he has actually returned to the site of the battle. He does not wish to take part in its re-enactment, quite understandably, and I am surprised that as many people who were there do turn up to take part. All goes very well, with the occasional difficulty of trying to yell "cease fire" or "cut" because the assistant director does not believe in megaphones. You begin to understand how ceasefires break down so often, once everyone is wired up and deafened. We will be relying heavily on the FIDF for their invaluable co-operation; they are not happy with some aspects of their depiction within the film so I am going to take on board what they say and make changes if necessary to the script. Something that surprises me greatly is that very few, if any residents, turn up to watch. Although it is past midnight by the time we get down to action this is a film about their history and yet they seem totally ambivalent. This sort of sequence attracts crowds in the UK. But the Islanders are on the other hand most sensitive and quick to take offence. I portray them with sympathy as living in a forgotten time, a world of their own unfettered by the conventions we take for granted. Yes, it is comic at times but then every group portrayed in this film comes in periodically for comic treatment. If they call the script condescending then they have misunderstood it. TV companies do not spend circa 1.4 million to make fun of the Falkland Islanders.

Friday 6 March – The day begins late for Brad whose Land Rover gets bogged down when he goes running around Gypsy Cove in an attempt to see penguins. He fails to find the birds and on his return finds his vehicle half-submerged in quicksand. His jog turns into a half-marathon as he reaches the airfield to enlist the help of Gerald Cheek (an FIDF officer who plays himself in the film) and the fire crew who rescue the vehicle amidst much leg-pulling. Our work continues at a tough and furious pace; up to eight minutes a day including action/effects stuff (for which even in TV you do not reckon on shooting more than three minutes a day). We have to contend with ferocious weather, lack of the most basic local amenities a film crew needs – for example, no white paint for a police car, no letters for an "RN" number plate, etc. Even no nails at one point. Perfect sultry, windy weather when we want it today; normally in film-making you get the opposite of what you want. Patrick Watts, who has hitherto been most helpful to us, appears to be cranking the village pump on the radio. There are reports that we shot a scene of Dennis Middleton and his horse racing through town in which he yells "The Argies are coming!" and that we had young Falklands lasses frolicking naked on a beach with sheep. Wow. Still, the sight of our extras in Argie uniform brought tears to the eyes of one old lady so we must try and remember the trauma of this community, which accounts for their sensitivity.

Sunday 8 March – One of the hardest filming days I have experienced in eleven years of directing. We are using sixty non-professional extras, working in two languages (some of the people playing Argentines are Peruvian fishermen dragged off squid jiggers), with a minimal crew. The Argentine flag has to get ripped off by the wind at exactly the right moment in the flag-raising during which they are singing. The extras have to perform military drill, sing a national anthem they learned minutes before, and react to commands they cannot hear because I have no megaphone and am the only one who speaks Spanish. Plus we have most of the principal cast in the scene and certain principals get very upset at being made to wait; indeed one principal actor throws a very loud tantrum (though he later apologized). Although we fall two scenes behind, we get some excellent material and a wonderful tracking scene when we assemble the cheering "mass" of Argentine troops on the seafront, chanting "Ar-gen-tina" as Admiral Büsser passes. The scene is scalp-tingling, because we have wonderful emotion in the foreground action, a great spirit among the extras and pretty well every piece of surviving Argentine equipment in it (even though an armoured car is being pushed on a steel bar to make it *seem* mobile). The emotional counterpoint in the foreground is that despite defeat, Dick Baker in the white flag party is almost weeping with relief at the thought of seeing his children again. Wind and rain tonight for the second phase of the battle. Mike Norman watches Bob Peck relive the moment that he took cover behind one of Government House's ancient cannons, ducking fire and quaking uncontrollably with fear before getting a grip on himself. (He is to tell me later that this was the most difficult moment for him of the shoot).

Monday 9 March – Another flag-raising day, but this time it is the British flag that is going up for the film's epilogue (the retaking of Stanley). Although it is much easier to recruit Islanders to play Paras and Marines, today is a working day and many of the people playing Argentines have now left. So we send drivers round in a desperate trawl of the harbour and recruit the crew of a Chilean squid jigger and a Whitbread round-the-world yacht – quite a social mix but unlike the Islanders the dark ones don't mind playing Argies (though some of the local *Chilean gastarbeitern* have taken a lot of stick for playing the enemy). By getting our Argie POWs to walk round the camera in a circle they look sufficient in number. We are so pressed for time that I have to run two cameras simultaneously throughout – one of them being the apparent "news crew" visible in shot. Although that was a severe compromise, we had the wintry weather we wanted which was perfect. Poor Peter Chapman, the cameraman, kept worrying about image quality (rain on the lens, wobbly shots etc.) but I'll need it to look awful to match into the rest of the news footage we are using for the nightmare-style end sequence. The rest of the film is shot in a very classical style with no handheld whatsoever, part of the 1950s feel that I am going for (since Stanley in the eighties resembled the fifties elsewhere). In the West Store we had the real Don Bonner play a character greeting his screen alter ego on a shopping trip with his mistress. During the unusually calm evening we actually had spectators – two children who watched us shooting some action scenes for a while before trundling off. A crew member asked them if they were bored already but they replied "no, our mum told us to keep an eye out and report back on what we saw". I think the locals view us with suspicion.

Tuesday 10 March – An early morning meeting is held with the FIDF to accommodate their views on how they should be portrayed. Their written statement on why they did not actually engage the enemy that night is unsigned. Major Norman remains sceptical and unfortunately the man who holds all the answers is now dead (Major Phil Summers of the FIDF). He is alleged to have ordered blanks to be issued on account of cost. I am not including this simply because I do not wish to insult the FIDF. Today it is a very efficient force but in those days even the current commander (Phil's son Brian) admits it was a "bit of a Dad's Army force" and that is, in a lesser degree, how I am going to show it. We arrive at a compromise because there seems to have been some breakdown in their chain of command from the Governor which would explain why they were not defending the ridge as requested by Major Norman (the ridge from which the handful of Argentine Commandos kept Government House's defenders pinned down until the armoured column encircled them). For our beach scenes today the weather is simply appalling, which is what we wanted; horizontal rain, sixty-knot winds that often blow the boom swinger and other people over. My hat flew straight into the sea, and as I charged across the lovely sand to get it I heard fragmentary yells through the gale. They were reminding me (too late!) that this beach was not proven to be mine-free and the Bomb Disposal team who had agreed to make it safe for us had not done so. Surely this can have nothing to do with the Air Vice-Marshal's directive to his forces not to assist us in any way. Mines sometimes get washed up on the tide. Still, the risks were probably minimal as locals seem to use the beach without exploding. We continue into a night of equally relentless gales and rain. I pity the three actors who prepared for months to film these scenes, who had modelled performances in the quiet rehearsal rooms of Acton, only to face a tempest from Greek mythology. Not a single complaint from them or the crew, I have to say. Most would have given up and gone home. Morale boost of the evening was when I laid hands on an image intensifier from the FIDF and discovered the normally ever-active producer Brad, fast asleep in a warm dry Land Rover. They all queued up for a good laugh but in fact this was most unlike Brad. (He never lived it down). He soon got woken by the gunfire that ensued, when we used the night-scope to direct live tracer bullets out to sea, taking care there were no passing ships and avoiding a cormorant's nest that was near the line of fire. We will put the reverse (i.e .incoming) tracer fire on with optical special effects.

Wednesday 11 March – We film the touching and amusing scene where islanders sing "Auld Lang Syne" as the Governor drives off to exile in his maroon taxi. Our cameraman Peter gets quite overwhelmed and tears come to his eyes. Next stop is the Bakers' house, where we stage the mock execution of the FIDF men which the Argentines put on for some photographers. Mavis Hunt looked down from the window and genuinely thought they were going to be shot, as did two of the people against the wall both on the actual day and, today, Gerald Cheek and Marvin Clark. A bizarre feeling doing this, because we ourselves have to go through the various stages – fear, confusion, and finally laughter as "the joke" manifests itself. Marvin Clark joins us later tonight on the Government House ridge playing one of the Argentines. Horizontal rain in torrents is interspersed with horizontal hail. But somehow, playing one of the Argentines myself, I get really into the whole thing and am able to ignore being soaked. Firing down over those rocks (even if they are blanks), calling on the Governor to surrender (even if he's away on holiday at the moment), one nevertheless has some inkling of what it must have been like. The dreadful weather helps, and the heavy radio on my back. Indeed, I get so stuck into the spirit of things that when we dive for cover in one take, I hit the rocks with such force that I actually crushed the metal radio in several places! A great cheer goes up from the crew at my antics. Less heroically, I slip on a rock some time later and an accidental shot from my sub-machinegun nearly hits Peter Chapman in the face. This could have been fatal. Although I knew full well that the gun was not pointing at him, it was nevertheless a deeply unsettling moment, particularly as Peter dropped to the floor yelling with shock. This probably would not have happened if I had done some of the military training which I inflicted on cast members, but in the crazed run-up to filming there had not been the time At the end of this sodden night of action my feet were squelching in my boots, I was covered in aches, cuts and bruises and was limping (like several others who followed me) from landing heavily with my knee on a particularly sharp rock. And I had nearly shot my cameraman. But I felt fantastic; it is hard to describe the feeling in not only directing but acting out these events behind the bullet-scarred rocks the Argentines fired from (indeed I had to forget directing and concentrate on delivering Spanish in an Argentine accent). Even odder for Marvin Clark who, though playing an Argentine Commando tonight, was an FIDF man on the actual night, pinned down by fire from these very rocks! But we have completed one of our most challenging days in the most dreadful weather. Just tomorrow to go.

Thursday 12 March – Gerald Cheek calls us from the airfield in the morning to say that a Hercules will be taking off shortly. They normally swoop low over Stanley every day but since we arrived they have been conspicuously absent and the airbase knows we want some swooping low-level passes for the scene where the Argentine Air Force buzzes the Marines. Two problems follow: firstly Peter Chapman heads off with his camera to Mount Pleasant (the wrong airport) forty-five miles away; secondly the Hercules inexplicably fails to take off soon after Mount Pleasant is informed that the BBC are waiting to film it. We failed on this occasion but we did get a marvellous pass of two Chinook helicopters which we very much wanted, while they were practising for Mount Pleasant open day. We begin with a scene on the football field near Government House where Marvin Clark and others were pinned down at various times. Because of the weather and scheduling problems we have had to borrow the goalposts several times from up the hill. For although this has recently been replanted with grass it is not actually in use and we have had to keep "moving the goalposts" and releasing them for match kick-offs when we failed to get to the location in time. The real Major Mike Norman makes a wonderful FIDF man in his acting debut, together with excellent first-timer Gary Clement, who also fought in the war as a Marine. Mike has come through with flying colours, displaying commitment, an immediate and profound understanding of the production process, and boundless energy during the difficult night schedules. Our worst day in terms of lack of extras: having milked two hundred of the locals to appear (that's a quarter of the Stanley population) the novelty value is wearing off and rumours continue to abound about the script being unfavourable to the Islanders. We drag some people off an Antarctic survey boat to play Marines only to find (just before we begin the scene with them) that their vessel is about to leave. After a certain amount of begging we discover that it is only their meal-break they will be missing and the problem is resolved by our feeding them later. But "Argentines" remain thin on the ground (I should explain that we could not cast any Argentine actors as I had wanted to because their nationals are banned from the Islands. As enlightened as the Arabs' policy towards Israelis). Pretty well all the crew are dressed up as Argies today including the girls. The sight of the Argentine flag on the pole finally made the good citizens' patience snap even though we were filming it being ripped off. We were ordered to take it down by the Council after complaints . We complied, despite the fact that we were entitled to insist on our agreement with the Governor. To add to my woes, the FIDF, having promised to supply the old men who volunteered to fight that night but got turned away, present only a phalanx of very warlike young men. A trawl of pubs fails when the old boys refuse to play ball. And our attempt to arm the FIDF with the kind of primitive weapons which we know some of them had is rebuffed; they claim we are ridiculing them yet they themselves told us how they lost half of their automatic weapons or magazines to the Marines that night. When designer Steve Hardie produces a flintlock rifle he is told that these do not even exist on the Islands but he obtained it down the road. We put it away. They were at pains to show how disadvantaged they were that night but are worried about being portrayed as a rabble. We show them neither in a cowardly nor a heroic light but certainly apportion no blame to civilians faced with a massive surprise attack supported by armour and aircraft. Indeed, Major Summers says that the re-enactment of the telephone call, when his late father told Rex Hunt that their HQ was surrounded, touched him and was very much like he imagines it must have been. The FIDF have been very good to us. I have moderated their image in return, for the Marines are very scathing about their performance that night. Anyway, this night we complete our Falklands shoot in the face of so many difficulties. Only one short exterior scene lost which can easily be recreated in the UK.

Friday 13 March – This is our pack-up day and we venture out to

Mount Pleasant to try and sneak some over-flights of aircraft from beyond the perimeter fence but unfortunately their Open Day (for which pilots have trained for months) is cancelled because of the poor weather. Meanwhile Steve and the design team frantically clean up the destruction at Government House, restoring it to the status quo ante bellum. Fortunately the Governor and his wife are slightly late back from holidaying in Chile on the same little Otter that I flew on. We are actually towing the last Argentine prop (an armoured car) out of the back drive as Mr and Mrs Fullerton are driven by Don up the front drive in their official car, GH1. (We learn later how Mrs Fullerton was very distressed at the sight of her flower beds, which of course cannot be restored until next season). Returning to the penguins at Gypsy Cove, we try to achieve the wide shot where a penguin is mistaken for an Argentine in the dark. It fails, so we resort to Brad's expedient of me dressing in black-peaked cap, white scarf and black clothes waddling down the tussac grass to the beach, deliberately underexposed. – (Note: the shot worked perfectly well in rushes when several people did not even realise it was a trick until the exposure opened up and the penguin metamorphosized into a director chortling with laughter. It is sad to be leaving the Falklands, which many of us have come to feel very attached to. It is such a unique place and yet I can't imagine I will ever come back here again. Indeed if peace – true peace – ever breaks out then Mount Pleasant, this expensive airbase in the middle of nowhere, will soon get overgrown with weeds and the Islands will revert to their previous state of virtual isolation. But the minefields will probably remain unclearable forever.

Friday 20 March – A day of antics and melodrama. Fortunately all's well that ends well, for this is a production with luck on its side so far. Somehow the MOD directive that we should not be given assistance has failed to reach every unit in the country and we are "somewhere in the UK" at a base whose commander is perfectly willing to assist us. Thank God that these people and the (nameless) regiment that lent us a tank and crew yesterday are willing to help. Meanwhile one of our camera crew acted on a tip-off that some Hercules aircraft would be taking off from a nearby base (Major Mike Norman had been drinking in the hotel with a Yank air crew who just happened to be flying a Herc back to the States). We get one great low-level pass before the cameraman is arrested by the Military Police. But because he is perfectly within his rights, being on public land, they have to let him go. To boost the look of the film, we have hired a former Soviet amphibious Armoured Personnel Carrier at great expense, to come up tonight out of some water which represents the South Atlantic. Unfortunately, the men operating this vehicle leave a valve open and it promptly gets flooded, sinking right in front of the beach which we are using as our location. The novice tank crew are lucky to have got out but will have a lot of explaining to do to the collector who recently acquired and imported this twenty-one foot beast from Czechoslovakia. Thank God we have already filmed the scenes with it shooting up the replica of Government House's yard yesterday afternoon, since the engine compartment is now flooded. If we cannot shift it then not only do we lose the APC from the story but we cannot film at all because we need the beach clear for scenes before the main Argentine landing – the APC's side is still poking bizarrely up above the surface. But God (and the commander of this military unit) is on our side and an engineering tank is sent to the rescue, towing the stricken behemoth from its watery grave and even positioning it nicely for the later scene to make it look as if it has come out onto the beach under its own steam. Thousands of gallons of water pour out from the vehicle for half an hour. The Army boys lend their own APC to come charging out of "the sea" and hey presto, our armoured vehicle scene has suddenly got double the numbers. Military boats churn up the water to make it as choppy as the South Atlantic just before each take. An exceedingly heavy day but we got, in the end, more than we could have planned or budgeted for!

Wednesday 1 April – Ten years to the day from the start of our film's story. And what could be more fitting than a visit to the set by Sir Rex and Tony Hunt? He professed himself astounded by the precision and eerie familiarity of Steve Hardie's Government House interior. Publicity photographers snapped away, and whereas Rex had been perfectly civil in meeting Fulgencio Saturno (who plays Rear-Admiral Büsser) he refused to shake his hand for the cameras in any kind of reconciliation in this, his reincarnated office. Ian Richardson was rather uncomfortable with the idea of Sir Rex staying around for the climactic surrender scene. Fortunately Rex has to go off for his book launch soon, and will just have time to view the first assembly of some of the scenes at the film's opening. According to Brad it was an absolutely bizarre and even uncomfortable experience showing these scenes to people who actually lived the real thing, particularly because they did not necessarily view it this way or agree with everything we showed. We took many of their points on board. Tony Hunt maintains that he was never quite such a tearaway and therefore we will cut some of these scenes. But that is the point: each person who participated in these events can only recognise their specific role and shape their memories accordingly. I believe that as the only dispassionate observer who has recently met nearly all of them I can arrive at something like an objective truth. Meanwhile I was shooting the surrender scene, in which Fulgencio and Ian were both brilliant as the Rear-Admiral and the Governor. Very difficult for Fulgencio, working in a foreign language, but he was the perfect counterpart to Ian and reminded me a great deal of the real Rear-Admiral Büsser.

Thursday 2 April – The last day of shooting, and no one is more conscious of what was happening ten years ago (almost to the minute in the case of one scene) than Mike Norman. He keeps glancing at his watch as we come up to lunchtime, and it is not because of hunger. "It was now" he says, full of his own thoughts. For this was the precise moment (GMT) of the surrender. A poignant day for Mike and for us, after six action-packed weeks. Lots of horse-play, some of it quite necessary. For example, three Venezuelan lads are playing the Commandos who hid in a servant's bedroom until they were flushed out. An alarm clock goes off, shattering their nerves. Try as they might, they could not master a shocked reaction. I decided drastic methods were necessary and took a leaf out of director John Frankenheimer's diary on "Grand Prix" (when the crowd did not react enough to an imaginary crash off-screen he blew up the canteen truck). As the alarm clock struck, the armourer let off a burst off automatic fire behind their heads, which they had not been expecting. The reaction was utterly convincing, the soundtrack was changed, and they took it in very good spirits. We end the day by firing rocket grenades into archery nets for close-ups of the weapons that will be cut in to the Government House exterior ridge from which Argentine Commandos are bombarding the Marines. Steve has built a fake ridge out of plastic and the result is brilliant for a night sequence. I don my Commando uniform and spout Argentine Spanish for the last time. Ricardo, playing Lieutenant Lugo, has the misfortune of tumbling backwards off the "ridge" just before he is due to deliver a line but fortunately lands safely – the laughter on these occasions comes before it is known if the victim is capable of standing up. So, we come to the end a few minutes before schedule. Some two and a half hours of completed film and not a single scene lost, which is most unusual, but then this was a most unusual crew and cast. They even managed to cram in some extra scenes that I penned as we went along. The very last shot is a surprise. I had written a stage direction – "we see half the Argentine fleet in an aerial view, alternatively, a stock shot". And there, laid before me was half the Argentine fleet but on something like plastic sheeting and the fleet looked for all the world like models on plastic sheeting. But what the hell, we wasted some precious film on it. Must find a better shot later. To make the film I have travelled scores of thousands of miles in seven countries; completed some two hundred and twenty scenes – many involving gunfire, explosives and stunts; pulled sailors off round-the-world yachts to play Argentines; sunk an amphibious personnel carrier.... and all with no injuries except for a broken nose sustained by a crew member in a fight and the death of a chicken accidentally crushed by a flying stuntman. Most importantly it was completed on time and (I believe) on (a modest) budget.

The Pilgrimage

Mike Seear

*Earth is high and low, broad and narrow, far and
near, steep and level, death and life.*

Sun Tzu, 6th Century BC

I am a Kenyon Team Member as well as a Kenyon Associate[1] for crisis management training. My home base for more than two decades has been in Norway's capital of Oslo. However a quarter of a century ago I was a British Army officer who fought with the 1st Battalion, 7th Duke of Edinburgh's Own Gurkha Rifles in the 1982 Falklands War. Through the Internet early last year I learnt that a Pilgrimage to the Falklands for British war veterans was being planned by the South Atlantic Medal Association and Combat Stress organisation to commemorate the war's twenty-fifth anniversary. This event would take place from 4-14 November. Having spent an accumulated eight years writing a book on my "before, during and after" war experiences that had been published by Pen and Sword Books in 2003 (*With the Gurkhas in the Falklands: A War Journal*) and, four years later, becoming co-editor with an Argentine Malvinas War veteran of a second book (*Hors de Combat: The Falklands-Malvinas Conflict Twenty-Five Years On*) published by CCC Press, I was consequently determined to become a pilgrim and experience the Falklands, not least its remarkably unique terrain, for the last time in my life.

Despite initial worry about being placed on a reserve list, my application finally succeeded. But like many other pilgrims, I became anxious about returning to the site of past trauma as 4 November drew closer. How would I cope with confronting the reality of this after twenty-five years? What would my fellow pilgrims be like? Will I find everything I was looking for in that harsh, yet strangely beautiful, environment that had become such a personal life-event? And how would the Pilgrimage experience affect me and my future outlook on life?

Arriving in London, I made my way to the Union Jack Club adjacent to London's Waterloo Station where the pilgrims would congregate and stay overnight before travelling by coach to Gatwick Airport and the specially chartered Monarch Airlines aircraft that would fly us to the Falklands. I checked in and was immediately handed a special "Falklands 25" bag full of Pilgrimage information. However after

---

[1] Kenyon International Emergency Services is the only full-service disaster management organisation in the world with a global operational capability. A much-shortened version of this article was first published in Kenyon's monthly client newsletter for June 2008. However so profound was the Pilgrimage experience that the author has now written four chapters about this event for his next book.

emptying out the contents in my room, I also found these contained a paradox. A DVD and accompanying brochures described the current affluence of the Islands as a direct result of the British victory in 1982. The 1986 declaration and implementation of a 150-nautical mile Economic Exclusion Zone around the Islands and subsequent annual sale of international licenses for the fishing of squid has become the big income earner. But there was also a contrasting sombre brochure from Combat Stress, the Ex-Services Mental Welfare Society. It both warned and gave advice:

> Whilst you are in the Falkland Islands some of you may well experience anxiety, apprehension, sadness and grief, others will have intrusive memories, nightmares and flashbacks. Hopefully most of you will experience none of these. Don't isolate yourself. Talk to others on the Pilgrimage … Do try to find places when you can be quiet and alone and use any relaxation techniques that you have been taught … Don't brood. If you feel angry find someone to talk to … Don't feel you have to visit the battlefields … Do feel OK if you become emotional, cry or even breakdown, everybody will have similar feelings … Do find the Combat Stress staff to help you if you feel you need help when you return from the battlefields or memorial trips. Many of you will be accommodated with the Falkland Islanders in their homes. You may find this difficult at times especially if you have problems sleeping at nights. You may be embarrassed if you wake up with a start and make a noise or sweat heavily (or even wet the bed) … Don't forget that good communications is the best way to deal with most problems and will prevent embarrassment.

Perhaps I should have paid closer attention to these pearls of wisdom prior to attending the official cocktail reception that evening when several announcements were made by the Pilgrimage organisers. We would not only be accompanied by Combat Stress nurses, but also some bereaved next of kin and a three-man British Forces Broadcasting Service TV camera crew, with the total party amounting to 253 persons. Afterwards some VIPs arrived, but there was only one of real significance attired in her traditional blue dress. The pilgrims closed in around the frail former British Prime Minister whose strategic management of that national crisis in the South Atlantic proved so effective. Baroness Margaret Thatcher remains their darling, and I was determined to present my book to her. Pushing into the pilgrim scrum surrounding the Iron Lady, I tapped my finger on the arm of a nearby aide and showed him a copy of my book.

"No, no. She'll sign that later," he exclaimed.

"But I want to give it to her!" I protested.

He understood my request, took her gently by the arm, and she turned to face me. I opened the book to my hastily scribbled standard inscription of: *I hope you enjoy this universal story of a soldier before, during and after a war*, as she listened attentively to my rapid explanation. Her determined chin slightly stuck out as she read the inscription carefully. Then she looked at me and in a deliberate manner intoned, "I shall read this book not once, but twice." My séance with her had lasted not more than a minute, but nonetheless it was an unforgettable personal experience with a lady who had, all those years ago, dictated our destiny for those ten extraordinary weeks.

The sixteen-hour flight ended on the morning of 6 November as the 219 veterans that included sixty-eight combat stress patients, landed at Mount Pleasant Airport on East Falkland. We were driven by bus to the small capital of Stanley (whose population of 2,000 has doubled since the war) and, after an official welcome, all pilgrims met up their hosts who would provide accommodation for the week. The programme had started. It was packed with events: a reception at the Governor's residence in the trips to the numerous war memorials dotted throughout East Falkland, a visit to the little settlement of Goose Green which had been the Gurkha main base during the war and to Blue Beach 2 at San Carlos where we had landed, parades, church services, and even a band concert. Yet it was the personal requirement to return to the battlefield across which I had traversed with the Gurkhas on the war's final night that was uppermost in my priorities.

Those subsequent accumulated four days of tramping around the Two Sisters-Goat Ridge-Tumbledown-Mount William area, however, proved not enough to view everything. Walking in daylight across the terrain is crucial for any combat veteran to confront those past dangers successfully. It was important to carry out such an activity slowly whilst getting to grips again physically and mentally with the unique terrain of multiple stone runs and jagged rock formations. The Islanders have deliberately not cleared up the battlefields, preferring to leave them as they were from 1982 in memory of those that fought for their freedom. It was therefore like walking in an open-air war museum at times, where I would often come across shell and mortar craters, discarded military equipment and empty ammunition boxes.

Another major aim of mine was in locating the many defensive positions once occupied by our opponents, the Argentine 5th Marine Infantry Battalion. It was not difficult as both trenches and stone-walled sangars are in abundance. I have visited Argentina four times in the past five years in my efforts to become acquainted with "the other" veterans. Eight months before, on my latest visit to Buenos Aires, I actually met the 5th Marines' retired 81mm Mortar Platoon Commander and some of his conscripts. It was a most extraordinary "reunion" after quarter of a century during which Suboficial Segundo (2nd Petty Officer) Elvio Ángel Cuñe had told me about his experiences during this final battle of the war and indicated on a map the location of his mortar pits from where his platoon had engaged us and the Scots Guards.

So disappointment in not having seen everything on this battlefield, was tempered by my discovery of Cuñe's platoon position carefully sited in dead ground on the easterly side of the eastern saddle linking Tumbledown and Mount William. Conversely I also managed to locate that particular deadly area on the Tumbledown's north-west slopes where Gurkha hearts had once leapt into mouths as we came under a ferocious hour-long night bombardment from the Argentine artillery and Cuñe's mortars, prior to our attacks that would have to be carried out in broad daylight on the long north-east spur and daunting 1,000 metres of open terrain southwards onto Mount William where 150 Argentine Marines were waiting for us. Luckily we only took only nine casualties on that last night and morning of the war, and I am lucky to be able write about it.

Thus walking in daylight, as opposed to marching at night, and actually seeing the terrain again is crucial for any combat veteran to come to terms again with those twenty-five year-old pent-up impressions. A good parallel can be drawn to survivors of aircraft accidents when re-visiting the accident site provides, for most, a soothing therapeutic effect. Some pilgrims camped out on the Tumbledown battlefield during their second night in the Falklands to confront their past trauma in more intimate way. Others would experience intense emotion elsewhere as many war memorials were visited whilst those three ubiquitous Scots Guards pipers would play a spine-chilling lament on their bagpipes to the fallen. For example, who could forget that cold sunny morning on 8 November at the four war memorials of Port Pleasant and nearby tiny settlement of Fitzroy where, so many years before, fifty men had died on board two British ships from Argentine Skyhawk air strikes?

We would return to Stanley in the evenings and stay in the private homes of Stanley residents. But then I experienced that my personal shortfall during this time whilst trying to digest each day's impressions, was not in having a conversation partner to whom my thoughts could be articulated and who could understand my war experiences of all those years ago. With the benefit of hindsight I should have read that Combat Stress brochure more carefully and been more proactive in seeking the company of other pilgrims to prevent those occasional "creeping" depressions.

Space prevents me writing a full account of those strangely surreal seven November days which, without being life-changing, did assist me in some ways with reliving my war experiences. There were more questions than answers, but a seven-month aftermath of e-mail exchanges with three other pilgrims captured their riveting stories and lifted my total Pilgrimage experience into a new stunning dimension. It will be incorporated into the sequel to my first book that I have embarked on.

The best way to end this account is with a moving poem recited by a pilgrim during the Remembrance Sunday Service in Stanley's Christ Church Cathedral on 11 November. Gus Hales was not part of the official programme that day. However when Derek Twigg, the UK Under-Secretary of State for Defence and Minister for Veterans, had finished reading the lesson, Gus seized his chance and strode purposely up the aisle to interrupt the Cathedral's Minister who was poised to deliver his sermon from the pulpit. A short preamble from the former Para Engineer who has since become a Prison Buddhist priest, included an estimated figure of 308 British Falklands veteran post-war suicides, more than were killed during hostilities. Afterwards the congregation would give Gus a standing ovation for then articulating his carefully composed and rehearsed poem that blazed like a beacon in an otherwise dull service where the ordinary soldier had not been mentioned. The intervention was a highlight for many pilgrims of this memorable trip:

> Every year on Remembrance Sunday
> I sit in the corner of a British Legion bar
> dressed in blazer, shirt, regimental tie
> polished shoes with my head held high.
>
> But deep in my mind
> where nobody goes
> I see a wooden cross
> where the wind of victory blows.
>
> Three cheers for victory
> I heard the politicians say
> but they never asked me about my victory
> and if they did, I would have explained it this way
>
> It isn't the flags or the emblems of war
> or the marching of troops past the palace's door
> It isn't Mrs Thatcher on the balcony high
> re-affirming her pledge to serve or die
>
> But it's the look and the pain on a teenager's face
> as he dies for his country in a far off place.
> It's the guns and the shells and the phosphorous grenades
> the dead and the wounded, the freshly cut graves
>
> Or a grieving wife with a fatherless child
> whose young tender life will be forever defiled.
> Or the alcoholic soldier with a shattered mind
> who takes the suicide option for some peace to find.
>
> Well that's my victory
> but no one knows,
> for it's deep in my mind
> where nobody goes.

Oslo, July 2008

Meeting the Iron Lady – "I wouldn't repeat it if I were you."

Diego García Quiroga

I cannot be more thankful for Nottingham. It was great, though it proved to be just the tip of the iceberg. I emerged from it deeply impressed, grateful for having met all these fantastic people. For it took greatness to be there, greatness of soul to gather in respect, showing care and compassion for each other's experience, extending a hand. November 2006 was, in many ways, a dream come true.

Before leaving the UK I paid a visit to Victoria Cook and Victoria Main from the Research and Information Department at the Imperial War Museum in London. They had approached me earlier at the suggestion of Mike Seear, in order to see whether I could somehow contribute to the exhibition that the museum was staging throughout the summer of 2007 to mark the twenty-fifth anniversary of the conflict. Needless to say, they were extremely kind and interested in my story, so that I ended up being invited to the exhibition's opening. Though I was keen to provide them with an item for the exhibition, in the end this was not possible.

This was how I ended up appearing at the Imperial War Museum on 14 May 2007. I was greeted there by the Museum Chairman Air Chief-Marshal Sir Peter Squire and was immediately charmed by his warm welcome. To my delight, I was then introduced to other former opponents some of whom I was able to recognise at first sight, having seen their faces in pictures before. There were Rick Jolly, the intense and humane combat medic who made no distinction of sides when it came to help the suffering; Major-General Julian Thompson with his irresistible sincerity and warmth and his subordinate Lieutenant-Colonel Peter Cameron, a man of enormous sympathy and arresting friendliness; Admiral Sir Alan West, whom I recognised from pictures I had seen with mutual friends in Argentina; the brave and silent Sergeant Bill Belcher; Nicci Pugh, the festive nurse; charming Peter Holdgate and Lieutenant-Colonel Ewen Southby-Tailyour. I had wanted to meet Ewen from the first time I heard of him and always found it grim to be on opposing sides, for all I heard about him could tell me that we had many interests in common. Needless to say, my expectations fell short. These were fantastic people and they made me feel extremely welcome. This was the day for interviews, so I had the pleasure to meet Cliff Caswell from *Soldier* magazine as well as to talk to BBC radio, *The Sun* and the *Daily Telegraph*. BBC TV and BBC History also asked me about my story and how I felt twenty-five years after. After these meetings and having toured the Exhibition, most of us gathered at a nearby pub to celebrate with a few pints. It was unforgettable. All I can say is that moments like those are what make all life worth it.

The evening ended at "the Rag" – the Army and Navy Club in St James – where we all sat to dinner under the gaze of impressive-looking portraits of uniformed heroes. After dinner there were spirits and cigars at the bar of this venerable institution. Another dream come true.

The following day we arrived a bit late, blame it on London traffic for beginners. As we were ushered to the hall where the opening ceremony was to take place, I found my friends already involved in conversations. Rick Jolly came forward and introduced me to the late Major-General Sir Jeremy Moore, also informing me that Margaret Thatcher was present. It was only then that the phrase whispered at our arrival by one of the staff girls ("the Baroness has just arrived") made sense to me. I shook the old warrior's hand and he seemed pleased to meet me. This gentleman, many years my senior, had received my commander's surrender. He looked a little frail twenty-five years later as he stabbed the air with his walking stick – alas, he would pass away in a few months – but it was easy to tell I was in front of serious soldiering.

Suddenly and as I was turning to face Julian Thompson, who had appeared at my side, an energetic giant spotted me from the other end of the room and approached with large steps and an immense grin. "I've been looking for you!" he almost shouted, his arms wide as he offered his hand and hugged my shoulder. It was Major Mike Norman, the officer who led the Royal Marines defending Government House in Stanley that distant morning, the guy who ordered his men to open fire on us, the man whose orders resulted in the first Argentine casualties of the war. He merrily led me to meet Sir Rex Hunt, the former Governor of the Islands and his wife Mavis. We all shared a great moment, not the less cheerfully when Lady Mavis scorned me for trampling on her rosebushes during the morning of our attack.

Sir Peter Squire was now up on the stage and the voices quickly died away. As Museum Chairman, he introduced the Exhibition offering a short account of the conflict and its circumstances, the challenges met and the bravery of the British forces. For the first time in the morning I realised that I was the only Argentine on the premises, a discovery that I met with both sorrow and pride. When his words praised Baroness Thatcher's steadfastness and thoroughness I was delighted to hear isolated voices around me shouting Aye! or Yes!, the feet stomping the floor in support of the speaker's statements with apparent disregard of etiquette. This fantastic expression of the British spirit of individuality has always sparked my imagination, for I imagine it comes to us from ancient feudal times when semi-barbaric warriors vowed their support to their sovereign.

Shortly after his words, Sir Peter joined us, tactful and smiling. He then whispered to me: "The Baroness is aware that you are in the room and wishes to know if you would care to approach." Not only the invitation, but the way it was worded, redoubled my impression of reviving an era I thought did not exist anymore.

Soon he was back to guide me towards a sitting group amongst whom Baroness Thatcher was present, her back to the assembly. At a sign from one of her companions she rose and turned towards us, her hand extended. I was a trifle stunned. Slightly taller than me, she was exactly what I expected, elegant, pale and measured. Almost like a Gainsborough I thought, to the Reynolds that would have been a better brush to Sir Jeremy Moore who was sitting beside her. We shook hands and she said she was pleased to meet me and see me there. She added that the conflict had been a sad occasion but "very convenient for the kingdom". I did not comment, but instead replied something along the lines of having regretted Sir Rex's rejection to my invitation for tea that distant morning. The lady is bright. Smiling dangerously, she said "But they told me you hadn't brought the tea! In any case," she added, "I wouldn't repeat it if I were you. Please don't do it again." She then asked me about the veterans in Argentina, how were they received and taken care of after the conflict. Then she inquired on how and why I had come to the Exhibition, about my present life, and what it was like to live in Norway. It was all very polite, quite jolly indeed. As I was about to take my leave she asked how did it feel to have come back alive. I told her it felt great, though sometimes I missed the excitement. She was holding my hand in hers when she replied: "I do too…".

Twenty-six years after the conflict, I am old enough to look back on it as the memories of a world already gone. We had a way then, an understanding of things, of relations between people that has changed dramatically since. It is natural that it happens this way, but it is nevertheless somehow unsettling to behold. Most of the characters of this fantastic adventure that began in Nottingham lived through that world. They remember it, too. It held something which made possible that former opponents share a laugh and be fearlessly human to each other, in a greater sense. Even the Iron Lady felt this, I know. And now that I have looked into her eyes, isn't it grand to think that she knows that I also do?

**Carlos Gamerro interviews Bernard McGuirk for *Clarín*
and reflects on his own treatment of the War
in the novel *Las Islas***

Clarín, 31 March 2007

Bernard McGuirk is author of the imposing *Falklands-Malvinas. An Unfinished Business*, the most complete and all-encompassing study of the impact of the War in the South Atlantic on the Argentine, British and world-wide cultural production, including narrative prose, poetry, theatre, cinema, graphic humour and television. Professor of Romance Literatures and Literary Theory at the University of Nottingham, he is working currently on another book that deals with the satirical treatment of the 1982 conflict on both sides of the Atlantic, *It Breaks Two to Tangle*: *Political Cartoons of the Malvinas-Falklands Conflict*.

*

CG.   It is usually said that the 1982 War had a great effect on Argentine culture and consciousness, while its effect on British cultural production was negligible. Am I right in believing you disagree with this view?

BM.   Yes. It was partly to adjust the perception of such an imbalance that I wrote *Falkland-Malvinas*: *An Unfinished Business*. The 1982 conflict has had a way of surging into the domain of literature and cultural production of all kinds. It has become the emblematic folly that has stubbornly made it its business to suffuse the international imaginary alongside subsequent instances of avoidable pain...or criminality. It is now a watchword of what not to do. Not only in the UK but elsewhere, too, the dilemma of what could or should have been done to counter the excesses executed in one regime by the however excessive intervention of the other, plagues the representation of the Malvinas-Falklands heritage with no less insistence than the repugnance at its ostensible fatuity.

CG.   Would it be right to say that the war was dealt with in Argentina by serious narrative literature, while in England it was mainly exploitation novels and best-sellers?

BM.   To some extent, what you suggest is true; but therein lies the perception of those English critics who dismiss the conflict as a 'little war' (Max Hastings) from which 'the blood spilled has left little cultural stain' (Mark Lawson). The English have perhaps perceived that the war has not 'permeated the consciousness of Britain's most prominent writers' (Nigel Leigh) because they have been looking – or reading, or viewing – in the wrong places. The English narratives have, indeed, been largely exploitation novels and best sellers yet, setting aside the notorious mono-lingualism that limits and bedevils dominant literary and cultural criticism in the UK, a disease that lamentably excludes much of Argentine literature from that reading public, there is, for example, another apparent blindness. The case of the Irish Colm Tóibín's *The Story of the Night* is emblematic. First, in my view, it is a remarkably successful novel in what has been termed 'the literary sense-making' of the war. Second, it succeeds by setting the short conflict in the broader and, consequently, deeper context of a quarter of a century's 'process' of dirty war, cataclysm and painful aftermath. If the terms seem ambivalent, it is deliberately so. For the resonance reminds us that for the UK, too, as Simon Jenkins has claimed, the 1982 War was 'a trivial conflict yet one awash with lessons. Put crudely, the British Establishment does not piss on victory, and future generations pay the price'. Jenkins's point is that the British military, its Government and, indeed, much of its population has come to expect a 'Falklands-style' capability, allowing ministers to 'play at Empire' in Afghanistan and Iraq. Analysis of cultural production that focusses only on the 1982 moment rather misses the point, and countless writers, as I insist in the book, touch on the War as emblematic of the way the Thatcher revolution – permitted by the 'victory' – was transformed into Blairism, and a dramatic political and cultural adventurism.

CG.   You try to avoid, in this book, *Falkland-Malvinas*: *An Unfinished Business*, and in your forthcoming one, *It Breaks Two to Tangle*: *Political Cartoons of the Malvinas-Falklands Conflict*, the idea of a symmetrical or tit-for-tat presentation of both sides. This is evident in, for example, your different treatment of the depiction of the enemy (i.e. abjectification versus demonization). Could you expand on that?

BM.   Yes, I do try to avoid such a lure. And when I deal with the literary and cultural representations of such as abjection and demonization, I attempt to do so ever in the markedly different contexts not only of Argentina and Britain but also of French, Italian, Irish, United States, Brazilian and other perceptions and representations of the Malvinas-Falklands effect, or effects. The very notion of 'enemy' is both brought into play and, ethically, interrogated as a perilously constructed ideological and culturally saturated device... ever differentially.

CG.   Could you comment on your relationship and work with both British and English war veterans?

BM.   In November of 2006, I organized, with Mike Seear, the first coming together of veteran ex-combatants from both sides in the context of a conference on post-conflict cultures. The experience was as uplifting as it was enlightening, lived in the calm and respectful sharing of memories and analyses of a harrowing past from which so many still suffer the dreadful post-traumatic consequences. They, no less than their dead comrades, can and must not be forgotten.

CG.   In terms of Britain's foreign – particularly war – policy, would you trace a straight line from the Falklands-Malvinas to Iraq?

BM.   In the light of my answer to your previous question, I have to say that not to trace such a line, although it is far from straight and is problematically interrupted by complex gaps and meanders, would be to repeat the mistake of those critics who have underestimated the real and the symbolic resonance of the 1982 conflict – its 'Unfinished Business'.

2 April 2008. The dialogue continues...

Dear Bernard:

This text began with an error that the Orwellian flow of the computer allowed me to delete at once but which, in my memory, as in that of Winston, refuses to let pass as if it had never been. I wrote: *April 1982. The dialogue continues.*

Can it be, then, that the time of trauma is always the present, that the unconscious is a cinematech where films do not grow old (and from which we can only draw snippets), and where the passing of time and concomitant memory are only another name for repression?

At the colloquium at which we came to meet each other for the first time, in London on 17th March 2007, I took meticulous notes on every one of the interventions of Major Mike Seear. All of us had gone there to speak about or to listen to *representations* of the war, yet he showed the marks, the scars, and the (literal or figurative) stumps (the meaning of war is just that: a stump of language. An amputated language). I was again surprised, too, that one night, a single night of advancing under artillery fire, not in hand-to-hand combat, just one night, could change so much the life of one man and his perception of the world.

I say that I was *again* surprised because I had already seen this in Argentine ex-combatants when I was interviewing them for my novel. I understood that I had to complete a famous phrase of Walter Benjamin in "experience and poverty": "Men come back silent from the battlefield". Yes, they came back silent, but *only for those who had not gone*. Amongst themselves, communication is not marked by remaining silent but by being laconic. Their words are the same as ours, but they do not mean the same: "cold", "bullets", "explosion", are words of a secret code. Perhaps because of that, paradoxically, it is not necessarily those who come back from war who are its best narrators: they cannot, – they do not wish to – speak with those who *do not understand*:

> *"Me dijo también: 'hay otro monje con el cual yo puedo hablar sobre esto, porque él ha tenido esa experiencia; a usted no puedo decirle nada'. Claro, yo entendí: toda palabra presupone una experiencia compartida, porque si usted está en Canadá y habla del sabor del mate, nadie puede saber exactamente cuál es."* ["He also told me: 'there is another monk with whom I can speak about this, because he has had that experience; I can say nothing to you'. Of course, I understood: every word presupposes a shared experience, because if

you are in Canada and you speak about the taste of *mate*, nobody can know exactly what that is".]
Jorge Luis Borges: *Diálogos* con Osvaldo Ferrari

In his exemplary chronicle "What I Saw of Shiloh", Ambrose Bierce, after reviewing the futility and fear of one of the most bloody battles of the first modern war, ends on this unexpected note: "*Is it not strange that the phantoms of a blood-stained period have so airy a grace and look with so tender eyes? – that I recall with difficulty the danger and death and horrors of the time, and without effort all that was gracious and picturesque? Ah, Youth, there is no such wizard as thou! Give me but one touch of thine artist hand upon the dull canvas of the Present; gild for but one moment the drear and sombre scenes of to-day, and I will willingly surrender an other life than the one that I should have thrown away at Shiloh*". Who can be surprised that the man who wrote these lines decided to end his days, at the age of (we suppose) 72, losing himself in the Mexican Revolution? We only hope that he found what he was looking for.

I had not read this text by Bierce when I wrote *Las Islas*. Only because of that do I dare to transcribe the following fragment. Without passing judgement on its dramatic or literary merit, I must confess my surprise at the power of the fiction: suddenly my character was saying words that were not mine, that I could not have said out of my own body and my own life, because they belong to the order of untransferable experiences:

–Todos soñamos con volver. Es difícil de explicar. Yo no volvería ni loco. Pero sueño con volver –hice una pausa–. Ustedes también.
–¿Nosotros?
–Los que nunca estuvieron. ¿Para qué nos buscan, si no? Nos buscan y nos tienen miedo. Suponen que sabemos algo, que no les queremos decir, y que ustedes no quieren saber; nos envidian porque conocemos el camino y temen que se los revelemos. Dejamos un espacio preciso cuando nos fuimos, pero allá cambiamos de forma, y al volver ya no encajábamos, por más vueltas que nos dieran, en el rompecabezas; volvimos diez mil iluminados, locos, profetas malditos, y ahí andamos, sueltos por las cuatro puntas del país, hablando un idioma que nadie entiende, haciendo como que trabajamos, jugamos al fútbol, cogemos pero nunca del todo, en algún lugar siempre sabiendo que algo nuestro valioso e indefinible quedó enterrado allá. En sueños, al menos, todos volvemos a buscarlo. ¿Entendés? No es el criminal el que vuelve al lugar del crimen. Es la víctima, bajo la tiránica esperanza de cambiar ese resultado injusto que la dañó. Andá preguntale a los ingleses. ¿Cuántos te crees que quieren volver? Somos nosotros, los perdedores, los triturados, los que gritamos volveremos volveremos cada vez que hay alguien que quiera escuchar. ¿Qué puede interesarle la revancha al ganador? El infierno nos marcó de tal manera que creemos que volviendo lo haremos paraíso, y a la noche nos despertamos llamando papá a los demonios que nos clavaban arpones riendo. ¿Sabés por qué todavía, diez años

después, seguimos disfrazándonos de esta manera, reuniéndonos para organizar expediciones imposibles, reconstruyendo hasta el segundo cada uno de aquellos días que lo mejor sería olvidar? Estamos infectados, entendés, las llevamos en la sangre y nos morimos de a poco, como los chagásicos. ¿No las viste, que son iguales a pólipos? Cada año que pasa, se extienden un poco más, como esas manchas en la pared. Trauma de guerra, trauma de guerra, no es tan fácil. Estamos enamorados hasta la médula, y las odiamos. Fetichistas, adoramos una foto, una silueta, una bota vieja. No es verdad que hubo sobrevivientes. En el corazón de cada uno hay dos pedazos arrancados, y cada mordisco tiene la forma exacta de las Islas.

["We all dream of returning. It's hard to explain. I'd be crazy to want to go back. But I dream of returning." I paused. "You guys too."
"Us guys?"
"The ones who didn't go back. Why else would you be after us ? You're after us and afraid of us. You think we know something we don't want to tell, and that you don't want to know; you envy us because we know the way, and you're afraid we might show it to you. When we went to the Islands we left behind a particular space, but we changed shape over there, and when we came back we couldn't fit into the jigsaw puzzle any more, no matter how many times they turned us over. We returned: ten thousand enlightened ones, madmen, damned prophets, to wander to the four corners of the country, speaking a language no one can understand, pretending we work, play football, fuck, but never entirely; somehow knowing there was something precious and indefinable we left behind, buried back there, on the Islands. In dreams at least, we all go back to look for it. Don't you understand? It's not the criminal who returns to the scene of the crime. It's the victim, driven by the tyrannical hope of changing the unfair outcome that marred him for good. Go ask the English. How many of them do you think want to return? No, it's us, the losers, the broken ones, who shout "we will return, we will return" whenever anyone will listen. Why would the winner need a second chance? Hell has branded us so deep that we believe it'll become paradise on our return, and at night we wake up calling out daddy, daddy to the devils that harpooned us, laughing out loud. Do you know why, after ten years, we still dress up in these ridiculous clothes, get together to plan impossible expeditions, re-create down to the second every one of those days it would be best to forget? We're infected, don't you see, they're in our blood and we're slowly dying of them. Haven't you noticed how they resemble cancer polyps ? Every year they grow into us, like the damp stains on these walls. War trauma, war trauma, it's not as easy as that. We carry the love of them in our bones, and the hatred as well. Fetishists that we are, we have replaced them with a picture, an old boot, a silhouette. There were no survivors, let me tell you. In every one of our hearts, two pieces have been torn out, and each bite is the precise shape of the Islands".]

This logic of deep imaginative participation in the experiences of other individuals and other peoples must be the one which rules the imaginative output, for the present scant but ever increasing in number and, more important still, richer and more valuable, literary texts, written by foreign authors, in foreign languages, about the dark years of Argentine dictatorship and war. After the bad start of *Imagining Argentina* by Lawrence Thornton, which is offensive from the publication itself, with its cover of cheap tropicalism (the illustrator took too much to heart the word *Imagining* of the title) and its tired magic realism, and with its profusion of prophets guessing at the whereabouts of the disappeared and gauchos on horseback rescuing kidnapped youngsters from the claws of policemen in Ford Falcons, came *The Story of the Night* of Colm Tóibín and, recently, the book that you recommended to me: *The Ministry of Special Cases* by Nathan Englander, that I am reading at the same time as we indulge in this our ongoing conversation.

The weight of the dictatorship, the war and the disappeared is too great for but one language and but one literature. Welcome are those companions who accompanied us and helped us, to bear it, to overcome it...

Afterword

The Management Committee of the Centre for the Study of Post-Conflict Cultures of the University of Nottingham and the organizers of the International Colloquium *The Falklands-Malvinas Conflict Twenty-Five Years On* acknowledge their contributions and express their gratitude to veteran ex-combatants, professionals from various disciplines, academics and other delegates by reproducing here a selection of the comments received from those who took part in the first event of its kind in the quarter century since the war and one that inspired this collection of reflections *Hors de Combat*.

*

This colloquium has been of immense importance as a healing process between two nations where combatants were sent to war by politicians and then largely forgotten once the job had been done. The casualties of war are like a pebble thrown into a pond – the ripples spread to the horizon. So does the suffering, caused to those who died and to the living, spread to the far shores and rebound.

*

This meeting exceeded everything that could have been imagined of it in advance and showed the way if not to a definitive solution to our differences then the path to our reconciliations. It is to be hoped that every participant carries away to political, military and economic leaders of our respective countries and beyond the lessons and the warnings so poignantly absorbed at the Nottingham gathering.

*

I was apprehensive about attending. I felt that it might become an unpleasant return to matters from 1982 which it would be better not to revisit. I found instead that I learned of many events which took place of which I was unaware. This, I feel, has been a helpful event, a unique one, that has helped me come to terms with the Falklands-Malvinas War. I was most heartened to hear that my impression of a low long-term Battle Neurasthenia count among my unit has been and remains low according to "combat stress" figures.

*

It has worked well; particularly on the purely military side, which, of course, is my particular area. Political aspects were inevitable but usually kept in proper perspective. Emotion, additionally, and understandably, was not far from the surface. A good session and, probably against any preliminary thoughts, I enjoyed it, particularly meeting my old enemy.

*

Hors de Combat: the Falklands-Malvinas Conflict in Retrospect

I came with a degree of mixed emotions. My contacts with the Argentine Forces in 1982 were not extensive. How would we all feel on meeting with each other twenty-five years on? What really could the Colloquium achieve? How would my presentation fit with the sequence of the programme? I need not have worried. On arriving I was cordially welcomed not only by the organizers but also by those who had fought against us in the Falklands. Individual papers, given with honesty and integrity by so many different and gifted people on so many different issues relating to the conflict and post-conflict periods were both informative and poignant. The University has not only furthered the quest for knowledge but has also enriched and brought forward to a remarkable degree the processes of reconciliation and understanding between former enemies. Faith, core values, courage and patriotism were cherished by both sides.

*

A hugely brave and highly successful event which rapidly achieved common ground based on the pride with which all service personnel (and women) have in their armies, and in their men (and women) in particular. Many presentations and personal accounts clearly identified that neither Government is providing adequate care for those of its veterans who have become the long-term "casualties of war", suffering mental and physical disability coupled with social exclusion, unemployment, family breakdown, loneliness and penury. The services which should be being provided to prevent this situation occurring need to be veteran focused and delivered by people who understand veterans, otherwise they will not work. These services need to be funded by Governments.

*

By participating in this colloquium I have been given the opportunity to see undiscovered perspectives, to me at least, of the Falklands-Malvinas conflict. Especially personal stories have shed new light on the conflicts; a new focus that I shall implement directly in the Danish military officers' training. This invitation has been unique, as has the programme. I have gained a whole new perspective on the close-quarter battle. Finally I am impressed at the gap between the supposed image of intelligence on the battlefield and the actual image; this goes for both sides. The colloquium has finally confirmed to me that I want to write a study on this conflict.

*

The most important historical event to deal with the Falklands-Malvinas conflict *and* the post-conflict. For the first time, in either the United Kingdom or in Argentina, officers of both forces, and who were at the front, met each other and could share inseparably military techniques and human experiences. A complete academic and international

182

conference that clearly shows the *universitas* aims and freedom of the British university.

*

I was relieved that my initial reticence to exchange views with former adversaries was entirely unfounded. From the presentations and informal conversations I have learned that I was not alone in the emotions that I have felt since first learning that I must go to fight in the Falklands; that bridges can be built and enemies forgiven. The consequences of a marked lack of accountability in government is a tragedy over generations. "Combat stress" is a vital organisation – it *must* be run by ex-forces professionals and *not* reintegrated into the NHS.

*

There is an obvious need to prepare soldiers mentally for combat (education on coping methods, early signs of danger etc) and for training on psychological first-aid and early intervention, as well as training commanders on the leadership aspects of combat stress; also to strengthen training in National Health Service providers on war-related mental health issues. We must maintain and preferably expand the military medical and particularly the military psychiatric services for veterans, including also those who have returned to civilian life.

*

I found the period relating to Battle Stress and the meeting of ancient foes of particular value. Meeting my old adversary and discussing what occurred on a professional level has enabled us to develop both a friendship and a laying down of antagonism. I have made lasting contacts now with both UK and Argentine as well as with US and other European armies.

*

This colloquium probably represents one of the most important events regarding the Malvinas issue. Military Argentines and their British counterparts met, saw each others' human dimension and found out what really happened during the hand-to-hand bloody battles of Tumbledown and Two Sisters, among others. Medical doctors know about pain and the fact that war is hell. To be able to give a great hug to my erstwhile opposite number, with whom I had previously only had written contact, was a most rewarding and uplifting experience.

*

This is a fascinating experience, and in British Service History is probably unique. The mixture of social banter and serious presentation has been good, but in retrospect could perhaps has been improved by two factors: I think we would have benefited from longer sessions on particular subjects – until completely drained of all questions; next time let us have a wider audience. All the organisers need to be heartily congratulated – it has been a tremendous success and should be built on.

*

This encounter worked very well. Not only has it permitted an unprecedented explosion of warmth between people who had probably thought long about their own experiences of twenty-four years ago but it has also opened their minds to new possibilities that may very well exceed their personal interests. It also highlighted the yet unvoiced fact that most of us who have lived through the Malvinas-Falklands conflict have reached a maturity that allows us to think forward with optimism and humanity.

*

I think it was a most unusual opportunity to see and hear details of the Falkland-Malvinas War. Especially, the personal statements made a great impression, and actually to witness the two parties meet was fantastic. I have gained many contacts, and made new friends. I shall use the experience to optimise the training of Royal Danish officers and the Academy in Copenhagen. It has been a truly unique and special experience.

*

The crucial debate for me was less about the academic, military and political arguments of a sovereignty dispute between countries and more about the post-conflict debate that continues in the minds of those who actually fought. Twenty-five years on, many remain persecuted by memories of death, pain and meaningless survival.

*

The retired Rear-Admiral of the Argentine Navy made this announcement early on in the proceedings: "I am so glad to be here. We can have a dialogue that might finally bring a resolution to this conflict". Most applauded the general point, but the personal point will not have been lost on combatants still in conflict with themselves. It was the dialogue with those they fought against, rather than those they fought for, that offered the hope of resolution.

*

Il n'y a pas de hors-combat…

Diego F. García Quiroga Educated at a British school and then at naval secondary institute in Buenos Aires, he graduated as a Midshipman in 1977. Subsequently serving in the Argentine Navy for twenty-two years, his tours of duty included Antarctic support ships, fleet units, the Navy's tall ship school, a cargo ship and the Special Forces. He was a member of the Special Forces group whose mission was to re-take the Malvinas Islands on 2 April 1982. In the course of the action that day he was severely wounded. He later served as instructor at the US Naval Academy; Commanding Officer, Naval Special Forces and Commandant of Midshipmen at the Argentine Naval Academy. He retired from the Argentine Navy in 1999 with the rank of Capitán de Fragata (Commander) and now lives in Oslo with his Norwegian wife.

Mike Seear Originally commissioned into the Royal Corps of Transport, he transferred to the Light Infantry in 1971. He served in numerous emergency tours of duty in Northern Ireland counter-terrorist operations during that decade and, having been seconded to 1st Battalion, 7th Duke of Edinburgh's Own Gurkha Rifles in March 1982, was Operations and Training Officer in the Falklands War. Serving also in other parts of the UK, Malaysia, Hong Kong, Canada, Germany, USA and Norway, he retired from the British Army in 1988 with the rank of Major to join Scandinavian Airlines in Norway as Head of Security and Emergency Response. Since 1996 he has been a crisis management consultant, and is the author of *With the Gurkhas in the Falklands: A War Journal* (2003).

Nicolás Urbieta Served as a Support Section Commander of 2 Platoon (Pérez Grandi's), C Company, 4th Infantry Regiment in the Malvinas War and at the Battle of Two Sisters. Since the war he has served with the United Nations in Cyprus and Bosnia. Currently he is a serving Suboficial Principal de Infantería (Infantry Warrant Officer) with the 24th Mechanised Infantry Regiment at Río Gallegos in southern Argentina.

Jorge Daniel Pérez Grandi Serving as 2 Platoon Commander, C Company, 4th Infantry Regiment in the Malvinas War, he was severely wounded at the Battle of Two Sisters. After rehabilitation, he retired from the Argentine Army with rank of Teniente (Lieutenant) and has since become a successful practising lawyer in Buenos Aires.

Mike Scott Commissioned into the Scots Guards in 1960. After regimental service in London, East Africa, Germany, Northern Ireland, the Falkland Islands (during the war) and Cyprus, where he commanded 2nd Battalion, the Scots Guards, he became General Officer Commanding (GOC) Scotland, Governor of Edinburgh Castle, and, finally, Military Secretary. Retiring in 1997 with the rank of Major-General, he now deals with complaints against barristers.

Carlos Hugo Robacio Commanded the Argentine 5th Marine Infantry Battalion in the Malvinas War and at the Battle of Tumbledown. He also served as Commanding Officer of the Infantería de Marina's 1st Brigade, and has been both Assistant Director of the Directorate of

Naval Welfare, Head of the Infantería de Marina's General Staff and Commanding Officer of the Infantería de Marina. He retired from the Argentine Navy with the rank of Contraalmirante (Rear-Admiral) IM (Infantería de Marina – Marine Corps). A Professor at the Armed Forces' War Colleges and the Joint Chiefs of Staff College, he is the internationally honoured author of Desde el Frente (From the Front Line), a book about his unit's operations in the war. He has also collaborated on the work Chile's Presence in Argentina and Globalization.

Simon Price After commissioning, he joined the Scots Guards at Windsor in October 1970 as a Platoon Commander. He started the Army's Section Commander's Battle Course in 1975, and took over Command of Right Flank Company of 2nd Battalion, the Scots Guards in October 1981 as an Acting Major. In this appointment he served with the Battalion in the Falklands War and at the Battle of Tumbledown. Retiring from the British Army with the rank of Major, he now works as a grade two staff officer (retired) in a consultant capacity.

Eduardo Villarraza Graduated as Midshipman in the Infantería de Marina (Argentine Navy) in 1972, he was N Company Commander, 5th Marine Infantry Battalion nine years later and, in 1982, served in the Malvinas War at the Battle of Tumbledown. His further appointments have included command of the Marine Corps 4th Battalion at Río Gallegos, Chief of Operations Marine Corps and Military Chief of the Navy Board at the Argentine Navy HQ. He retired from the Navy in 2003 with the rank of Capitán de Fregata IM (Commander). Currently he works in a system for Armed Forces' welfare.

Alan Warsap BM BCh FRCGP Serving in the Royal Army Medical Corps from 1962-1995, his previous appointments include Senior Lecturer in General Practice, Royal Army Medical College, Senior Medical Officer, Royal Military Academy Sandhurst, Director, Army General Practice, and President, 5 Division Permanent Standing Medical Board from 1995-2004. He was the Regimental Medical Officer of 2nd Battalion, the Scots Guards from 1980-84, which included service in the Falklands War and at the Battle of Tumbledown. Retiring from the British Army in 1995 with the rank of Brigadier, he is currently a Medical Member of the Tribunal Service.

David Morgan Commissioned into the 7th Duke of Edinburgh's Own Gurkha Rifles in 1959, he served in Hong Kong, Malaya, Singapore, New Guinea, Borneo, India, Nepal, Ghana, South Korea and the United Kingdom. He commanded the First Battalion of his Regiment throughout the Falklands Conflict. Retiring from the British Army in 1994 with the rank of Brigadier, he became the Custodian of Glastonbury Abbey for eight years. Now retired, he is the Chairman of SSAFA Forces Help in Somerset and Secretary of the Gurkha Welfare Trust (Western Branch).

Angus Smith Commissioned into the Royal Army Chaplains Department in 1972, he served in Germany and Scotland before being posted to 2nd Battalion, the Scots Guards in 1979 to become that unit's Chaplain. He served in this appointment during the Falklands War and at the Battle of Tumbledown. Two further UK postings followed until retirement from the British Army in 1991 as Chaplain to the Forces

Class 2 with the rank of Lieutenant-Colonel to become Chaplain to the Oil Industry for fifteen years with a work-base at Aberdeen, Scotland. He has now retired and lives in Edinburgh.

Jeremy McTeague Served in the Falklands War as 10 Platoon Commander, D Company, 1st Battalion, 7th Duke of Edinburgh's Own Gurkha Rifles. He retired from the Army in 1985 with the rank of Captain, spending the next three years with Barclays Bank International in the UK and South Africa. He then became a lobbyist working for UNITA to bring about an end to the civil war in Angola, and continued to work in the communications field until 2005, when he joined a philanthropic foundation in Geneva.

Eduardo C. Gerding MD Served in the Argentine Navy, where, amongst other appointments, he was the Chief of the Medical Department of the Batallón de Infantería de Marina de Comando y Apoyo Logístico (Marine Corps Logistic Battalion) and then the 5th Marine Infantry Battalion (1987-1990). Retiring with the rank of Lieutenant-Commander, he is now the Medical Coordinator of the Malvinas War Veterans at the Instituto Nacional de Servicios Sociales para Jubilados y Pensionados (INSSJP) and also writes research articles on naval history for *The Buenos Aires Herald*, *The Southern Cross* and medical articles for the *International Review of the Armed Forces Medical Services* (Belgium). Author of *The Quest of David Jewett*, published in the USA.

Martin Reed Served as the First Officer on board SS *Canberra* (The Great White Whale) throughout the Falklands War, and post-war was the Executive Officer on board SS *Uganda*, the former British Task Force Hospital Ship. Retiring with the rank of Captain (Merchant Navy and RNR) in 2000, he has since become the Chairman of the South Atlantic Medal Association 82.

María Isabel Clausen de Bruno Born in General Roca, a small town in Córdoba province, Argentina, she has been a teacher, politician and writer. While a primary school teacher, she discovered that the Malvinas subject was very important to her and so organized and conducted acts and events in her town with many authorities and ex-veterans. An author of four books (*From Heart to Heart* [1999], *Between Your Hand and Mine* [2003], *Leaves of the Wind* [2004], and *Reflections (reflexions) from the Soul* [2006] – a book of poems), she participates in workshops and Book Fairs. As an active member of a Literary Workshop in the city of Inriville since 1992, she has organized conferences to spread the importance of this topic and help the Malvinas veterans.

Mark Sandman After serving as an infantry sniper with the 101st Airborne Division in the Vietnam War, he became a civilian psychologist and has worked with traumatic stress since 1969, when he started a support group for reforming gang members of the Chinese Gang Wars near San Francisco. While training Combat Stress Teams in Eastern Europe and Asia, and PTSD treatment teams for in-patient military hospitals in Europe, the Arab Gulf Region and Africa, he has provided on-site psychological intervention services for natural and human-induced disasters in thirteen counties. He has created and trained hospital-based crisis intervention teams at four Level One Trauma Centre hospitals in California. He has also trained and created several US Police and Fire Peer Teams. Currently he is focussing on Veteran Peer Support Team training for community-based efforts aimed at supporting combat veteran readjustment.

Lars Weisæth MD Norwegian Psychiatrist and Professor in traumatic stress, he is a world authority on the psycho-traumatology and psychosocial support aspects of war and major civil disasters. His renowned research work in this field has led to him writing countless books and articles on the subject. A household name in Norway, he has also an extensive international background, having led United Nations World Health Organisation missions to post-1991 Gulf War Kuwait, Lebanon and all the Balkan wars in the 1990s. He is Research Director for the Norwegian Centre for Violence and Traumatic Stress Studies, University of Oslo, and is also Head of the Norwegian Armed Forces Psychiatric Service.

Lucrecia Escudero Chauvel Argentine critic and semiotician and Paris-based academic, she has a Ph.D in Semiotics from the University of Bologna and MD in Language Sciences from the University of Paris. She is a Professor of Theory of Communication at the University of Lille and Chief Editor of *DeSigniS*, the Journal of the Latin-American Semiotics Federation. Author of *Malvinas, el gran relato: Fuentes y rumores en la informacion de guerra* (Gedisa, 1996) and *Media truth: fiction and rumors in war news* (Toronto University Press, 1996).

Sophie Thonon-Wesfreid French Barrister at the Paris Bar, she has been responsible for bringing to court the case of the disappearance and torture of French citizens during the Argentine and Chilean dictatorships.

María Fra Amador Argentine academic and researcher who has taught at the University of Bologna in Buenos Aires, she is a political scientist specializing in anthropology and psychology. She has also worked at national and international level in government affairs and in the development of social guidelines and the organization of indigenous and peasant communities.

Bernard McGuirk Professor of Romance Literatures and Literary Theory and Director of the Centre for the Study of Post-Conflict Cultures, University of Nottingham. Author of *Falklands-Malvinas: An Unfinished Business* (2007).

Jean Andrews is a poet and translator. She has published in British and Irish poetry magazines. Her first collection, *In an Oubliette* (Arima) came out in 2005. She translated the Cuban poet, Nancy Morejón (Black Woman and other Poems, Mango Season, 2001).

Stuart Urban, since 1982, has made highly regarded, award-winning popular TV drama and movies that have sold around the world, winning him two BAFTAS (*Our Friends in the North* and *An Ungentlemanly Act*). In 1997 he established Cyclops Vision Ltd, producing and directing successful feature and documentary films including cult comedy *Preaching to the Perverted, Against the War* (a collaboration with Harold Pinter), the thriller *Revelation* starring Terence Stamp and Udo Kier and most recently the feature documentary *Tovarisch I Am Not Dead*, released in UK cinemas, winner of several international awards and shortlisted for Britain's Grierson Award.

Carlos Gamerro was born in Buenos Aires in 1962. He has studied and taught Literature at Buenos Aires University (UBA). In 2007 he was Visiting Fellow at Cambridge University. His publications include the novels *Las Islas* (Simurg, 1998; Norma, 2007), *El sueño del señor juez* (Sudamericana, 2000; Página 12, 2005), *El secreto y las voces* (Norma, 2002) *La aventura de los bustos de Eva* (Norma, 2004; Belacqua, 2006), the book of short stories *El libro de los afectos raros* (Norma, 2005) and the books of essays *El nacimiento de la literatura argentina* (Norma, 2006) and *Ulises. Claves de lectura* (Norma, 2008).

List of Abbreviations and Glossary

AFP Agence France-Presse (French global news agency).

Agrupación de Buzos Tácticos Naval Tactical Divers Group (APBT) based at the Mar del Plata Naval Base.

Agrupación de Comandos Anfibios Amphibious Commando Group (APCA) under Marine Corps Command.

ANSA Agenzia Nazionale Stampa Associata (Italian News Agency).

AP Associated Press (US news agency).

ARA Armada de la República Argentina (equivalent to HMS).

ATC Argentina Televisora Color (State TV).

Battalion Infantry brigade sub-unit comprising three rifle companies (four in a Gurkha battalion), support company, HQ company and battalion HQ, totalling about 650 men (1,000 in a Gurkha battalion) commanded by a lieutenant-colonel. There are variations to this organization and its strength regarding Argentine Army infantry battalions and Marine battalions.

BBC British Broadcasting Corporation.

BIAC Batallón de Infantería, Artillería de Combate (Marine Field Artillery Battalion.

BIM5 Argentine 5th Marine Infantry Battalion Ec. Ec. means "Escuela". The unit was organically defined as a "school" battalion, meaning that the majority of its soldiers were conscripts who were sent there to be trained, as opposed to a unit composed mainly of regulars where conscripts were only attached for the purpose of carrying out support and administrative tasks. A "school" battalion is supposed to train this otherwise supplementary manpower into a fighting force capable of going into combat successfully.

Blue-on-blue An engagement between friendly forces by accident, i.e. "friendly" fire. So-called because friendly forces are marked in blue on a battle map, as opposed to the enemy who are in red.

Brigade A formation comprising three infantry battalions, supporting artillery, cavalry, engineer and logistic units, and Brigade HQ and signals squadron totalling about 3,000 men, commanded by a brigadier. There are variations to this organization and its strength regarding Argentine Army infantry battalions and Argentine Marine battalions.

CGT Confederación General de Trabajo (General Labour Confederation).

CNN Cable News Network

CO Commanding Officer of a major unit (e.g. infantry battalion) with the rank of lieutenant-colonel.

Company Infantry battalion sub-unit comprising three platoons and HQ, totalling about one hundred men commanded by a major. Similar-sized units of other arms are squadrons, batteries, etc. There are variations to this organization and its strength regarding Argentine Army infantry companies and Argentine Marine companies.

DYN Agencia Diarios y Noticias (Buenos Aires).

EPE Spanish news agency.

Exocet French-built anti-shipping missile capable of being fired from the air, sea and, in the case of the Falklands-Malvinas War, land.

FAP The 7.62mm FM (Fabricaciones Militares) FAP (Fusil Automático

Pesado – Heavy Automatic Rifle) is a heavy barrel version (with bipod) of the standard issue Argentine 7.62mm FM FAL – Fusil Automtico Liviano (Light Automatic Rifle).

Franks Report The Franks Committee was convened by the British Government to examine alleged British Government failings with regard to intelligence and diplomacy prior to the war. The Committee published the subsequent Franks Report on 18 January 1983, exonerating the Government from blame.

HMS Her Majesty's Ship.

INSSJP Instituto Nacional de Servicios Sociales para Jubilados y Pensionados (National Institute for Social Services for the Retired and Pensioned).

IPSA International Political Science Association.

ITN Independent Television News.

LAW 66mm Light Anti-Tank Weapon.

MAG The FN (Fabrique Nationale) MAG (Mitrailleuse d'Appui Général) was the Argentine 7.62mm General Purpose Machine Gun.

Milan An infantry anti-tank wire-guided missile with range of 2,000 metres.

MV Motor Vessel.

NATO North Atlantic Treaty Organisation.

NCO Non-Commissioned Officer.

OAS Organisation of American States.

OC Officer Commanding (a sub-unit).

Operación Rosario The Argentine amphibious operation launched on 2 April 1982 that re-took the Malvinas Islands.

Operation Black Buck Royal Air Force Vulcan bombing operation flown from Ascension Island against Port Stanley airfield.

Operation Corporate The overall British Task Force operation to re-take South Georgia, the Falkland Islands and South Thule.

Operation Paraquet The British Task Force operation to re-take South Georgia.

Operation Sutton The British Task Force operation to carry out the main amphibious landing at San Carlos Water.

Orders Group Otherwise known as an O Group. The Commanding Officer's formal Orders Group where he gives out operational orders to subordinates. This information is then, in turn, passed on down the chain of command.

Para A title given both to individual paratroopers of the Parachute Regiment and used as shorthand for individual battalions of the Parachute Regiment, e.g. 2nd Battalion, the Parachute Regiment (2 Para).

Platoon Infantry company sub-unit comprising three sections and HQ, totalling thirty to thirty-five men commanded by a lieutenant. There are variations to this organization and its strength regarding Argentine Army infantry platoons (forty-five men) and Argentine Marine platoons (fifty-five men).

Puerto Argentino The Argentine name for Port Stanley.

PTSD Post-Traumatic Stress Disorder.

RAP Regimental Aid Post.

Rattenbach Commission The Argentine Junta's Commission of Enquiry into the conduct of the Malvinas War.
RFA Royal Fleet Auxiliary.
RMO Regimental Medical Officer.
RMS Royal Mail Ship.
Royal Military Academy The British Army's training establishment for young Sandhurst officers at Camberley in the English county of Surrey.
SAMA 82 South Atlantic Medal Association 82.
Section Platoon sub-unit of eight to ten men commanded by a corporal. The Argentine equivalent has twelve men.
SLR British Army 7.62mm infantry Self-Loading Rifle.
Special Forces Specially trained combat servicemen who undertake exceptionally hazardous military operations.
SS Steam Ship.
Start Line A natural feature on the ground which marks the start line for a battalion or company attack and which is crossed at H-hour.
STUFT Ship Taken Up From Trade.
TÉLAM Agencia de Noticias de la República Argentina.
UK United Kingdom.
UN United Nations.
UPI United Press International (US news agency).
USS United States Ship.